Brothers

Cynthia Cockburn

Brothers
Male Dominance and
Technological Change

NEW EDITION

Pluto Press
London • Concord, Mass

First published 1983 by Pluto Press
345 Archway Road, London N6 5AA
and 141 Old Bedford Road
Concord, MA 01742, USA

Second impression 1984
This edition first published 1991

British Library Cataloguing-in-Publication Data
A catalogue record for this book
is available from the British Library

ISBN 0 7453 0583 0 pb

Printed and bound by
The Cromwell Press Limited,
Broughton Gifford, Melksham, Wiltshire

To the memory of Jane Payne, the first woman
to become a member of
the London Society of Compositors, 1892

Contents

Acknowledgements / 1

Introduction / 3

1. **Craft, class and patriarchy** / 14
   The pre-capitalist printer / 14
   Capitalism and the growth of unions / 19
   A man's craft / 23
   The iron comp / 26
   A divided working class in printing / 31

2. **Hot metal: craft control** / 36
   The 1950s / 37
   A generation of hot-metal compositors/ 43
   The hot-metal labour process / 46
   The balance of power in work / 52
   The turn of the tide / 55

3. **Technological innovation** / 61
   Cold composition crosses the Atlantic / 64
   Developments in the 'regional' press / 67
   Desperation on Fleet Street / 74
   A stay of execution / 83
   Why new technology? / 86

4. **Cold composition: change in the labour process** / 93
   Text input: 'a glorified typist' / 95
   From metal to paper: 'lick and stick' / 104
   Integrated working: 'all singing, all dancing' / 108
   Skill and 'deskilling' / 112

5. A man among men / 123
   The compositor and the Natty / 126
   Death throes of craft identity / 129
   The politics of masculinity / 132
   Class in turmoil / 140

6. Women: stepping out of role / 151
   A crusade against women / 152
   Women's disadvantage in print / 159
   Women in the NGA: stirrings of change / 163
   The case against women: then and now / 171
   'She couldn't do it' / 174
   'She shouldn't do it' / 181

7. Class and sex: two power systems / 191
   Seeing a sex/gender system / 193
   The economics of male advantage / 199
   There's more to 'material advantage' than money / 202
   Ideas and their effects / 205

8. Men and the making of change / 210
   Contradiction: the motor of change / 211
   Technological innovation as catalyst / 216
   The family, sexism and the right-wing option / 219
   The alternative option / 223

Afterword / 234

References / 253

Index / 279

Acknowledgements

The research on which this book is based was funded by the Social Science Research Council. The City University, London, accommodated me as a research fellow in the Department of Social Science and Humanities. The National Graphical Association, the union that represents compositors, was hospitable in numerous ways, helping me to make contact with compositors, to understand the traditions of the craft and the new departures in union policy. The Fathers of Chapel and members of those chapels that were the subject of the four case studies were generous with their time, both in interview and in reading and commenting on drafts. The London College of Printing, where I was a student of old and new technology for a year, continued their support into the period of research by allowing me to use the resources of the library and giving me access to staff for consultation about technology. The librarians of the St. Bride Printing Library were helpful in finding historical material.

I would like to thank many friends for patiently reading and commenting on the story in draft. The following helped me with particular chapters and themes: David Albury, Elizabeth Bargh, Michèle Barrett, John Child, Marianne Craig, Anna Davin, Lucy de Groot, Tony Elger, Trevor Evans, Jane Foot and Jonathan Zeitlin. The following read the entire draft with much expense of time and goodwill: Anna Coote, Megan Dobney, Frank Elston, Andy Friend, Pat Longman, Anne Phillips, Liz Sullivan, Hilary Wainwright and Paul Willis. I am specially indebted to Geoff Hayward, Education and Training Officer of the National Graphical Association, for his thorough and painstaking comments on the manuscript and to Richard Kuper of Pluto for his experienced editorial help.

To all these people I am very grateful. They are not, any of them, in any way responsible for the shortcomings of the book. But without their help it would not have been begun, let alone completed.

Introduction

This book began as a study of the human impact of technological change. It has ended as a study in the making and remaking of men. It is also about the uses to which men put work and technology in maintaining their power over women.

The particular men on whom the study focuses are compositors in the newspaper industry in London. They are a group who, until very recently, were skilled, well-paid and secure in their employment. The tradition in which they were apprenticed as lads differed little from that of their fathers, uncles and grandfathers, many of whom were also in the print. It was a patriarchal craft culture, with a strong trade-union identification.

In the 1970s the corporations that own the newspapers began a sweep of modernisation which the trade unions are experiencing as a technological offensive. Computerised photocomposition is swiftly replacing the 'hot-metal' technique of preparing type for letterpress printing. Many composing jobs will be lost and opportunities for entry to the occupation will become scarce. The unions, however, are strong enough to retain the right of many existing compositors to the transformed job: the men in this study have been retrained for photocomposition.

The upheaval in printing has only just begun. The 1980s promise turmoil in the class relations of the craftsman. His position with regard to the employer is weakened, his relationship with others in the industry, with editors, reporters, technicians as well as with the semi-skilled and unskilled men he has been used to classing as his social inferiors, all have to be re-assessed. New technology is also disrupting gender relations. The men find the new work less manly. Women are entering typesetting, once the unique preserve of the craftsman.

Can anything be learned that is of general interest from the instance of the compositor? It is true that in many ways the tenacity with which the compositors have held onto their craft identity makes them untypical of male workers. They are survivors of processes within capitalism that have dismantled the craft organisation of other skilled men – the millwright, the toolmaker, the cabinet maker, the mason. Certainly the craft compositor's employer has long regarded him as a dodo that wilfully refuses extinction. This high profile makes the compositor untypical perhaps, but it enables us clearly to detect the kind of changes that dissolve craft away and some of the effects of that dissolution.

Similarly, the London news compositor is not typical of all comps. The news industry has traditions that differ from those of the general printing trade, and London has always been an exceptionally well-defended fortress of craft regulation. The crisis is more acute for these men than for most others in the industry. It is helpful to a researcher, however, in that the distress they are experiencing makes London news comps especially ready and willing to give voice to their feelings and to reassess their position.

Although they may be a special case in some respects, compositors are at one with many other categories of secure worker in established manufacturing firms in being dispossessed by the recession and by the restructuring of British industry. A crisis such as this shakes up old prejudices and opens up new possibilities and new dangers. What alternatives are open to such men? What sense do they make of what is happening to them? What will influence their political decisions and trade-union strategies? These are the broad questions that underlie this study.

Research into the workplace, 'the sociology of work', has until recently been characterised by two things. First, most of it has been about men, giving pre-eminence to men's experience, assuming that the relation between capital and labour is one between bosses and men.[1] Recently, however, women researchers and writers have begun to listen to women workers and to tell their story – acknowledging the fact that 40 per cent of the people in paid employment in Britain are now women.[2] Why, then, another study of men? This time the analysis is a feminist one: the subjects are seen not just as workers but also as males. This invokes the second shortcoming of workplace studies. They have examined in meticulous detail the class relations of the protagonists, especially the labour and wage relations of work, but have neglected gender relations, whether these are lived at work or at home. The experience of class cannot be understood without reference to sex and gender. In this study I try to introduce that second dimension. I use both a marxist analysis of class and a socialist-feminist analysis of sex. As a result, it has been a complicated story to write and may prove so to read.

There is a revival in marxist work of the practice of seeing capital not just as an economic category but as a relation between human beings.[3] This book uses and develops that idea. In one of its aspects the story unfolds as an analysis of the power relations linking employers and workers, the relations of the labour process and the struggle for control of work. It is also about relations betwen groups of people *within* the working class. Many people hope and believe that capitalism will one day give way to a more rational, equal and caring society. Socialists see the working class as the main actors, as well as those who would mainly gain, in such a transformation. But the working class is deeply divided: well-paid against low-paid, waged against wageless, white against black, men against women. Marxism has often skated over these cracks, preferring the prediction that the expansion of capitalism reduces the working class to an oppressed and therefore united revolutionary mass. The truth is, however, that the working class is continually changing, dividing, recomposing. As Richard Johnson has said:

> These internal divisions – within factories, within industries, between occupations, between the sexes and between the employed and the reserve armies – ought to be an object of any primary theory of the working class. We need to start, indeed, politically and theoretically, not from the assumption of simplification and unity but from that of complexity and division . . . Socialist strategies are not at all aided by the rooted belief that such divisions must somehow pass away, or be easily transcended in the name of some essential unity.[4]

One of these divisions in particular, that between men and women, marxism has explained in a way which has been misleading: the sexual subordination of women has often been reduced to a by-product of class processes.[5] Marxism tends to explain the disadvantaged position of women at work as the result of a simple desire by capital to exploit cheap labour, and of men to protect themselves against capital. Such a theory overlooks the economic, social and political benefits accruing to men of all classes from women's long subordination. My analysis therefore employs a second theory, the feminist theory of sex/gender relations, to throw light on such things.

Using a historical and materialist *method* that does not differ from marxist method, we can nonetheless model the world in an alternative way. Marxist historical materialism speaks of a mode of production. Feminist historical materialism proposes that there exists as well, as in all societies, a *sex/gender system* which determines the social categories that people of different sexes fill.[6] It orders these categories in a hierarchy of power relations. Economic, social, physical and ideological initiatives in all societies seem to interact to produce a sexually-differentiated power system of great scope and influence. It is not only class, it is also sex, that determines our chances in life.

The gender we live socially, ('I am a man', 'She is a woman'), is not a natural phenomenon like the sex features we are born with. Gender characteristics such as clothing, style, personality – even physique – are moulded by experiences of childhood, youth and adult life.[7] In our society the definition of biological sex is, from the outset, sharply dichotomised: a baby is officially registered as male or female, and if the physical attributes are ambiguous, as they sometimes are, an arbitrary but firm decision is made one way or the other. As we know, some people feel they have been pushed into a sex that doesn't fit them. The sex of a person as recorded at birth strongly determines the gender they are expected to live: male children are brought up to be manly and female children to be feminine.

In principle, a sex/gender system *could* accord scant significance to biological maleness and femaleness. It *could* organise humans into more than two sexes, allowing social space for people who do not readily fall, biologically or psychologically, into either male or female category. It could confer power on women. Our sex/gender system, however, makes a sharp distinction between male and female. It does not tolerate sexual ambiguity, and homosexuality is deplored. It is a society dominated by men.

It seems that male-dominated sex/gender systems are very long-lived. Though the form of their domination has changed, we know that men have dominated throughout at least three modes of production: slave societies, feudalism and capitalism. Many feminists use the term *patriarchy* to signify our present-day form of the male-dominated sex/gender system. That convention is used in this book, though it will become apparent that the patriarchs that flourished in the Victorian age may now be on the wane, their rule giving way to a more diffuse form of male domination which, before the end of the twentieth century, may deserve a different name.

As Edward Thompson has said, one class can only exist in relation to another. 'We cannot have two distinct classes each with an independent being and then bring them into relationship with each other. We cannot have love without lovers, nor deference without squires and labourers.'[8] In the same way, it is clear that we cannot have masculinity without femininity: genders presuppose each other and are relative, as classes are. Furthermore, classes are made in the course of history. 'The working class did not rise like the sun at an appointed time. It was present at its own making . . . Class is defined by men [*sic*] as they live their own history.'[9] In this book I suggest that genders should be seen as the product of history too. In other words, we are not looking at timeless monolithic structures, capitalism and patriarchy: such a view is indeed unproductive of any insight into the relation between the two. Instead we are looking at what Raymond Williams called 'constitutive processes'.[10]

In the course of the story I explore some historical and recent events which play a part in the two processes of mutual definition: that in which men and women are locked and that in which classes are historically engaged. Capital owns technology. Labour sets it in motion. Through a struggle over its design and manipulation each contributes to the formation of the other's class character. In the same incidents, powerfully-organised workers can be seen forging their social identity in interaction with those less organised and less skilled. And the struggle over skill, technology and trade unionism is part of the process in which men and women can be seen as defining each other as genders. Neither the formation of class nor of gender is a balanced process. Through its ownership of the means of production the capitalist class has the initiative over those who work in order to live. By securing privileged access to money, organisation, capability and technology, men hold the initiative over women. In each case, one party gains the power to define another as inferior.

There are differences within feminist theory on the relation between class and sex/gender hierarchies. Some suggest that the most useful model to work with is one of a single social system combining both mode of production and sex/gender system. Our society would be termed a capitalist patriarchy.[11] Others suggest that we must suppose the existence of two systems in continual interaction: capitalism and patriarchy. This has come to be known as the 'dual systems' theory.[12] It will become clear that I find the latter more useful and continually refer to the class relations of capitalism *and* the gender relations of patriarchy and their bearing on each other.

The book is based on research carried out between mid-1979 and late 1981. The backcloth to the study has been the restructuring of the printing industry and its labour force, including the introduction of several new technologies, since the second world war. Four newspaper companies were singled out for special study. In each of them hot-metal techniques had given way to computerised photocomposition. Two are Fleet Street firms, producing national papers. In terms of organisation the other two firms are 'regionals', though each serves part of the London area with a chain of local weeklies. In each of these houses I studied the composing room – the composing 'companionship' as it is called – and its response to technological change. I interviewed management, technicians and FOCs (Fathers of Chapel, the name given to shop-floor union representatives in printing).

The heart of the study consisted of in-depth interviews with a sample of 50 craftsmen drawn from the four chapels (union 'shops'). Some of these conversations lasted as long as four hours, the average was perhaps one and a half. The questions on my schedule covered 11 major themes: apprenticeship, the old technology, the new technology, the firm, women as competitors and colleagues, union policies, relations with less-skilled men, feelings about class, home-life and domestic relationships, the newspaper as product, and the future of work for compositors. In 15 cases I was able to talk with the craftsman at home, to see his house and sometimes to meet his wife. All other interviews took place in a private room at the place of work. Besides the craftsmen who are the main focus of the study, I also interviewed a number of women. Some were members of the compositors' own union, the National Graphical Association (NGA). Others were members of the National Society of Operative Printers, Graphical and Media Personnel (NATSOPA) which represents less-skilled workers in the industry. I also sought the views of some male members of NATSOPA so as to learn something of the way the compositor is seen by other men.

In the newspaper composing room, the men who were apprenticed to the inclusive craft of composition for print used to specialise to some extent as *linotype operators* (setting the type), as *piece case hands* (handling the large characters for headlines), as *stone hands* (organising the type into page form) or as *readers* (checking proofs for accuracy).[13] Once retrained and working on the new technology, some of the men became *keyboard operators*, some *paste-up hands*, some *computer or photosetter operators* and others did integrated work involving several processes. Here and there I came across a man working in new technology who had been not a comp but a stereotyper – casting printing plates. Conversely, a man now working on the new process of platemaking may once have been a comp. I interviewed two men whose colleagues had moved to the new composing area, leaving them to await their own move. The 50 men therefore had varied backgrounds and occupations. The two consistent factors were their experience of the hot-metal processes of type preparation for letterpress printing and their experience or anticipation of the transfer to computerised photocomposition and its related tasks, sometimes now known as 'pre-press work'.

It should be remembered, however, that important groups are absent from the study. Some compositors have been shed from the labour process altogether because they failed to adapt or because they were too costly. Even further from my sample are those young people who might have become compositors but will not now get access to this work because of narrowing job opportunities due to the greater productive capability of the new technology. The redundant compositor and the unemployed school-leaver are ghosts that hover round the new composing area and they are never very far from the minds of the men who work there. They are the 'industrial reserve army' that weakens the worker's bargaining power and urges him to accept the new discipline. On the other side of the coin, however, and equally absent from the composing room and from this study, are those (comps and others) who have trained for and found different and better work as the new corps of higher-paid, technical and managerial workers who minister to the computerised system.

What people experience, the way they deal with events and the meaning they make of their lives, is the bedrock of history. The institutions that create the content of the newspapers, television programmes, education and official policies predominantly express a view that is antagonistic to working-class interests. It is important, therefore, to broaden the range of expression, to set up situations where working-class people represent their own experience and their own case, and give voice to their understanding of the world and the ways they would like it to change. Much of this account therefore stays close to the spoken word of the interviews. Individuals, however, do not act in a free and unconstrained way to produce political effects. Unfortunately theories of ideology say little of the links that connect material circumstances with ideas, or connect the widespread philosophies that find expression in books, media, political parties and movements, with the individual making up her or his mind. On the whole the theories stay at the upper level.[14] Yet it is the individual who experiences the dilemma and who also, in the end, takes action and makes change.

While the limits of ideological change are set by material conditions, I believe the mechanism that prompts a break, a redirection, in either a person's practices or ideas, is the mechanism of *contradiction*. To grasp contradiction we need a dialectical way of thinking. The dialectic in the work of Hegel and its application in marxist historical materialism emphasises the idea of *process*. Events unfold and one form replaces another, denying it yet developing out of it. The dialectic proposes that all phenomena contain their opposites, that there is a tension within them. Outside events, acting upon them, may bring about a rupture, but it is the form of the contradiction itself which will determine how and where the break occurs. In resolving the conflict between opposites something new occurs: a *synthesis* which in turn develops its own contradictions.[15] The dialectic emphasises inter-connectedness and therefore rejects a simple one-way movement from cause to effect. In this way it proposes a theory of the relation between knowledge and the world and between phenomena and the sense we make of them, that is foreign to mainstream sociology.[16]

If sociology has found it difficult to take account of contradiction, in real life people are only too painfully aware of it. People are uncomfortable when their ideas are in contradiction with their practices, or when they harbour conflicting feelings. As the tension increases, so they seek to put matters right – they change what they are doing, move their position or abandon one set of ideas in favour of another. They are strictly limited in what they are likely to be able to feel or do by their class position, their sex, and perhaps also by their age, race, life experience and many other factors. But these material circumstances can never be totally determinant because they suggest conflicting meanings. Current ideologies coming to the individual from the state, the trade union and other individuals, bid for attention and invite a following. And nothing stands still for long: new decisions are always required.

It was with the importance of contradiction in mind that I designed the research method of this study. The 50 compositor interviews were based on a schedule of 72 basic questions. However, since I felt free to pose these in any order and usually began with a request for the story of how and why the compositor came into the trade, his apprenticeship or 'the old days', the interview took on the character of a conversation or exploration.

It is usual in social science to seek to code and tabulate responses, even in interviews of this kind. Does the respondent prefer the new technology to the old? Yes/No/Don't know. Of course there are advantages to this method. It enables detailed correlation between replies. There are some questions to which the answers can sensibly be handled in this way. It is useful to be able to say, as I can without hesitation, that 30 out of the 50 compositors had fathers who had been in skilled manual work. Past mistakes have shown me, though, that to enter a field of experience such as this with the idea of emerging from it brandishing a handful of 'yesses', a bunch of 'noes' and a few 'doubtfuls', all adding up to 100 per cent, leads to asking the wrong questions, hearing the wrong replies and seriously under-estimating the intelligence of informants.

Instead, I tape recorded all the compositor interviews and transcribed them carefully. The hesitations and silences tell as much as the words. A speaker changing pitch, shifting in his chair or lighting a cigarette often denotes tension. People have certain phrases to voice conflicting ideas: 'I have mixed feelings', 'you are really torn', 'but then again', 'on the other hand'. Only the unconfident or the bigoted answer complex questions with an unproblematised 'yes' or 'no'. A thoughtful statement will be the unpacking of a contradiction. Often indeed the contradiction is so intense or suppressed that it does not get unpacked at all and results in an illogicality or a *non sequitur*. In the course of a two-hour interview a contradiction may weave its way through the discourse, coming clearly into view only after many different topics have been touched upon.

The contradictions that crop up in this story are of several kinds. The compositor might be recounting two contradictory practices. For instance, he may be active within the collective solidarity of the union, yet operating in conformity with the sectional interest of piece-workers. More often he will be describing two contradictory thoughts or feelings: I don't want to be left behind in a dying trade, but I don't like the prospect of training for new technology. Or he may be conscious of contradictions existing between what he does and what he thinks or says: I operate the keyboard as fast as I can because I enjoy working to top performance. But in the chapel we agree it is not in the collective interest to establish too high a standard.

I tried to see contradictions not as problems to be ironed out, ('How shall I decide whether he is saying 'yes' or 'no'?), but as the *goal* of the research. Such elaborations of paradox and confusion are painstaking and often painful. But it is precisely out of the process of bringing such contradictions to consciousness and facing up to illogicality or inconsistency, that a person takes a grip on his or her own fate. Politically it is of vital importance that we understand how we change. This perhaps will explain the free-rein given in this narrative to contradictory accounts and feelings, my large tolerance of indecision.

It is easier to be tolerant of the contradictions expressed by others when you are aware of those in your own life: I write from the point of view of a woman, a socialist, a feminist, a worker, a mother, a trade unionist. Not all of these categories sit easily with each other.

1. Craft, class and patriarchy

The sights, the sounds and smells of an old letterpress printshop evoke an image of working relations that are two hundred years out of step with the rest of British industry. It is furnished with worn wooden cases of metal type, lead shavings litter the floor. There is a characteristic smell of ink and paraffin. In one corner a linotype tinkles away, in another an old Heidelberg platen press hisses and thumps as it turns out sheets of print. Until 15 years ago there was little reason for the master of such an outfit to consider change, since its technology was still unchallenged. Now, every week another shuts up shop.

Most of the printers I talked to in the course of this research entered the trade between twenty and forty years ago as apprentices in such jobbing shops, expecting that this historic craft environment would surround them for the rest of their working lives. They were wrong. All of them today are employed in light, modern offices, where the loudest noise is the background hum of air-conditioning. They see no ink, handle no lead, lift no heavy weights. Their materials are paper and film. And into their labour process, the terrain of control contested by the management and the trade union, has entered a new organising principle: the computer.

In order to understand the impact of such change on the individual and on his trade it is necessary to step backwards in time and see where the compositor and his union have come from.

The pre-capitalist printer

Caxton assembled the first printing press to be used in England in the almonry of Westminster Abbey in 1476 AD.[1] Like the new technology of today, Caxton's innovation displaced a skill, threatening the scriveners and textwriters who had controlled the written word since civilisation began. Simultaneously he drew into existence two twin crafts: that of the *compositor*, who arranged the separate pieces of movable type to form words and lines of text; and that of the *pressman*, who applied ink to the printing surface and pressed paper against this to produce an image. These two crafts are the backbone of the National Graphical Association (NGA) today. The first is the subject of this study. For two centuries, however, though printers were culturally important, they did not amount to more than a handful of men among the thronging trades of London. A hundred and fifty years after Caxton's press was founded there were still no more than 22 printing houses in London, probably with one press apiece.

The relations of this labour process in pre-capitalist days were intricately entwined with those of the patriarchal family. The medieval master printer was governed by membership of his guild, incorporated as The Stationers' Company in 1557 AD. His status, as well as the printing establishment itself, was often handed down to the oldest son. A master would set up his workshop near or within his home; his apprentices (and even some qualified journeymen) used to live in his house, provided with 'meate, drinke, lodging and wasshinge of his lynen' by the master's womenfolk and servants.

Though increasingly his own head of household in the late sixteenth century, the journeyman seldom rose to be his own master. The statutory limitation on the number of printing presses prevented upward movement and had the effect of creating a permanent class of skilled journeymen.[2] Though the journeymen nominally belonged to The Stationers' Company alongside their masters, and in theory enjoyed equal rights and status, the Company became increasingly undemocratic, controlled by the wealthiest masters. At periods it acted as an arm of the state itself.[3]

The apprenticeship contract is a paradigm of the unity of home and work in a fully patriarchal and pre-capitalist world. When a young man was bound over to a master printer to serve his term of seven years, the formal deed was signed by three parties: the parent or guardian, the master and the boy. The boy left his own home and went to live under the roof of his master who then, *in loco parentis*, fed and clothed him (often scantily) and was held responsible for his misdemeanours. The apprentice was not paid, but often borrowed from his master, finishing his time in debt to him and so open to yet more exploitation. 'In some unhappy households the wretched apprentice, as well as being the drudge, was cuffed and whipped by every ill-tempered adult.' The boy was committed 'to a kind of bond slavery from which he could hardly escape, except to the prisons or the gallows'.[4] The power of the master was a patriarchal ascendancy that spanned employment and domestic life.

On the other hand, the apprentice who survived this induction and became a journeyman printer obtained his status as an artisan and a passport to citizenship: he became a Freeman of the City. The butterfly that emerged from the chrysalis of apprenticeship could never again be confused with the mere grubs of the labouring world. This process of youthful suffering to win manly status is still very important to compositors today, as we shall see.

The union shop to which a printer belongs is still known as a *chapel* today. 'Every Printing House is by the Custom of Time out of Mind, called a Chappel' wrote J. Moxon in *Mechanick Exercises* in 1683, 'and all the Workmen that belong to it are Members of the Chappel; and the Oldest Freeman is Father of the Chappel.' Decisions were made democratically, by a 'plurality of Votes in the Chappel. It being asserted as a Maxim that the Chappel cannot Err.'[5]

The printer's chapel is often idealised for its workshop solidarity, egalitarianism and mutual responsibility.[6] The direction of my study, however, is not only to look at what this kind of organisation secures for those who are within it, but also to examine its implications for those who remain outside. There were always fewer apprenticeships than those who desired them. The sons of men already in the trade were normally, perhaps naturally, given precedence. Since a printer had to know how to read and write, the son of a labouring family had little chance to become a recruit. Within the male working class, as it emerged from the feudal strata, printers became a self-perpetuating, differentiated group. Along with other skilled men they were an elite among workers.

This is not to say that they were always high earners or secure in their employment: frequently they were not. But the key strategy they developed in their struggle – control over entry to the craft and the job – set them apart from the mass of unindentured labour.

For every apprentice compositor with his foot on the bottom rung there were a hundred likely lads clustered around the ladder. Equally to the point, there were one hundred and one *girls* who were not considered likely at all and for whom the ladder was out of sight. There was only one way for a person to enter print other than by apprenticeship and that was by inheritance of a master printer's family concern.[7] Felicity Hunt cites records that show a number of widows and daughters taking on a printing business and employing journeymen in their own right, in the seventeenth and eighteenth centuries. It is unclear, however, how many of them were personally skilled and proficient compositors.[8] Certainly by the nineteenth century, as printing moved away from the home and the joint stock company gradually took over from the pre-capitalist printshop, even this avenue, narrow and unfrequented as it was, closed to women. As to the rituals of apprenticeship, it was unthinkable that a girl should pass through a process so clearly designed to produce a free *man*.

Let's look at some of the chapel customs of the eighteenth century and try to imagine a woman in place of a man. The initiation ceremony was bizarre:

> When a Boy is to be bound Apprentice, before he be admitted a Chapellonian, it is necessary for Him to be made a Cuz or a Deacon, in the performance of which there are a great many ceremonies. The Chapellonians walk three Times round the Room, their right Arms being put through the Lappets of their Coats; the Boy who is to be made a Cuz, carrying the wooden Sword before Them. Then the Boy kneels, and the Father of the Chapel, after exhorting him to be observant of his Business and not to betray the Secrets of the Workmen, squeezes a Sponge of Strong Beer over his Head and gives him a Title, which is generally that of Duke of some Place of least Reputation near where he lives . . . Puddle Dock, P–ssing Alley and the like . . . Whilst the Boy is upon his Knees all the

> Chapellonians . . . walk round Him, singing the Cuz's
> Anthem, which is done by adding all the Vowels to the
> Consonants in the following Manner: Ba-ba; Be-be; Ba-be-bi;
> Bo-bo etcetera and so through the rest of the Consonants.[9]

Similar arcane procedures accompanied the 'banging-out' of the apprentice as journeyman printer. To the boy it says he is different from other boys. To a girl it clearly says: you have no business here.

The chapel had many rules governing members' behaviour. Misdemeanours included swearing and fighting, and lack of diligence in work and over the care of materials and equipment. 'Solaces' or punishments were imposed by vote of the chapel. Normally, they were money fines. Newcomers to the chapel were also expected to contribute a 'benvenue' and accumulated funds were usually destined for drink.

Beer drinking was an important component of chapel life. In the office where Benjamin Franklin worked as a young man there was an ale-house boy in constant attendance and a printer might drink 'a pint before breakfast, a pint at breakfast with his bread and cheese, a pint in the afternoon about six o'clock and another when he had done his day's work'.[10] There is still an institution known as the 'wet chapel' today. Chapel meetings are frequently held in pubs and a decision is made as to whether or when the chapel becomes wet, that is to say members may drink. The result of hard drinking on a Sunday was the frequent observance of Saint Monday: absenteeism on the first day of the week. Another social custom among printers was to demand of the employer an autumn feast or 'wayzgoose' on pain of refusing to work after nightfall. At this celebration, which lasted well into the present century, the employer 'not only entertains them at his own House, but besides, gives them Money to spend at the Alehouse or Tavern at Night'.[11]

Solaces sometimes took the form of corporal punishment. The workmen took the wrongdoer by force and 'lay him on his Belly athwart the Correcting-stone and held him there while another of the Workmen, with a Paper board, gave him . . . eleven blows on his Buttocks; which he laid on according to his own mercy. For Tradition tells us that about fifty years ago one was Solaced with so much violence that he presently Pissed Blood and shortly after dyed of it.'[12]

From such rituals it is clear that the exclusion of girls from apprenticeship, women from print, did not need to occur through closing a gate or through formal banning. It would have been an odd family that was willing to see a daughter enter so male-oriented a life. The exclusion is inherent in relations between workers in the workplace and practices that were designed, maintained and adapted over time precisely to create a close identity of interest among a fraternity of men who defined themselves as masculine, a universe away from women.

Occasionally in this history of compositors one catches a glimpse of woman the way the men see her. For instance, among the misbehaviours cited as being punishable in a certain chapel is the instance of 'a Workman or a Stranger saluting a Woman in the Chappel'. And again, 'if a journeyman marry, he pays half a Crown to the Chappel. When his Wife comes to the Chappel, she pays six pence: and then all the Journeymen joyn their two Pence apiece to Welcome her.'[13] Women, clearly, were perceived as something different.

Capitalism and the growth of unions

The means to reproduce and circulate written material are a boon to political activists – as the duplicator and the small offset presses of the twentieth century have proved. During the ferment of the English revolution of the 1640s and 1650s, presses sprang into existence to print tracts and pamphlets. With the restoration of the monarchy in 1660, however, there was a new clamp-down. Through a Licensing Act in 1662 and the good offices of the guild, The Stationers' Company, the state reimposed control. And just as there was no free market in print, neither could labour power be freely bought and sold. The Statute of Apprentices continued to restrict employment in printing, as in other skilled occupations, to men who had served their apprenticeship.

Such devices could not, for much longer, however, hold back the growth of capitalism, seeking free scope for enterprise and a free labour market. In 1695 the licensing laws were allowed to lapse and

newspapers began to flourish. Between 1696 and 1709 the number
of London weekly papers rose from 9 to 16. Although the growth
of the press was impeded by an Act of 1712 which imposed stamp
duties on newspapers, nonetheless by 1785 there appear to have
been 28 regular papers in London, including 19 dailies. Printing
was also now spreading from London to the provinces. By 1785
there were no fewer than 50 provincial newspapers. The Stationers'
Company waned in influence and it became increasingly difficult
for the state to keep control.[14]

The late eighteenth and early nineteenth centuries were a
formative time for capitalism in printing. Iron presses replaced
wooden presses around 1810. The steam-driven press was first
introduced, at *The Times*, in 1817. The scale of the industry grew
fast. In the period 1750–1825, the number of London compositors
trebled and the number of apprentices quadrupled, in spite of the
journeymen's energetic resistance. Provincial presses began to
threaten the London trade with their low prices. In 1813 the Statute
of Apprentices that had protected craftsmen since Elizabethan
days was swept away and the journeyman compositor was thrown
onto his own resources:

> While he could witness with philosophical detachment the
> servile status of the domestic servants, the ill-paid toil of the
> manual labourer, or the monotonous drudgery of the factory
> operatives, the attempt to lower his own status – to substitute
> the impersonal cash nexus for the social-economic relationship
> of the old order – seemed to him an offence against justice and
> decency.[15]

Women and children, who had characteristically worked and
earned within a family context, were increasingly drawn into
employment in factories and mines. Here they came under the
control of a rival authority – the capitalist employer. Men felt their
masculine familial identity, along with their class identity,
threatened by the changes. With the end of the Napoleonic Wars,
unemployment became serious for printers. It enabled the employers to force through wage cuts in the following period.

During these early decades of the industrial revolution the

journeyman compositor needed more than ever before the strength to be derived from workshop organisation. As John Child puts it:

> [though] *laissez faire* was coming to be regarded as the almost divinely inspired doctrine of social organisation, the chapel sustained in the ranks of the journeyman printers the spirit of industrial comradeship and endured to form the basis of the new organisations in which they could recover their sense of common purpose and unite to resist a depression of their traditional standard of life in the bleak age of industrialisation.[16]

These new organisations were trade societies, the forerunners of trade unions. In 1793 the London comps first formed a committee to represent their interests. This Union Society, as it later became, was cautiously active in the early years of the nineteenth century, though inhibited by the Combination Acts of 1799 and 1800 which made such initiatives illegal. It was not until the repeal of the Acts in 1824–5 that the societies of London compositors and, separately, the newsmen, began to shed the cloak of 'friendly society' and develop as trade unions, precipitated into a struggle with the new class of capitalist employers. Printing did not industrialise on the scale of many other industries – textiles or engineering, for instance. Throughout the nineteenth century printing had a dual nature, many old-style small jobbing shops persisting alongside larger and more modern joint stock firms. But gradually in many companies managers and foremen were inserted between the owner and his workforce. The thrust of the employer was continually to weaken the craftsman's grip on the labour process and to cheapen the value of labour power.

In their own defence the compositors redoubled their efforts to control the labour supply, defining printing unambiguously as a craft, staking exclusive claim of members of the societies to practise it and limiting entry to the societies. They insisted on a seven-year period of apprenticeship, tried to fix and enforce ratios of apprentices to journeymen, and laid down rules to govern the kind of work that apprentices could be put to so that they could not be used to steal the journeyman's job. These regulations the employers continually attempted to evade.

An important device in the journeymen's strategy was the control of the unemployed. The societies raised subscriptions to enable payment of strike allowance and out-of-work relief to prevent men on the streets from under-cutting their brothers at the frame. They organised a 'call book' which unemployed journeymen signed daily and which enabled them to be given jobs in rotation. Later in the century London compositors combined into unofficial exclusive clubs known as the 'Gifts', which cornered certain printing offices and gave access to employment to their own members only. The Gifts were active in Fleet Street until the 1950s and show the printers at their most exclusive and unpopular. One mechanism devised by craftsmen to reduce the reserve of unemployed men competing for work in any particular town was the 'tramping system' which prevailed in printing from around 1700 to 1840.[17] Unemployed men were paid an allowance to travel along an agreed route that often spanned the British Isles, looking for temporary work. They held a society tramping card and would be given a small sum of money and a bed of straw in the attic of any society 'house' (usually an ale house) at which they called.

The journeyman's great fear was always the outsider. Non-apprenticed, unqualified rivals to the trade were traditionally called 'foreigners'. Because printing was originally introduced from the continent many of the fifteenth-century compositors and pressmen were from the Netherlands and other European countries. These printing workers from across the channel were at first specifically exempted from the restrictions on entry to the country that applied to other categories. But in 1557, by which date the masters had sufficient English printers to satisfy demand, restrictive legislation was brought in to stop the flow. Control of 'aliens' from abroad was often cited as a problem at this time, and such chauvinism echoed on into the nineteenth century.[18] 'Rat labour', 'illegal men', 'foreigners' . . . these were the terms that compositors used to contrast the inferior status of those outside the self-definition of the craft with their own legitimacy.

Here we can begin to see how the compositors' key strategy, control of labour supply, drawn from them by the forward drive of the capitalist class, played a part in dividing the newly-emerging working class against itself. If capital seemed an enemy to many a comp, 'foreigners' and 'the demon of boy labour' seemed another, and one to be fought no less energetically. Later this divisive strategy would hit back at the craftsman, who had inadvertently helped to form a pool of unorganised, unprotected labour which capital could use to undercut him and whose loyalty he had forfeited. Meanwhile, as capitalism advanced, upward progress to independent self-employment became less and less realistic a possibility for journeymen. They were being formed as a distinct class stratum and, in turn, were moulding those below them into another.

A man's craft

Women, meanwhile, were becoming (in their working lives) a component in that 'other' working class with which the compositor often saw himself in conflict. Histories of printing in the nineteenth century tend to group three separate activities within the term 'the printing trades': bookbinding, paper manufacture and printing itself. Women did establish, and have maintained, a substantial presence in the first two. But from printing they have been notably absent. It is interesting to contrast the position of women in relation to bookbinding and to composing. By 1851 there were 3,500 women in bookbinding, 7,000 by 1871 and 14,200 by 1891.[19] They often did skilled work, but their skill did not win them the earnings that a craftsman could command. Often their conditions and pay were appalling.[20] Women filled distinct, segregated occupations within the binderies, mainly folding the printed sheets, collating the sections and doing the preparatory stitching. These tasks were tacitly acknowledged by the journeymen as 'women's work' and it was only after 1840, when a growing demand for books led to mass production and eventually to mechanisation, that demarcation problems arose between men and women in the binderies.

In contrast, of the employees in the printing industry proper, no more than one in a hundred was a woman: in 1851 they numbered only three hundred. The figure was still only seven hundred in 1871 and 4,500 in 1891. Besides, of these females in the print, very few were doing compositors' work. The great majority were at their traditional tasks of folding and stitching, where print shops had expanded horizontally to undertake these finishing operations. Ramsay MacDonald, writing early in the twentieth century, pointed out that the aspects of the printing trades which women tended to enter were those requiring nimble fingers, jobs which were quickly picked up. He emphasises the distinction between trade skill and single process manipulative ability as 'a fundamental consideration in every problem concerning the woman wage-earner . . . Only in a very few cases is the beginner, whether an apprentice or not, thoroughly taught every process of her trade. The manual dexterity she may acquire is in no sense genuine trade skill.'[21]

Felicity Hunt points out that by the time the rather late industrialisation of printing had created a potential demand for cheap female labour, the printing trade societies were already strongly organised to defend the men against it. They were reinforced in their resistance by the Victorian ideology of 'a woman's place is in the home'.[22]

Press work was an undeniably heavy and dirty occupation (though no more so than hauling coal in the mines, which women were currently doing). Composing, on the contrary, was relatively light and could have been a profitable source of employment for women. Craft organisation and social sanctions together, however, effectively barred women from such a possibility. Child says, 'The employment of women on typesetting was not a very grave threat to the hand compositors, for long training was necessary for all-round competence as a compositor'.[23] Long training, yes, and that training could only be acquired by passing through the strongly masculine ritual of induction to the all-male societies. It would have been a hardy woman who set herself out to gain acceptance as a craftswoman – sharing in the ale-house conviviality of the compositors, tramping the country in search of work or sleeping rough on the straw of the societies' houses of call.

Some resolute employers did bypass the societies' regulations and put women to work at the typesetting case. The *Woman's Gazette* for November 1876 reported 'at the present time women compositors are employed in several firms in London. We may mention Messrs. Bale and Sons, Messrs. Danks, and Messrs

Boldero and Foster.' The *Women's Union Journal* for November 1879 contains a letter from the firm of Smyth and Yerworth in which 'about four or five years ago we commenced to employ female compositors and as we found the advantages of so doing we increased the number from time to time'.[24] A deputation of comps from the trade society, however, resulted in the craftsmen withdrawing their labour from this firm when they failed to unseat the females. More typical instances ended with the removal of the women instead.

A number of mechanical inventions, none very successful in technical design, were introduced by employers in the latter half of the century in an attempt to bypass the craftsman's costly labour. Most of these machines separated the operation of setting type from that of distributing the used characters. The 'dissing' task, tedious and unskilled, had always been claimed by the craftsman, intent upon keeping common labourers out of the composing room. On the machines, girls were often set to work the disser. For a few years in the 1840s a number of firms operated the Young Delcambre machine, using female labour in this way. Later, in the 1860s, some newspaper owners introduced the Hattersley composing system, employing girl and boy labour on the dissing mechanism. The compositors of course 'blacked' firms that engaged in this practice, with more success in London than in the provinces.

What small success women did have in composing work was due less to the economic processes of industrialisation that brought women into bookbinding and into the textile and other industries in such numbers, than to a politically-conscious movement of middle-class feminists. In the mid-nineteenth century more than one-third of women in their twenties and thirties were spinsters. Only one-fifth were in paid employment. The reformers were seeking to open up work opportunities for women, especially employment that might be suitable for middle-class women. The Victoria Press, set up in 1859 by Miss Emily Faithfull, was supported by the Society for Promoting the Employment of Women. In Scotland, the following year, a similar body founded The Caledonian Press. In 1876 the Women's Printing Society Ltd. was formed and by 1895 was employing 40 women, mainly on printing work connected with women's interests and the suffrage societies. These projects proved

– had there been any doubt – that women were quite capable of doing composing work, but they were too small to create any panic among the trade societies, who simply dismissed them as 'a wild scheme of social reformers and cranks'.[25] The very idea of women seriously undertaking to achieve the competence of craftsmen was easily ridiculed.

The iron comp

The replacement of the flat press by the high-speed rotary press in the 1870s and 1880s greatly increased the output of the newspaper pressroom. Hand composition thus became a bottleneck and the productivity of the composing room a matter of renewed concern for the newspaper owners. For the compositor, the problem was increasingly one of resisting the intensification of work and, where this failed, improving his share of the increased earnings. The introduction of more scientific management methods by employers was everywhere meeting active resistance from craftsmen in their struggle to maintain control of the labour process. The comps' primary strategy of control of the labour supply was progressively reinforced by elaborate provisions concerning participation and reward in work.

By now the local trade societies of the past had united into three regional bodies that were to all intents and purposes trade unions: the London Society of Compositors, the Typographical Association (in the provinces) and the Scottish Typographical Association north of the border. The societies engaged with the employers in many attempts to negotiate standard rates of pay. Some compositors, called time hands, were paid by the hour, others by output. For the former, the societies sought uniform 'established' (or 'stab') rates and maximum hours of work. For piece-workers they sought continually higher rates per unit of output, and guaranteed minimum hours of work. The rules and rates prevailing in piece-work were embodied in the London Scale of Prices, so complex that it needed an expert to decipher it. The first edition of this bible, a paradigm of craft regulation, was issued in 1785 and, with many enhancements, it exists to this day. By such means, though the craft went through periods of unemployment and was continually under attack from employers, compositors maintained a relatively firm grip on printing work, blocking the aspirations of the owners, until the last decade of the nineteenth century.

By then, capital had succeeded in cutting labour costs in many industries by restructuring skills, sometimes diluting them, sometimes superseding them. Even in print, the machine minders of many of the new rotary presses had been transformed into new-style engineers. The former craft pressmen had permitted the entry to the pressroom of teams of semi-skilled assistants (a brake hand, a sup hand, a reel hand, a couple of fly hands), none of whom were apprentice or journeyman printers.[26] The inroads of the non-craft labourer in this period are reflected in the dominant position in some newspaper pressrooms today of members of NATSOPA, the union of unskilled/semi-skilled print workers. Compositors, in contrast, had been continually vigilant against any division of labour within their craft. They had vigorously opposed attempts to redefine parts of it as jobs for boys or girls. This vigilance was rewarded in the critical years of the 1890s when printing capitalists turned their modernising attention from the pressroom to the composing area.

The employers had found little profit in the use of the early models of mechanical typesetter. At last, the invention that every British newspaper proprietor had dreamed of arrived. Ottmar Mergenthaler acquired the patent for his 'linotype' machine in 1886 in the USA. His achievement was to do away once and for all with the problem of distributing the used type. Linotypes cast type anew from molten alloy for each and every use. The metal itself is melted down for re-use, but the type is used only once. So successful was this machine that by the time its patents expired in 1913 it had penetrated throughout the newspaper industry. It has continued to be the standard mechanical typesetting system in the news trade, challenged only by computer-aided photocomposition today. Between 1893 and 1968 Linotype sold 74,000 machines worldwide. Intertype, a subsequent competitor, sold 38,000 to 1968.[27]

British print masters had to wait some years to get their hands on the 'iron comp', as it was called. The first linotype to be imported from America was installed in 1889 in the *Newcastle Chronicle* offices. By 1894 there were six in use in London papers, including

the *Daily Telegraph*. The British Linotype Company began manufacture in 1893 and was soon producing 500 machines a year. The
company's annual profits shot from £11,000 to £69,000 in two
years. The risk capital had been well invested: linotype was clearly
a winner. 'The greatest and most prosperous invention of this
century, if you except electricity' as the company's deputy chairman put it.[28] The question was, of course, whose prosperity was
assured and whose was threatened?

Linotype threw the compositors headlong into their first ever
real crisis of craft control. They would not meet another like it until
our own day. The newspaper owners' ideal would have been to do
away with the craft compositor in typesetting altogether. Fortunately the design of the new machine conspired with union strength
and employer disarray to betray this hope. Though the mechanisation of typesetting introduced a sharp division within the labour
process of the hand compositor, separating typesetting from the
subsequent composition of the page, linotype setting was itself
necessarily a whole operation, requiring one operator only, with a
fair degree of know-how.[29] Unlike the preceding short-lived inventions it played into the hands of the craftsman. Indeed, the
Typographical Association (TA) wrote to the manufacturers to
congratulate them:

> The Linotype answers to one of the essential conditions of
> trade unionism, in that it does not depend for its success on the
> employment of boy or girl labour; but on the contrary,
> appears to offer the opportunity for establishing an
> arrangement whereby it may be fairly and honestly worked to
> the advantage of employer, inventor and workman.[30]

The unions made it clear that they stood by the absolute right of
skilled men to the machines, to a fair share of the financial returns,
to shorter hours and to training at the firms' expense. And they had
the muscle to press such demands convincingly, especially the
London Society of Compositors (LSC) with its militant rank and
file and a left-wing general secretary, C. Bowerman. 'The Typographical Association was an army of guerrilla bands' writes John
Child. 'The LSC was a panzer division.'[31]

The craftsmen, once in command of the machines, of course had influence on speed of operation and organisation of work. The operators deliberately restricted output in order to shelter the hand compositors. 'We have not . . . at all reached a possible or even creditable output in England in machine composition' complained a manager of the *Manchester Guardian*. In certain Society houses, he said, men were working at 4,000–5,000 ens per hour while in non-Society houses other men were outputting 7,500 ens per hour.[32]

In contrast to the craftsmen the employers were an undisciplined band, starkly competitive and unpractised in collective bargaining. As a result they failed to withstand the societies' claims to the keyboard, backed where necessary by strike action. Indeed, the first 'machine-scale' addition to the London Scale of Prices in 1894 grossly underestimated the productivity of this new force of production, and yielded phenomenal earnings to the operator. 'This prince of working men will receive in London or Manchester on a morning newspaper some 70s or 75s a week. This is higher income than a graduate of Oxford or Cambridge with first-class honours can often obtain in the scholastic market.'[33] Print employers in the USA, even using the original craftsmen, had quickly made 60 or 70 per cent savings in their wage bill. Such gains proved elusive to British capitalists. Sir E. Lawson of the *Daily Telegraph* complained that the practices of the comps 'hampered and handicapped the machine to a terrible extent'.[34] The Linotype Company, seeing the advantages of their brain-child brought to nothing by the comps, trained their own scab operators and used them as strike breakers. They were believed by the union to have engineered an attempt to split the LSC by setting up a rival linotype operators' union. A short-lived National Free Labour Association, inspired by the employers, set up a 'free labour bureau', registering compositors who were prepared to work in 'unfair' shops and guarantee not to strike.[35]

The history of this tumultuous period has been recounted in detail by Jonathan Zeitlin.[36] He analyses the divergent histories of compositors and engineers in the 1890s. Capital exerted a similar pressure on the two groups, attempting a new division of labour by deskilling, thus aiming to destroy craft control. The engineers' organisation was usurped in part by this tactic, but that of the

compositors held firm. Zeitlin suggests that the failure of the one
and the success of the other hinges on the outcome of the class (and
gender) struggle of the previous few decades. Unskilled and
semi-skilled assistants had been allowed to penetrate the engineering workshops, and these were now used against the skilled men. In
contrast, the compositors had continued to insist on the right to
even the undemanding chores of the composing room. The protective legislation of 1867, restricting the employment of women on
night work, had limited the usefulness of women to newspaper
proprietors long before the advent of the linotype. Through this,
and their own vigilance, compositors had averted any potential
threat from female labour. There were thus no unskilled rivals for
the machine waiting at their elbow. Though many hand comps,
particularly the old, did suffer redundancy, as a species the
compositor survived strengthened into the twentieth century. The
machines were introduced during a period of rapid growth when
the demand for print was snowballing. Employers' profit margins
could afford some laxity in labour costs. By the end of the century
most of those thrown on the 'call book', if they had not retired or
changed their occupation, had been absorbed by growth. The
census shows employment in printing, paper, books and stationery
to have risen from 94,000 in 1871 to 178,000 in 1891, and 253,000
by 1911. The union leaders had waged their struggle shrewdly:

> [They] established their principles but they knew when to
> turn a blind eye to an irremediable breach. They modified
> their rules, educated their members, bargained with the
> employers, gave way when the opposition was too strong.
> Neither the TA nor the LSC suffered even a temporary
> setback to the steady growth of membership.[37]

Indeed, union control over the labour market gradually increased.
Pockets of non-unionism were steadily cleaned up and casual
labour declined. By the first world war the conflicts over the
introduction of composing machines – both Linotype in newspapers and the subsequent Monotype in the book trade – had been
resolved in favour of the craftsman.

The advent of the iron comp had been a politicising experience
for compositors. By 1900 there were many in the trade unions who

would have called themselves socialists. The TA was quick to affiliate with the Labour Representation Committee, forerunner to the Labour Party, when it formed in that year. Some members of the LSC were inspired by the 'new unionism' of the 1890s and encouraged the formation of a union for the unskilled in print.[38] The TA leadership was active in helping form a national Printing and Kindred Trades Federation to unite the unions.[39]

A welcoming hand to women workers was not, however, among the gestures of even the most progressive printers. Women were never in the running for the Linotype. In Chapter 6 we shall see the campaign the compositors waged against women working on the Monotype. Yet large numbers of literate and eminently capable women were ready and waiting for such work. So much is clear from the rapid feminisation of clerical work that accompanied the introduction of the office typewriter.[40] The male clerk of course was less well organised to defend himself against female encroachment than the unionised comp. In skilled composing work, however, the prestigious and better-paid aspect of printing, women's participation continued to be kept to a minimum. The composing room, now housing the mechanical typesetter, continued an all-male preserve and lost none of its traditional atmosphere of masculine camaraderie. Indeed, as we shall see, to many of the men, the clatter and clunk of the linotype if anything enhanced the manly qualities of the occupation. In turn the craft has contributed something to our conceptions of masculinity.

A divided working class in printing

Looking back on their own history, printers today often describe themselves as having been men of status. 'Top-hatted gentlemen, weren't we.' 'You were a printer, you were a king.' The compositor's work required fluency in reading and writing, and at a time when literacy was not common in the working class this earned him respect and standing. Historians, too, often locate printers within the mid-Victorian 'aristocracy of labour'.

The serviceability of the concept of an aristocracy of labour was extensively debated during the 1970s, particularly by socialists who are concerned to know why and in what circumstances a working class is quiescent or revolutionary.[41] Though complex and painstakingly argued, this debate has lacked a dimension. The demands of capitalism and the manner in which the processes of capitalist development structured the working class it drew into existence are analysed. Less often remembered is the active part played by the working class itself in the process of its own formation, and less often still the imperatives of patriarchy in that history.

The working class is not an inert mass manipulated into shape by capital. Working people have contributed to history.[42] Their actions and reactions have had a bearing on the way capitalism itself has developed. Capital's continual division and redivision of work into detailed tasks, its restless revolutionising of its factories, can be seen in part as attempts to outflank an actively resistant labour force.[43] Its alternations of management style, now the tight control of Taylorist efficiency, now job-enhancement and invitations to 'participation', can be read as responses to the unruliness of workers.[44] This active view of the printer was expressed to me by a compositor in interview. 'Because they were literate and had connections with intellectuals,' he said, 'they were able to grasp the changes in society first. They were in the forefront of change and set the pattern in some respects for trade-union improvement.'

The history recounted above will have shown the degree of conscious activism among printers. In his study of chapel organisation, A.J.M. Sykes suggests that 'the unity and cohesion of the chapel is enjoined by the belief that there exists a state of conflict between printers and their employers'.[45] It was the vital sense of unity against the employer, he suggested, which led to the printers' willingness to subordinate their individual rights to freedom of action and to accept the group decisions of the chapel and later of the union.[46] The self-definition of compositors as craftsmen, superior to and different from the remainder of the working class, was part and parcel of the conflict between capital and labour, not a sign of its absence.

The pressure on the craftsmen came from the capitalist class in its thrust to lower the value of their labour power. But the craftsmen made choices. They chose union practices which included the carving-out of a uniquely defensible identity that was skilled, white and male.[47] With the benefit of hindsight, it is possible to see today that there is more than one way of organising resistance to capitalist exploitation. The dockers, for instance, who, like printers, retained an extraordinary measure of control over the labour process in the period after the second world war, did so not by craft separatism but as teams of equal semi-skilled workers.[48] Class responses are not totally determined from without.

Perhaps the wrong questions are being asked in the debate over the political possibilities of the working class. To ask what responsibility the skilled working class bear for the failure of a revolutionary movement to arise in Britain is interesting, but insufficient. A more relevant question may be – what sort of a revolution would it have been if such men had led one? For they were deeply implicated in advantages accruing from the hierarchical relations of patriarchy: their trade unions were male power bases and they gained much of their standing and comfort from their authority over women at work and at home. Their radicalism never came near relinquishing – or even questioning – that power.

It is easier to grasp the extent and location of male political organisation in historical perspective than to pinpoint it in the more diffuse society of today. Thomas Wright, a nineteenth century journeyman engineer, describing the fraternity of trade clubs in his craft, wrote: 'Its members are numbered by tens of thousands . . . I can turn into it in any part of England, Ireland, Scotland or Wales . . . it still awaits me with open doors and a brotherly welcome.'[49] Likewise, the compositors' trade unions were the institutions in which their solidarity as a group was forged, in which their ideology developed and their battles were waged. The Typographical Association, the Scottish Typographical Association and the London Society of Compositors did not have explicit written rules barring women. They did not need to. That there was an effective, informal exclusion is evidenced by a curious event in 1886. At an exceptional conference of the three societies held in London, the compositors discussed measures for dealing with the threat from women compositors in Edinburgh. (This incident is discussed at length in Chapter 6.) The societies found themselves caught between contradictory needs. One was to keep women out of the craft altogether. The other was to ensure that, if they entered it, their rates of pay were brought up to the men's level to avoid undercutting. Under the stress of this tension, they passed an illogical resolution:

> That while strongly of the opinion that women are not
> physically capable of performing the duties of a compositor,
> this Conference recommends their admission to membership
> of the various typographical unions, upon the same conditions
> as journeymen, provided always the females are paid strictly
> in accordance with the scale.[50]

This was studied hypocrisy. As Sidney Webb pointed out soon after, the compositor could rest assured in the knowledge that no employers would take on women at equal pay with men, 'with the limitations that the Factory Acts place on her . . . some possible hostility of the men and other considerations that her working with the men might introduce'.[51] And this indeed proved the case. It seems that no women joined the Typographical Association in the wake of the resolution and only one held, for four years, membership of the London Society of Compositors. The unions continued to be male clubs and their procedures and customs, language and ideology to be the cultural and political expression of manhood as much as of labourism.

Men of the skilled stratum were emphatic believers in the undesirability of women leaving the home for paid work. A man was no man if he could not keep a wife at home to minister to his comfort: 'Among the working class the *wife* makes the home . . . The working man's wife is also his housekeeper, cook and several other single domestics rolled into one; and on her being a managing or mismanaging woman depends whether a dwelling will be a home proper, or house which is not a home,' wrote Thomas Wright, the engineer, in 1868.[52] He complained of the shortage of suitably competent women for such a man as himself to wed and proposed a system of education to qualify girls for the role of wife. The ideal would be for a female to step directly from the patriarchal control of one man to that of another: 'The best wife that a working man can get is one who is the daughter of a family which from its numbers or some other cause has necessitated her being kept at home to assist in its management.'[53] The relationship should be one of authority and discipline as well as affection and care. Wife-beating in the area in which he lived was looked upon, 'if not exactly as a proper and commendable practice, at least as a very commonplace one and one which no person of a well-regulated mind would be guilty of interfering with'.[54]

The compositors held fiercely to the ideology of 'the family wage'. Their demands to employers were couched in terms that made it clear that the norm they wished to establish was that of a family dependent upon a single male breadwinner.[55] (Many men expressed this same ideal to me in interview in 1980.) The very character of the trade societies as supportive clubs running insurance schemes and paying sick benefits was designed to maintain family income in times of trouble.

The desire of a man to 'keep' a wife, hemmed within the home, in a strictly sexually-polarised social division of labour, and on his wage alone, is not something that can be explained by class theory. It requires reference to a sex/gender system.[56] It is men as men who benefit from personal rights over the domestic labour, sexuality and reproductive capacity of a wife. It is in the light of this fact that the militancy of printers has to be assessed. It is true that one should not inscribe the trade unionism of the nineteenth century with possibilities it may never have had. However, if we are to formulate new trade-union strategies for the future (as I invite in the final chapter of this book), we need to be clear at least as to what trade unionism has *not* been in the past. It has not had within it that feminism and egalitarianism which informed some other social movements – including aspects of the English revolution of the seventeenth century[57] and Owenism in the 1830s.[58] The struggle to keep women competitors out of work and to wrest from the employers a wage sufficient to keep an entire family may have seemed to the men at the time, as it is often represented today, a necessary class struggle, pure and simple. It was, nonetheless, also a struggle by men to assure patriarchal advantage.

2. Hot metal: craft control

In the twentieth century, the grip of men on many skilled male occupations was prised open by the labour shortage created by two world wars. Government-enforced 'dilution', which normally meant the introduction of women trainees at less than craft rates of pay, contributed to the long-term erosion of craft control. In printing, however, the craftsman's monopoly was barely touched by these events. In the first world war, though a dilution agreement was eventually signed by most print unions, it was not widely used and the London Society of Compositors (LSC) evaded it altogether. First the Society brought in unemployed and retired men, then it relaxed overtime limits, had hand comps trained up rapidly for the machines and encouraged members to do overtime in second offices (a practice known as 'smooting').[1] Under pressure the Society did agree in 1916 to two women graduating from handsetting to monotype, thus bringing their female membership to eight (all paid craft rates). This was the most the London craft was obliged to bend, though losing close on three thousand members to the fighting services. Far from being weakened, the union gained financially by the war due to the drop in unemployment benefit it was required to pay.[2] It used the war as an added argument for 100 per cent unionisation in print. A leaflet challenged suspected blacklegs:

> Have you considered what *your* position is likely to be after the war? Do you know that non-Society employers are engaging and training girls and women to work as compositors – case and machine? Are they doing this for *your* benefit? When the boys come home, will *your* position be better or worse? . . . play the man and join [the Society] now.[3]

In the second world war the shortage of craft compositors was more acute. By 1941 composing rooms were manned only by the infirm, the elderly and the very old: three hundred retired members were wheeled back to man the barricades against women. The employers pressed the government hard and obtained a dilution agreement for printing. A number of women entered and trained mainly for work as mono and lino operators. Employers were warned that, while they could rely on the attitude of women, 'taking it for granted that they will feel honoured by being allowed to do any work ordinarily performed by men', they would need to use propaganda and influence to overcome 'the prejudice and ignorance' of the men on the composing-room floor.[4] The compositors' journals did indeed ridicule the idea of 'frocks at the frame', but were met, however, by women's response that many dilutees quickly became competent workers while not a few craftsmen 'remained passengers for life'.[5] The dilution agreement was hedged by a guarantee that dilutees would be the first to be dismissed when the labour supply picked up and a strong rhetoric of 'jobs for our boys and women to keep home for them' ensured that few females remained to work at craft jobs after the end of hostilities.

The 1950s

Many of the compositors featured in this study were apprentices during the post-war decade. For them the 1950s are 'the good old days'. The patriarchal structure of the unions and the patriarchal assumptions within the workplace culture remained surprisingly intact and helped to form the boys' ideas about printing and skill, class and gender. The lads were often indentured to a small family firm in which the owner was known personally by the men.

As the masters of the printing industry entered the fifties they saw markets opening up invitingly. Print demand had increased massively after the war and seemed set to go on growing. Book production was up and periodical publication was booming. The press was prosperous too, particularly the provincial newspapers, though impeded by official rationing of paper. The industry was buoyed up by a spectacular growth in advertising.

As the print masters saw the situation, however, there was one leash restraining them from making hay in this sunny climate: the shortage and cost of skilled men. They were getting nowhere in their efforts to create a long-overdue free market in labour, the pre-requisite of a virile capitalism. Government-sponsored delegations of printing industrialists went to the USA to see what could be learned. They came back impressed by the dynamism of American managements, the fluidity of labour power and the supine posture of the trade unions.

In British printing, in contrast, the unions had the whip hand. It was a seller's market for labour, skilled manpower being critically short. The London compositors, for instance, had succeeded in holding down entry to the trade in the postwar years so effectively that in 1950 the total was still one thousand men fewer than before the war began. Each demand for increased pay was met by employers with a counter-demand for relaxation of the labour supply. Some bitter disputes resulted, in a period that was more generally characterised by working-class quiescence. The pay round of 1949–50 saw a dispute between the LSC and the London Master Printers Association (LMPA) which led to an overtime ban followed by a lock-out. The conflict ran for four months and involved suspension of three thousand workers. In the mid-fifties there were many shop disputes, particularly in the provinces, concerning 'over-manning',* demarcation, pay differentials and the right to organise. Often it was clear that the compositors felt they had an enemy on either hand, the employers and the members of other unions. In 1955 the apparently untouchable Fleet Street was brought to a halt, not by the printers, as it happened, but by another small skilled section, the engineers. In 1956 there was again a six-week concerted lock-out by the London print masters.

The outcome of all these struggles was a gradual widening of the fortified gateway that apprenticeship represented for entry to printing. All the unions, even the LSC, were obliged to concede a reduction in the apprenticeship period from seven to six years,

---

* 'Over-manning' is the term used to denote the practice of employing more workers than strictly necessary per machine or per department. In the case of newspapers, it is inappropriate to quibble with its use on grounds of sexism, since all the workers in question are in fact men.

more generous apprentice ratios and exceptional block intakes of over-age youths as apprentices. The LMPA and the provincial employers were obliged, however, to pay a high price for this relaxation of craft principle. Official wage concessions combined with firms' widespread practice of paying extra 'merit money' (actually shortage money) to craftsmen carried the cost of labour to new high levels.

The tensions in the industry came to a head in 1959 in a national stoppage of six weeks over wages and hours versus productivity, to which the employers had now shifted their attention. In fact, production in the industry had risen by 90 per cent in 12 years, against an increase in the labour force of only 51 per cent.[6] But increasing the size of the work force against the resistance of the unions was proving a slow remedy for output. The employers' productivity drive resulted in 'the longest and most widespread stoppage in British industry since the General Strike of 1926'. One hundred thousand men and women came out, four thousand firms were affected and a thousand provincial newspapers closed – for '40 hours and 10 per cent now'.[7]

Meanwhile, the shape of the industry within which compositors were doing battle was changing. Takeovers and mergers began to hint at a coming consolidation of capital in printing, a rationalisation that was occurring in many areas of British industry. Within the firms the familiar forms of patriarchal authority were being questioned. There was a new rhetoric that appealed to the tougher imperatives of corporate management which were less concerned with the human factor. As the decade wore on, employers began casting around for technical innovations that could increase productivity with or without the co-operation of skilled men. Photogravure, rotary and web printing, colour technology and new methods of photo-engraving were crossing the Atlantic from America. A few British trend-setters began to convert from letterpress to offset litho. Compositors were hearing rumours of photocomposing systems, now in the experimental stage. There were 'so many inventions rumbling beneath the surface of the printing world that it hardly seems exaggerated to talk of a revolution. The aristocrats whose heads are in danger are the comps, the lithographers and so on, whose skills are being superseded,' wrote a far-sighted trade journalist.[8]

Labour in printing, embroiled in conflict with its employers, was simultaneously engaged in civil strife. The stronger, to give themselves leverage in their push against capital, pressed down on the weaker. The weaker sometimes hit back, unsure at times whether to regard the employer or the craftsman as their main enemy.

There were 16 separate unions representing print workers in 1950, and the labour force was divided in several other dimensions as well. The first was territorial. The LSC defended London as though it were its private fortress, continually fighting to restore or retain its customary wage differential over the provinces. The Society restricted the movement of compositors inward from Typographical Association areas and 'blacked' provincial work to discourage the use of cheaper sources of labour than its own. The print masters protested that the compositors were 'segregating London from all other parts of the country by drawing a union ring around it like a new customs barrier'.[9] To escape the high cost of London labour many printers, especially book firms, moved to greener fields. As London employers complained, the craftsmen's earnings had always been liable 'to kill to goose that lays the golden egg, or at least force the bird to go and lay in the country'.[10] Even within the provinces there was conflict: during the decade the lower-paid towns succeeded in abolishing the much-resented grading system, bringing all provincial areas to the same rate of pay.

A second dimension of strife was between the newsmen and the general trade: the newspaper compositors had their own ferociously pro-craft journal and were discussing a separate union that would represent their (well-paid) interests alone. A third was rivalry between crafts. In 1919 a national agreement had assured craft parity, equality of earnings between stereotypers, binders, lithographers, machinemen and compositors. But wage cuts in the ensuing depression had soon upset the balance. Now the stereotypers were again in conflict with compositors and machinemen over their specialised skill differential. Even among the typographical unions there was continual tension between keyboard operators, compositors and proof-readers over relative advantage, and more generally between piece-workers and time hands. Proof-readers challenged the compositors as 'phoney aristocrats'. Operators justified higher earnings for themselves as 'the cream of the trade'. 'Clotted cream', sneered the compositors.

If there was bitterness among craftsmen, the abyss separating all of them from the semi-skilled and unskilled categories of printing labour was wide, deep and acrimonious. Continually at issue were the twin questions of pay differentials and demarcation: were the unskilled creeping into jobs formerly designated as skilled? A standardised but not immutable wage differential divided the three groups, but the craftsmen were correct in feeling that the unskilled were getting closer in this game of grandmother's footsteps. By the end of the decade the semi-skilled were getting 87½ per cent and the unskilled 85 per cent of the craft rate. 'I don't begrudge the unskilled man a living wage', wrote a typical comp in the Society journal, 'but in a craft industry craft must be entitled to a much bigger percentage of the wages bill.'[11] The General Secretary of the LSC wrote, 'If you are prepared to be apprenticed to a skilled trade, to work as you do in acquiring a knowledge which is necessary, for a miserable 10 per cent over the labourer's rate, you are not the man I think you are.'[12]

Men, of course, is right. The last, and in a sense almost invisible, rift in the fabric of worker solidarity in printing was that between men and women. Women were not included in the formalised class of printing labour but were a separate category of 'females' suspended below Class 3, unskilled men. They had started the decade with a wage of 54 per cent of the craftsmen's rate, moved up to 58 per cent by the 1955 wage-round and were in line for 66 per cent by 1959. The improvement in women's relative position was effected without direct challenge to the craftsmen, however. In a sense they rose up the scale in the wake of the upward thrust of the less-skilled men. Indeed the boom circumstances of the 1950s allowed all groups to gain something, even within this strife-ridden structure. But women continued to be almost entirely grouped within the separate unions of the semi- and unskilled, and in segregated occupations very similar to those they had filled in the nineteenth century.

The fact that there was no open militancy, no public position taken by women over access to skilled jobs or over wage differentials in this period should not lead us to overlook a difference of interest between men and women. Women were absent from the leadership of the trade unions. The women's movement of the 1970s was undreamed of and that of the suffragettes forgotten. A woman's struggle at this time was an individual one that barely surfaced in public. It was, in the first place, her attempt to leave the home, to modify singlehanded the dominant ethic of a 'a male breadwinner and his family wage'. Second, it was to find the personal courage to consider herself, let alone ask to be considered, as a candidate for training and education. Third, it was to think of herself as worthy of decent earnings and only then perhaps to demand an improved percentage of the male rate for the job.

The fifties saw the beginning of the great upsurge that brought many more women, especially married women, into the paid workforce. Around a million married women joined the workforce during the fifties and by the end of the decade, for the first time, a woman going out to work was just as likely to be married as single.[13] Overall, women stepped up from 30.8 per cent to 32.4 per cent of the occupied population between 1951 and 1961 and a further 4 per cent by 1971.[14] With this arrival in public life, women's attitudes and attitudes to women have both changed. But in the 1950s women were subject to the most contorted and ambiguous attitudes by men, both in the workforce and the business world. In the fifties trade-union journals of the skilled printing unions of course speak with a wholly and unselfconsciously masculine voice. The journal of NATSOPA, one of the unskilled unions, had a women's page. But the content was not then, as it is now, about women's work, women's disadvantage and women's rights. It was entirely concerned with fashion, beauty, housekeeping and etiquette tips. 'Are you one of those girls who firmly propels her poor partner where she want to go on the dance floor? The only cure for you is a strong partner.'[15] It is as though the many women working in the industry were seen by their male colleagues not primarily as workers but as characters from a domestic and sexual drama who had strayed onto the wrong stage. Their commitment to work, proved by the war, was overlooked.

In the printing-business press, women were used salaciously in advertising, then as now, but were also wooed by the newspaper and periodical industry and their advertisers as the new ideal consumer, vested with the power of the purse, bulging now not only with 'his' wage but with 'hers'. 'If you advertise in *her* evening paper,' advertised Kemsley Newspapers to its clientele, 'she cannot help thinking of *you*. We are the medium that can put you effectively into the housewife's mind.' Since the advertisers wanted women readers, more newspapers and magazines saw the advantage of employing a few women journalists. '*Times* woos women. A 28 year old ex-typist is editor of *Times*' new women's page.' 'Meet a new type of crime reporter – Jeanne Pinto. Jeanne has beauty as well. We like it better that way.'[16] Thus the thread of the exploitation of women runs through both the newspaper as labour process and as product, and binds together both home and work, labour and sexuality. It was the most anguished, if the least recognised, division within the working class in print.

A generation of hot-metal compositors

The 50 London newspaper compositors I interviewed for this study were all members of the National Graphical Association (NGA). Their ages ranged from 30 to 65, but a large proportion were clustered in the middle-age range of forties and fifties. Some had had their apprenticeships interrupted by the war, but most had begun or ended their 'time' in the 1950s. Consequently, they entered the trade in a period of high confidence. Never had compositors been more secure or self-satisfied. The electronic composing technology was as yet no more than a rumour, easily put out of mind. And if there had been a small relative deterioration in the position of printers in the league table of earnings, it was not yet severe enough to shake the printer's confidence in himself or his future.

The craft trade unions still had agreements with most employers restricting access to composing jobs to men who were already union card carriers: it was an effective pre-entry closed shop. Thus all these men had entered the trade straight from school by way of a long apprenticeship, as had their nineteenth century forerunners. They also stepped into a set of class and gender relations that were relatively unchanged.

Apprenticeship and chapel life remained a patriarchal affair.

Openings in print were still jealously guarded, and a boy was better placed if he had family connections. Of the 50 in my sample, 28 had had a member of their family in print before them. Fourteen had fathers in the trade. One man named four generations in the industry, including five brothers, two sisters and their husbands. The choice of career for a boy was often made by his father and printing was held to be 'a good number if you stuck at it'. The job had prestige among the working class. 'I came from the East End of London. For us, someone going into what was almost a *profession* – well, it was a gift from the gods and a chance you could not ignore.' Though it was uncommon by the fifties, before the war a father would often have to pay a premium of £50 or more to obtain his son's indenture.

The compositor's craft is situated deep within a dual set of tensions concerning work. The first is the polarisation between 'a man's job' and other forms of work that are seen as more effeminate and less appropriate for a man. One of the men I spoke to had begun a self-selected career as a ladies' hairdresser. 'There was quite a reaction to that. It didn't go down very well with the family. My dad, really, he thought it was a job for poufs (laugh), see, and er, I didn't take that point of view. I just thought of it as a job where you could do something a bit creative. But printing was regarded as, if you like, more of a *man's* job, and one that could produce a reasonable income later on.' By contrast, heavy manual jobs, though unequivocally manly, are exhausting and often low paid. Many men are understandably afraid of them. Some comps chose print therefore as a satisfactory compromise, escaping from a family tradition or local job market that threatened to suck them into the life of a miner or a deep-sea fisherman, yet still remaining safely within the accepted boundaries of a respectable man's work.

The second set of tensions is that surrounding the mental/manual division of labour and the class implications of that distinction. Print may have had high status among the working class, but there was no denying that it was a 'mere' manual job, inferior to those even more prestigious intellectual occupations that promised to take the working class boy entirely out of his class, as he and his family saw it. It seems, from what the compositors told me of their school days, that most had been deemed middle-runners, bright enough for a literate job like print – 'I always liked reading' – but not making the grade for higher education. 'I failed my scholarship, you see', or 'Well, academically I was pretty average I suppose.' In many cases, undoubtedly, the education system itself, because of its nature and because of their class background, had underdeveloped the boys' ability.

The apprenticeship was characteristically served in a small jobbing shop. (Newspaper apprenticeships were rare. They were in fact banned in Fleet Street.) Once an indenture had been signed by boy, parent and employer, there were penalties for a boy who broke the engagement. He would start as a general hand on 20 per cent of the craftsman's pay, slowly progressing from sweeping floors and making tea to the routine tasks of sorting leads and dissing type. Eventually the Printer would put him under the wing of a journeyman in the composing room proper. The comp would do his job and the boy worked alongside, taking notice. If this man were kindly and good it would make a big difference to the boy's experience. 'I learned from old pica thumpers and a clip round the ear was the accepted practice,' one remembered. But another said, 'No apprentice was ever *taught*. It was time-serving, that's all.' More often than not the men kept the cards close to their chest. 'It was pretty menial stuff. They didn't give you the opportunity to do what you felt you should be doing. Most of the guys there had the good jobs sewn up, because of the bonus schemes.' In the last year or two of his time the apprentice would be given a chance to learn the keyboard of the monotype or linotype machines. The union itself had (and has) no qualifying exam at the end of the apprenticeship period, but the boys usually studied for state technical qualifications at evening classes, in their own time. Luckier and later entrants had had some full-time or day-release courses. It was an all-round experience but slow, somewhat hit and miss. The apprentices sometimes complained in the union journal. 'Is the apprentice being taught his trade? No! Wake up you old'uns. Show us the roads you've travelled. We're willing to learn.'[17]

Some found the apprenticeship a hard grind. Those who had entered print for its semi-intellectual properties could feel quite demeaned by the rough treatment meted out to the boys, the degree of deference that adult chapel members demanded. The relations were quite literally patriarchal in the sense that they involved a hierarchy among the men, conferring authority on the older ones. 'The journeymen used you as a skivvy and a dogsbody. When I left school we were all A-stream material and they treated us apprentices as though we were absolute rubbish, very very badly.' It is interesting to read the apprentice column in the journal for this period. Members of the Guild of Young Printers speak with self-abnegation and subservience. The elders talk down to the lads ('hello chaps' they greeted them each month) in a tone that would scarcely be tolerated by young men today.

Most of the men, nonetheless, looked back on those days with some enjoyment. There was a pride to be taken in having started at the bottom and learnt a trade the hard way. 'To have been through it, to learn to become a full member of the production team, that gives you a shared experience.' It is like induction to a rather select club, it makes you part of an elite. So apprenticeship was a manhood ritual still. It tested and teased you, made you angry, and you emerged fighting, confident of belonging somewhere. Above all, it left you with a strong psychological need to see the skill that you had suffered so much to achieve as something of inestimable value.

The hot-metal labour process

It is impossible to understand the claims and counter-claims about skill without understanding the labour process on which they are founded. The work described here is that which the men in my sample had been doing immediately before retraining for photo-composition. It continues to be the working experience of many compositors whose firms have not yet abandoned metal technology.

The compositor's work in printing is made up of two major tasks – *typesetting* and *composition* – and a variety of smaller additional activities. All are comprised within the apprentice's training and fall within the demarcation that the union defends.[18]

Even in the 1950s, improbable as this now seems, much type was still set routinely by hand, a process that had changed little if at all since Caxton. All the men I spoke to had learned hand typesetting as boys and many had practised it for some years. It was the first thing I myself was taught at the London College of Printing as late as 1978. Characters cast in lead alloy were purchased by the printer from a type foundry. They were stored according to style and size in a series of wooden cases divided into partitions. An upper case contained the capital letters, a lower case the small. The art of the *hand typesetter* was to know the position of the characters in the case, to have the dexterity to withdraw them at speed and assemble them into words and lines in a metal slide or 'stick' held in the left hand. The nimbleness of a good hand comp is quite extraordinary and belies the myth that men are 'naturally' clumsy, while it is women who are dexterous. I have met elderly men, working on *Dalton's Weekly*, whose fingers and thumbs are physically flattened by a lifetime shifting type. The typesetter had to ensure that the line was evenly spaced and physically tight, up to a given measure, by use of lead spacing pieces. He needed good eyesight for reading the type faces, often minutely small, in reverse order, and had to be able to calculate in the 'point system' of measurement peculiar to printers.

In newspapers, however, to which all these men eventually progressed, text type was set on a linotype machine, differing little from the iron comp of the 1890s. Twenty-eight of my sample had been *linotype operators*. The operator sits at a wide keyboard on which 90 keys are organised in three banks, reflecting the lower and upper case of hand setting, and an additional alphabet of 'small capitals' together with digits and symbols. He also has a choice of magazines containing different type styles or sizes. Each keystroke he makes releases a small brass matrix, a tiny hollow mould of a single letter of the alphabet, from the overhead magazine. The matrices slide, one at a time, down a shute in response to the operator's keystrokes, collecting in an assembler where they may be read as a line. The linotype has a clever device of wedge-shaped spacebands that spread out the words to form a tight line according to the required width (measure), making possible a straight righthand edge to the column of text (justification). The operator must make a decision at the end of each line as to when to stop adding characters and whether and where to break a word, running it over to the next line (hyphenation). The collected matrices are then 'sent away' by pressing a lever. Molten metal is forced into the faces of the characters resulting in a solid slug or 'line o' type' about one inch high, which is ejected onto a waiting tray (galley). Here the lines, still hot to the touch, assemble, as the operator taps away, into columns of text. The used matrices are mechanically lifted to the top of the machine where, by a system of coded notches cut in the base of each one, they are distributed back, each into its appropriate channel of the magazine, to await re-use.

Operators set uncomplicated, straight matter at a speed of between five and ten thousand characters per hour. Because it is the first in the production line, and therefore a potential bottleneck to the flow of work, the linotype 'companionship' is often under pressure. Some matter is more demanding than others, but for an experienced man, setting becomes second nature as typing does for the typist. He may not even be aware of the meaning of some of the matter he sets. 'Somehow or other you don't take it in, it goes right over the top of your head. There seems to be direct connection between your eye and your fingers.' Most men can, to a certain degree, talk or let their minds wander while setting.

The linotype operator has (or had) an informed and interactive relationship with his machine – 'it was my little kingdom'. Many of the men I talk to had been accustomed to spending the first 15 minutes of their shift cleaning spacebands, hanging up new ingots of alloy, preparing the machine for work. They would regularly clean the plunger, change the moulds, adjust the blades that cut the slugs, and 'line' the pot. Sometimes they had to interrupt setting in order to sort out stoppages in the disser, the distributor of matrices. Often the men had their own set of maintenance tools. Some had taken machines to pieces and reassembled them. They often compare their relationship to the linotype to that of intelligent and informed car drivers to a car. They wouldn't handle a major breakdown perhaps, but they would maintain and service it, sensitive to all its quirks.

It is surprising, perhaps, that what seems to the outsider a rather repetitive and monotonous job is often experienced as challenging and satisfying by the operator himself. 'Complex setting, plenty of work, you are on the go all the time.' 'It has never felt boring to me. You are always trying to set cleaner than you did the day before.' Leaving the machine, walking over to lift each new piece of typescript from the 'block', was part of the rhythm that made the job enjoyable. 'You are up and down, up and down. Take and back, take and back.' Many of the men enjoyed the hurry, the continuity of the task. They liked being good at it. 'What did I enjoy? Just the pure effortless flow of stringing words and sentences together. How can I put it? I suppose it was a revelry, it was the ease and speed with which I personally felt I could get galleys of stuff out and when it came back from the reader there would be just one, maybe two mistakes in it, that's all.' 'You get the football results on a Saturday night, say. People are waiting for the job to be done and it depends on you, whether you can do it or not. I suppose it is a bit big-headed but . . . I get a kick out of it, out of being able to do it within the time alloted and to *my* satisfaction.' It became a kind of easy mastery. Above all, quality control was in the man's own hands. He identified with perfection.

The product of the linotype is not only visible. It is tangible. This metallic nature of the product is satisfying in itself. In addition the men insist that they had a degree of initiative within this task. They would read ahead and if necessary correct, sub-editing the words as they went along. 'If it was marked up wrong, looks wrong, you would change it. Use your wits on it.'

Most linotype operators in Fleet Street are still paid by output, according to the London Scale of Prices. These piece-workers earn substantially more than time hands. It has to be admitted that many operators are strongly money-motivated. That is what took them into the specialisation in the first place. They are counting as they work: counting output, errors, performance . . . and money. They feel that their earnings, the fact that they have learned an extra skill, put them above the common compositor. They put down the antipathy of others to jealousy – 'green eye'.

The material that flows through the newspaper production process, as fabric passes through a garment factory, is words (and associated picture images). They originate with the journalist, are adapted by the editor and arrive with the lino operator as a scruffy typescript. Now he has converted them to metal and they travel onward in this new form. Before they go far, however, the galleys are inked up and a proof-pull on paper is taken from the metal type which then goes for checking. The proof-reader's job is to mark any typographical errors, to detect stylistic aberrations or failures in sense, listening to his assistant reading aloud from the original. Three of my sample had spent some time as readers. One other had been a 'piece case' hand assembling manually the brass matrices for the large type of headlines and advertisements and forming the slugs on a Ludlow caster.

The word *'compositor'* has two meanings, one broad and one narrow. It refers to the ideal whole craftsman, as qualified through apprenticeship, even though he is perhaps in practice using only a part of his skill. Thus linotype operators are also 'compositors' in this broad sense. It is often used more narrowly, however, to designate the craftsman who is *not* setting type, but assembling it, once set, to form the printing surface. Fifteen of my sample had at one time been hot-metal comps in this more limited sense. In Fleet Street they referred to themselves as 'stab hands, because they are paid established hourly rates, not by output.

The linotype operator and the reader specialise in one job, but the compositor (in the narrow sense of the word) does a number of residual tasks, usually on a rota. One of the jobs he does lies upstream of the linotype operator. This is to 'mark up' the incoming typescript with the correct instructions for setting – the desired column width, type face and size etc. This job requires no manual skill, but a good confident knowledge of usage, newspaper typography and printers' signs is necessary.

The next task is that of 'random hand'. The first random hand collects the galleys, or trays, of slugs from the operators, organises them into correct reading order and takes them to the proof-puller – who in Fleet Street is likely to be a semi-skilled member of NATSOPA. He then passes the galleys to the second random hand, who places them in correct racks by page order ready for compositors to assemble. First and second random are thus occasional jobs on a newspapers comp's rota of work.

The comp's most characteristic task, however, is imposition of the type matter on the 'stone', or flat surface on which the 'pages' are created. Before the approach of the moment for sending the newspaper to press, while all is still calm in the composing room, type for advertisements comes to the stone hands to be made up into small individual sections and put aside ready for later use in the page. As editorial material starts to come down the pressure builds up. Sometimes two comps will work to each page, which may take 15 or 20 minutes to complete. Illustration plates, ready mounted to type height, now known as 'blocks', have to be located and associated with the correct galleys of text matter. The slugs and blocks are assembled by the comp, working with the characters upside down so that they may be read from left to right. A rectangular steel chase or frame is dropped over the whole and the material tightened into it with special wedges (quoins). 'You literally build up the page from these components.' Hundreds of these pieces of metal thus become one solid heavy mass (the forme) which can be lifted, with some difficulty, and moved away either to the press or for the moulding of duplicate stereo plates. The comp's tasks make demands on numeracy and literacy, aesthetic sense, dexterity and physical strength. 'You have to use your brain to make it compact, so you can lock it up tight. But it also has to look good, well-spaced.'

The men say they found work on the stone satisfying in many different ways. The variety was itself attractive to them. There was pride to be had in being able to do it well. 'No-one tells you what to do. It's down to you.' They liked the sense of completion, of a series of finished projects. 'Half the enjoyment is seeing the thing go off at the end of the shift and being able to say: I've done that.' Working with metal brings a special satisfaction. 'You could feel you were involved with a base material, creating something out of it, like a carpenter with wood.' 'There's a weight behind it. You lock up the frame, pick it up – it may weigh a couple of hundredweight. And you feel as if you have achieved something.' 'There is the actual physical effort of cutting up rules, figuring out the best way to do a thing, going and choosing type. It's artistic. A good comp is an artist as well as working with his hands, like Michelangelo I suppose.' Besides all this, there is a pride in knowing how to do physically heavy work without hurting yourself, 'mastering' the knack of manual labour.

The pace of newspaper life is itself a turn-on for many of the men. 'I enjoyed the cut and thrust of it. One minute you are standing around and doing nothing and the next minute it's hell for

leather and wanted five minutes ago. It gets heart-pumping sometimes. That's part of the enjoyment of it.' 'When edition time is due
you go like the clappers, you really shift it.' 'You know, on a
Sunday, when the whole of London is quiet, nothing seems to be
happening anywhere. And you come into the composing room and
there it is, all the clatter and noise, a little sort of embryo of
everything, belting away.' Many of the men compete with each
other – geared up as they are to edition times, revelling in speed
and performance. 'I do it just for that, I love to do it faster than the
next guy.'

Of course, this old metal technology had many disadvantages. It
was heavy work and tired you out. Often it was hot, dirty and
noisy. There were health hazards in working with lead, with
solvents and with machinery. The men quite rightly complained of
these things. But there was an ambivalence in their expressions,
because for many men these very factors were what made the work
manly:

> I like to do a man's job. And this means physical labour and
> getting dirty, you understand. To me, it must do. And I'm
> sorry if I might offend you in this way. I mean, women's lib is
> completely beyond me. I don't understand it, it's a different
> world to me. To me, to get your hands dirty and work is, you
> know . . . working brings dignity to people I think, they are
> doing something useful, they are working with these [he
> demonstrated his hands] that have been provided for that.
> That's what it is all about. Craftsmanship.

And another compositor said, 'At an animal level there is a lot of
noise, of heat. It's dirty, very dirty in fact. But that dirt and heat,
the noise, it can be a real wind-up, you know.'

The balance of power in work

The men felt positive about the hot-metal process. They had no
doubt that they had been apprenticed into a highly skilled craft.
'Not anybody could come in and do that job.' Chapel relationships
and loyalties, and at the smaller scale those of the working

companionship, fostered this sense of being in a club. This was enhanced by the intricate involvement of the chapel (which one sometimes forgets is in reality no more than a union shop), with the actual organisation of production in the hot-metal system. In comparison with the journalists and editorial staff 'upstairs', at one remove from the composing stone and the presses, comps felt themselves to be a kind of priesthood of production. They alone, better even than management, knew how to get the paper out.

In Fleet Street, this tendency was developed further than elsewhere. Even in 1980 it was accepted that the Fathers of Chapel (FOCs) should organise and co-ordinate the production job. They drew up rotas (e.g. for shifts and for holidays), placed men on various tasks to cover the work, and were responsible to some extent for discipline and welfare. If a man were ill or incapacitated, an FOC would send him home and arrange cover for him. The FOC allocated overtime in accordance with the requirements specified to him by the Printer (the floor manager). He likewise administered 'cut', by which men take turns to go home early when production allows. The same went for holidays: the chapel organised a list of dates and agreed it with the Printer. If a vacancy occurred in a staff job to which the NGA had rights, the Printer would inform the Imperial (overall) Father of Chapel who would circulate the notice among the men and organise a list of applicants. Disciplinary action from management had to come through the FOC. The chapel itself distributed the pooled piece-work payments at the week's end. In Fleet Street and to some extent in other papers the FOC was really leader of a work team as well as elected representative of the union. When these workplace roles are added to the fact that 'the Society' or 'the House', as the NGA regional office in London is still often called, acts as the sole labour exchange for its craftsmen through its 'call office', it can be seen why the organisation of printing labour in Fleet Street has sometimes been mistaken for labour subcontracting. 'Psychologically, if not legally, he works "The Lump" . . .'[19]

The NGA chapels do have a considerable presence in the management of production. It is an ambiguous presence. The manager may say: an FOC has the power to disrupt the shop floor, or alternatively to motivate the men to good work, but he does not *manage*. An FOC on the other hand may say: there are two people involved in production management, the Printer and the FOC. The Printer is there to ensure the job keeps going through. But in reality he could go home, because the men would see it done. Between these two positions there is tension. The precise articulation of control is continually contested by both sides in every news chapel.

The labourer may experience labour, according to the fine detail of its processes, as sensuous and satisfying, as tolerable or as torture. Hot-metal composing work had many of the qualities (most of them won or maintained by the men in struggle over the years) that make work enjoyable. The lino operator had the satisfaction of seeing, handling and measuring his output, an interactive and knowledgeable relationship with the machine, and little breaks in the monotony of setting – the adjustment of the line, the pressing of the lever, attending to the disser or lifting each new take. The stone hand had a subtle combination of manual and intellectual, physical and aesthetic elements in his tasks, a variety of work and a sense of project and completion. Above all, both had a sense of *knowing best* : not only knowing better than an outsider, but better even than their supervisors and managers, how to obtain (or impede) productivity in their own part of the process of producing a newspaper. These are the components of craft control in work. The compositor is typical of the craftsman whose 'work is his chief form of self-expression, the mainspring of his entire way of life', whose leisure time at home 'is not a refuge from his work but an adjunct to it, a time of recreation in the full sense of the word'.[20] They were the lucky (or clever) ones for whom, even in capitalism, a little bit of the human delight in making useful things still obtained.

Having said this, however, it is important to remember that waged work is waged work. It is not essentially performed according to the criterion of the enjoyment of the producer but the profit of the owner. The compositor never quite forgets that work for an employer is exploitative, that it steals his time and saps his strength. There is a constant tension between these two lived realities of work.

The turn of the tide

The experience of the British printing industry in the 1950s was consistent with that of the economy as a whole. The 1950s and early 1960s were a period of unprecedented economic vitality for the advanced capitalist countries of the world. The long boom, in the words of Andrew Glyn and John Harrison, 'saw the most rapid and sustained development of production in human history'.[21] But the British economy, although we 'never had it so good', was not performing as well as its competitors. British firms were failing to behave in the necessary cut-throat competitive way with each other that would assure that they could compete in turn with the thrusting enterprises of Japan and Western Europe. The nation had an adverse balance of payments and was in debt to the world. A fundamental problem was the failure of industrialists (printers among them) to reinvest their new high profits in productive new factories and machinery. The working class, supported by the relatively full employment which continued until the mid-sixties, had the strength to resist the introduction of new technologies on capital's terms. British employers responded to an acute labour shortage by paying higher and higher wages. The result: during the fifties and early sixties, wages rose more rapidly than productivity and profits went down. (The share of company output appropriated as pre-tax profit declined from about 25 per cent in the mid-fifties to around 20 per cent in the mid-sixties.)[22]

A Labour government, returned in 1964 after 13 years of Conservative rule, announced a new approach to curing the unprofitability of British industry. Harold Wilson invited the co-operation of the trade unions in a three-way partnership with employers and with a government committed to economic planning. The aim was to make British capital competitive in world markets. The government would assist rationalisation and concentration of capital, constructing large powerful corporations capable of competing on equal terms with the growing multinationals. 'Dead wood' was to be cleared from the boardrooms of industry. Technological innovation was to be hurried forward.

One of the Wilson government's measures was a planned incomes policy. A Prices and Incomes Board (PIB) was set up with the responsibility of achieving it. It was not long before the PIB threw an uncomfortable spotlight on printing craftsmen's earnings, particularly in the newspaper industry.[23] The Board asked, 'How has it come about that in this industry output per man hour has risen only slowly, earnings have risen rapidly, profits have fallen and prices have risen?' The health of the industry was causing official concern. There was worry over the decline of Fleet Street and closures of national titles.[24] The provincial press was proving 'economically vulnerable'. The printing industry generally was finding itself cheated of work by the growth of do-it-yourself techniques such as photocopying and small offset, provoked by its own high costs. A study by the British Federation of Master Printers asserted that 'manpower has been receiving more than its fair share from the industry'.[25] Now the print employers were able to say 'we told you so' as the government pointed an official finger at the unions, blaming them for 'overmanning', for artificially holding down output and for other restrictive ploys of the printing chapels. A Joint Committee on Manpower was set up, to look not only at the labour shortage artificially maintained by the craft unions, but also at ways of increasing productivity, including the introduction of new methods of printing.

The tide was beginning to turn against the print craftsmen. The outcome of the 1959 strike had been a compromise which tipped the balance against the unions. Fewer than half of their demands were granted and agreements were signed that markedly reduced craft control over the labour supply and the labour process. The agreement had been seen by the employers as clearing the way to the technological revolution that was looming on the American horizon, a revolution both exciting and alarming capitalists with its possibilities. The British Federation of Master Printers had written to its members after the settlement that the new productivity clauses 'may well prove the most important long-term outcome. Of outstanding significance are those covering the employment of craft skill to maximum effect, extra shift working, work study and incentive methods and the adoption of new processes and machines.'[26]

Once the new equipment was in, the old plant scrapped and, along with it, the old skills relegated to the dustheap, then technology itself would subdue and disorganise the men. 'The rate of progress of the industry for many years ahead is going to depend on the way in which employers and employees alike get down to the problem of making these new clauses work.'[27]

The aim of the employers throughout the fifties had been to achieve a national wage structure, with agreed and constant relationships governing the pay of all classes of work, together with a bilateral (united employers v. united unions) system of negotiating the regular wage round. Bitterly resisted by the unions at the beginning of the decade, this had become received common sense within the atmosphere created by the Wilson government in the mid-sixties.

Behind the innocent phrases 'a wage structure' and 'joint negotiation' lies concealed the whole question of division and difference in the working class. It was a contradictory issue, in the sense that both sides in the struggle had something to gain and something to lose by either outcome. 'Joint negotiation' meant that the unions should be loyally collective within the Printing and Kindred Trades Federation, negotiating with the employers as a body. A 'wage structure' implied that the differentials between occupations, regions, specialised skills and skill levels would be fixed permanently in a hierarchy of percentage difference. For the employers such a package offered an end to leap-frogging wage claims and stoppages caused by inter-union differential disputes. For labour it could mean greater solidarity than ever before, less risk of sell-outs by one group or another. For this very reason however, it might turn out to be against the interest of the employers by forging a more united labour force. But again, labour would be required to abandon the hit-and-run tactics it had employed so deftly, and those individually strong groups that had so often made the running in the wages-and-hours movements would have to sacrifice their sectional autonomy. On the other hand, those disadvantaged in the structure would forfeit the chance of regaining position.

The current of the sixties, however, was flowing strongly against craft unionism. The slowing of the boom reduced the power of 'wage leaders' to pull the rest of the working class along behind them. A different logic was beginning to emerge, and craft unions were obliged to move towards the mainstream of the labour movement. 'We are being forcibly thrust by the course of national economic and political developments into the main arena of trade union activity to a degree that has never happened before – and thus, if you like, into the main course of national and economic developments themselves,' wrote a leading representative of the compositors.[28]

This changing philosophy was reflected in a series of amalgamations among the craft unions. In 1955 the London Society of Compositors (LSC) had merged with the machine managers' union to form the London Typographical Society (LTS). In 1964 the LTS subordinated its differences with the provincial Typographical Association to create the National Graphical Association (NGA). And before long the NGA would be joined by the press telegraphists, the stereotypers, the litho printers and the Association of Correctors of the Press. Only the gulf separating the craftsmen from the rest remained unbridged – as it does today.

When I talked to them in 1980, the men were aware of many changes that had filtered through to the labour process since the 1950s. Over their working lifetimes, all had experienced a reduction in the amount of skill demanded in the performance of their work. They had felt a decline, too, in their control of the labour process and their job satisfaction. The machine had replaced hand typesetting in many more firms, industrialising as it came. Colour work, which demanded fine registration, had left their own, the letterpress, side of the industry and gone to litho. 'Quite honestly, if I had to go back to the letterpress general trade as it was and they were to say: look, we have a four-colour job coming up, say a travel agent's brochure, and we want you to go and whack those pages out, do a four-colour imposition, I would practically faint, I think. Yet I used to know how to do that.' Some jobs had been filched by other unions. NATSOPA, for instance, now had the right to clean and maintain the linotype machines. Newspaper work of course is characterised by being relatively simple, single-colour work in regular columns of solid setting. Being in the news trade, as opposed to the general trade, was a step downhill in skill, even if it was a step up in pay and status. 'Your craftsmanship is not necessarily compositor's work any more, if you understand. It is a production-line system. It is a harsher form of print.'

Despite chapel resistance, one comp had experienced an increasing division of labour imposed by management. As he put it in his own words the textbook instance of capitalist development was brought to life: 'I found they were chopping up the different duties. Like the Ludlow, casting the big type for headlines. We all used to take a turn at that. Then they began to say, you can't have a chap chopping and changing. The jobs were being put in compartments. It may, I don't know, from the boss's point of view be more economical, more financially rewarding. But I felt that we were getting, shall we say, in a small corridor doing one job.'

Because papers have to be produced fast and there is more and more competition between titles, especially in Fleet Street, there is a tendency to slap-dash work. 'You whack it in and if it doesn't fit in the chase you just spike the metal to tighten it up.' 'If it doesn't fit, hit it.' Basically, the men believe that the management in the news trade has no interest in standards any more, and standards are the craftsman's stock in trade. 'Thirty, forty years ago, when I just started,' a comp told me, 'you would look for a better product than you are getting now. It's not just in print, it's everywhere. Take motor cars, any big industry. There is pressure on management, pressure from the shareholders to show profits and to get the end result at the right price. Selling the product – that's what it is all about now.'

So the men were in a rather undecided frame of mind about hot-metal skill. On the one hand they very much wished to assert that their recently lost hot-metal work had been extremely skilled. On the other hand, they realised well enough that the occupation had already been degraded in various ways so that it fell short of the ideal compositor's skill as they had known it in the 1950s or before, 'when you could use your initiative. Vision, if you like'. So, yes, they were skilled. But perhaps there was an element of bluff in it now? Maybe there always had been? Many felt the apprenticeship period had been unnecessarily long-drawn out, mere time-serving. There was also a degree of deliberate mystification. 'Working with lead, we had our jargon. It was all hidden in mystery, all the point system of measurement we had. We'd use words like 'nomprul' and 'bujwa' [non-pareil and bourgeois, terms specifying sizes of type] and expressions like 'mutton' and 'nut' [standing for 'em' and 'en'] and we enjoyed being able to segregate ourselves like that. It was a code. I think that is how the theory of a really highly-skilled craft arose, because we made sure that people outside couldn't get hold of the fundamentals.'

All this gave a certain uneasiness to hot-metal compositors, especially the very high earners of Fleet Street, the more socially-aware of whom were embarrassed by their astronomical pay. Even before there was any question of new technology transforming the job, some compositors were beginning to wonder if their craft was being hollowed out from within, their skilled status taking on an element of bluff. Capital has more ways than one of breaking the craftsman's grip on the labour process and some were already being explored in the 1950s and 1960s. But the labour costs of printing would never be substantially reduced by whittling away at the margins of control in work. Capital needed a weapon that would strike at the heart of craft power.

3. Technological innovation

The weapon with which to smash the compositors, the new technology the British print employers needed, was being forged at that time in the USA. It would transform the preparation of type for printing, sweeping away all the metal technology on which the compositors had secured their craft control.

What is sometimes called 'cold composition' to contrast it with the hot-metal technology it replaced, was an innovation with two distinct phases. The first was the shift from molten metal to a photographic principle, which was well under way in the USA by 1955. The second was a further conversion to a totally electronic process. Where phase one was sometimes *aided* by the computer, phase two, following the first some 15 years later, was *governed* by the computer.[1]

Phase-one photocomposition had a forerunner. The first sign of things to come was the separation of keyboarding from casting, processes that had been combined in the linotype. In 'teletypesetting,' or TTS as it was known, a keyboard operator, usually working on a QWERTY keyboard, produced a punched paper tape. (Q–W–E–R–T–Y are the characters on the top row left-hand side of a conventional typewriter. The linotype's 90-key board had an entirely different lay.) The operator at this stage still made and tapped-in his own line-end decisions concerning hyphenation and justification (H-and-J). The tape could of course be used to drive a linecaster at any distance from the keyboard – in the next room or in another town, immediately or next year. One caster could be kept in operation to maximum capacity, fed by several keyboards. Tapes could be stored in a fraction of the space of hot-metal formes.

A further development of teletypesetting was the use of a small computer to H-and-J. In place of the operator's experience and judgment the computer was provided with a set of rules and a small 'dictionary' of those words for which the rules were inadequate. This left the operator 'free' to set matter in a continuous stream of words without regard to line-ends. The 'idiot' tape as it was called, was fed into the computer which emitted a new tape with H-and-J instructions for the linecaster. TTS was a very productive new division of labour but it was not yet photocomposition. The photo principle arrived when the tape-driven hot-metal linecaster was replaced by a tape-driven photosetter, using a film negative of the alphabet and a flash of light to produce not a slug of lead but a piece of bromide paper carrying black letters.

The method by which type is prepared for printing has to dovetail with the technology used for printing itself. As hot-metal technology is the partner of letterpress, so photocomposition is the ideal complement to offset lithography. Interest in photocomposition remained muted, therefore, until two other developments occurred. First, the shift to offset litho gathered momentum. Second, new techniques were invented that made photocomposition directly applicable to letterpress. This latter invention enabled letterpress printers to take everything that photocomposition offered without the cost of scrapping their existing printing presses.

The effect of this first phase of photocomposition on the compositor was to increase or reinforce the division of labour, to turn existing linotype keyboard operators into typists on 'idiot' boards and existing stone hands into paste-up hands, slicing and sticking the bromide print onto card lay-outs, according to editorial instructions. It also opened up the possibility of using semi-skilled labour in both those tasks where (as in many American newspapers) the employers had the whip hand.[2] We shall see the human implications of these changes in the labour process in Chapter 4.

If in phase one of cold composition the computer was edging its way in as an aid to typesetting, in phase two it became the ruling principle in an electronic composing system. Indeed it is more accurate to see phase two as an electronic information system, in which type for printing has become just one of a number of possible end products among other business uses. Phase-two technology began to enter the US printing industry in about 1970. It threatened to bypass the compositor entirely.

We should consider briefly both ends of the new process, the front end where type is put in and the back end where type is emitted. So far as *output* is concerned, phase two saw, first, advances in the science of light that introduced timed flashes precise to a millionth of a second and, ultimately, the laser. Second, systems of variable lenses were developed that increased the range of type sizes available and the speed with which they could be selected. Photosetters, however, were physically constrained to a limited number of type faces and sizes and mechanical movement put a limit on speed. Manufacturers of equipment moved on, therefore, to a digital system, in which the computer carries a programme that enables it to generate characters on demand in a great many different type faces: roman, italic or bold; in a wide range of sizes; and to produce them as images on a cathode ray tube or by laser at speeds, now, of thousands per second.

As to *input*, the most successful front-end system became the video display terminal. The VDT eliminates typed paper manuscript from the newspaper office and enables the complete integration of all aspects of production. Journalists, editors, accountants, advertising personnel, administrators and proof-readers, all have keyboards with associated video screens, all on-line to the computer. Any one of these may be used to tap in material, which may be corrected simply by overtyping errors as they are noticed. Stories may be called up and edited, classified adverts added to the computer's store, invoiced, recalled, updated or 'killed' as required. Work can be supervised and measured. Material which is required in type form for newspaper production is simply channelled to the digital typesetter by the press of a command button. Other matter may, for instance, emerge as a computer print-out for office use. In many modern business offices, typewriters are being replaced by electronic word processors which also use the QWERTY-lay board and the video screen. Many of these will soon be capable of interfacing with composition systems. Any modern office will be able to produce its own printed matter as readily as it produces a single letter.

It will be evident that the input methods described above are designed for 'direct entry'. That is to say, those who originate material for the newspaper, whether writers, editors, or typists, key in material which *bypasses* the composing room and goes straight to the computer and thence to output. The typesetting side of the photocompositor's job is thus immediately obliterated. So, potentially, is the page make-up side. More complex screens, known as graphics display terminals (GDT) or page-view terminals (PVT) enable the display of varied typesizes and faces and have a facility for shifting blocks of text around, inserting ruled lines and boxes, wrapping text around the shape of illustrations, enlarging or diminishing size. In this way display adverts and even whole newspaper pages can be made-up on screen and emitted as a whole sheet from the typesetter, so eliminating paste-up work. Text-and-tone systems are on the point of emerging from the experimental stage which will enable photographs and drawings, too, to be produced digitally and integrated with text on the screen.

We have looked ahead here only so far as we need to foresee the elimination of the *composing room's* craft personnel. Other technological innovations on the way will make irrelevant the photographic department, which at present reproduces the composed image and transfers it to the printing plate. The printing plate will be made by laser direct from the information on the page-size video screen. Even the massive rotary presses which churn out the finished print may one day be redundant as ink-jet printing enables a highspeed printed image to be produced, one copy at a time, direct from the computer memory without the use of a printing surface at all. Beyond that again, newspapers themselves may be made irrelevant in the not-too-far distant future by fully electronic media. We have seen the beginnings of teletext information services in Prestel, Ceefax and Oracle. Cable techniques will greatly increase the channels available to TV and satellites will open up media sources from all around the world. If cold composition is leading to a revolution in printing, electronics will make printing itself increasingly marginal to our information needs.

Cold composition crosses the Atlantic

To come back to earth and to the shattered composing room – the economic advantages offered to the newspaper employer by cold composition are dramatic. Take the example of the newspaper group Media General of Richmond, Virginia. In 1971, as hot-metal publishers, they had 185 skilled printers working in their composing room, each earning about $200 a week. By 1975, after the introduction of cold composition, the number of comps had fallen to 140. They were in fact no longer compositors at all, but an entirely different group of people, originally unskilled and now quickly trained up for the new job, earning only $125 a week. The cost of the equipment was no more than $900,000 while the savings from the changeover had been $800,000 in the first year alone and by 1975 were running at $1.24 million a year. Note that the gains were made *both* by reducing the number of people involved and by changing the nature of those workers: many more were women and many more were black. As the production director of the American Newspaper Publishers Association (pulling fewer punches than his British equivalents) said bluntly: 'Technology is useless without eliminating people.'[3] And time is working against the craftsmen. As, reasonably, they refuse to see their standard of living reduced, craftsmen remain costly. Meanwhile the cost of electronic equipment comes down every year.

The story of Media General was repeated all over America. The introduction of such systems had converted four-fifths of US daily newspapers by 1974 and weeklies moved even faster. Most newspapers going over to cold composition achieved a reduction of between one-half and two-thirds in the number of compositors. Between 1965 and 1978, the International Typographical Union (representing compositors) lost more than 34,000 members, one-third of its membership. They estimated that 80 per cent of this loss was due to cold composition.[4] By 1975 hot-metal machines were not being made in the USA any more. They were worth only their scrap value.[5] Many hot-metal comps felt themselves to be scrapped as well.

Meanwhile, the British printing industry lagged some way behind that of the USA. Far from embarking on the electronic revolution, the British printing industry in the 1950s was still only part-way through the *mechanical* revolution begun in the nineteenth century. There were many hand compositors still at work. Linotype and Intertype for instance were continuing to advertise their machines, barely different from the originals of the 1890s, as enabling the employer to 'free at least five hand compositors in every six'. Even in 1975, long after the USA had discontinued production of hot-metal linecasters, Britain remained 'the centre of world manufacture and trade in these obsolescent items'.[6]

In 1950 stories began to creep into the trade press about early models of photosetter – the Westover Rotofoto, the Fairchild Lithotype, the Intertype Fotosetter. Quick off the mark, the London Society of Compositors pressed the London Master Printers Association to sign an agreement giving them the right to the new keyboards. As in in the 1890s, the London craftsmen were determined to be the unchallenged contenders for the new process when it eventually arrived. However, despite scary rumours of the 'comp-less newspaper' in America, photocomposition remained long in the trial and error stage in Britain. In 1959, for instance, some Intertype Fotosetters on which London Typographical Society members 'had gained useful experience', had been installed and then removed from McCorquodales Ltd. It would be some years yet before even phase-one photocomposition began to affect the work and life chances of the average British compositor. Few gave serious thought to the possibility of displacement by women. Even Westover, one of the manufacturers, went on record as saying 'some American advertisements suggest that the competition will be between these male stalwarts and glamorous lady stenographers, but I am inclined to dismiss this as a case of wishful thinking'.[7]

The mid-sixties was a turning point. In 1965 the first book to be set in Europe by computerised photocomposition was announced. The firm that produced it, Rocappi Ltd., had been set up by two major British printers with US participation for purposes of 'research on computer applications in the printing and publishing industries'. The book in question was the proceedings of the Institute of Printing's Conference on Computerised Typesetting. In 1965 a new daily paper using computerised photocomposition – *The Reading Evening Post* – also opened. The NGA offered its first short courses for members in the new techniques. There were two hundred applicants for the 16 places. The pioneers were clearing a path that the majority of provincial newspapers and most of the general printing trade would follow in the seventies and eighties.

The four companies of which I made particular studies and in whose chapels I interviewed compositors for this research together provide an informative picture of this process of technological change in the British newspaper industry. Between them they represent many of the differences between newspaper firms. Three belong to conglomerates that are among the largest operating in Britain, and one is still a small family firm. Two began at the beginning with phase-one technology, and two went directly for more advanced systems. One made the break as early as 1968, and the other three not until a decade later. Two are Fleet Street firms producing national dailies and Sunday papers. Two, though situated near London and part of the London printing tradition, are more correctly seen as 'regionals', producing newspapers for local rather than national markets.

I will deal separately with the London 'regionals' and the Fleet Street 'nationals', recounting briefly the circumstances in which each of the companies made the technological leap, the reasons they appeared to have for taking the decision when they did, the choices they made and the resistance or co-operation which they met from their chapels.

Developments in the 'regional' press

The regional press comprises a (declining) number of morning and evening daily papers and more than a thousand local weeklies. It employs about ten thousand compositors. A prevalence of mergers and takeovers, already in progress soon after the second world war, continued unchecked in the fifties and sixties, in spite of frequent referrals to the Monopolies Commission.[8] Competing titles were persistently eliminated and Britain was parcelled out among large concerns with monopolies in their town or region. Of the 460 'independent' newspaper companies that existed in 1961, only 187 remained by 1974. Britain lost one-third of its regional newspaper titles between 1921 and 1976.[9] This concentration and slimming process helped the regionals to survive the competition from TV news and commercial radio and television advertising, and resulted in a moderately profitable industry by the mid-seventies.[10]

The newspaper owners of the provinces, however, felt themselves painfully handicapped by their production workers. Print labour was indeed relatively costly – wages were still above the manufacturing average. It was also, in the eyes of its employers, considerably too numerous: 'over-manning' was the frequent cry. Besides, competition and rivalry between crafts and between the skilled and unskilled, led to demarcation disputes that frequently disrupted production.

In the sixties the owners of the regional press flexed their muscles with the introduction of web offset litho. It was a conscious attack on labour problems and was accompanied by bitter industrial strife. The Newspaper Society, giving evidence to the Cameron Committee (1967), stated unequivocally that the only saving to be had from introducing web offset litho was that of labour. Without a reduction in manning it would not be worthwhile to pursue the innovation – web offset used more, not less, paper.[11]

By the seventies the industry was ready to push on with cold composition, offset litho's logical counterpart. By 1976 nearly half, and by 1980 two-thirds of firms had 'gone cold'.[12] Many systems are still primitive however and only one firm, the *Nottingham Evening Post* owned by T. Bailey Forman, has been prepared to move to direct entry, operating a 'black' house. The firm's managing director, however, does not expect to be alone for long and is urging on his colleagues and competitors a similar defiance of the unions.[13]

My first case study is of *King and Hutchings Ltd.*, at Uxbridge, now a division of *The Westminster Press Ltd.* In nineteenth century Uxbridge, two general printers, John King and Walter Hutchings, both extended their activities independently into the field of newspapers. In 1919 they amalgamated their businesses as King and Hutchings Ltd. Both families remained active in the firm during the first half of the twentieth century. Many of the older employees today can still remember the time when the two elderly patriarchs governed the family firm.

The path traced by King and Hutchings since the second world war reflects the process of consolidation of regional newspaper capital over the same period. From being a local family enterprise it has become a small component in a conglomerate operating on a global scale. In 1955 the company was taken over by Westminster Press Provinical Newspapers Ltd., a company incorporating provincial paper titles stretching from the northern counties to the south coast of England. In 1967 S. Pearson and Son Ltd., owners of Westminster, gathered all their publishing interests, including King and Hutchings, into one company, S. Pearson Publishers Ltd. In the following year, Westminster Press Ltd., 'for administrative and taxation purposes', took into corporate hands the operation of its wholly-owned subsidiaries and in this way King and Hutchings moved from semi-autonomy to the status of a division within the larger firm. Westminster Press, apart from its 25 newspaper businesses, owns a chain of two hundred retail newsagents' shops and has interests in general printing. It was one of the national chains that caused official worries on account of its propensity to monopoly, as it doubled its share of total weekly newspaper circulation between 1961 and 1974.[14] The parent firm, S. Pearson and Son Ltd., is 'one of the largest, most diversified and international companies in the world, having interests in banking, engineering, pottery, oil and property'. It also owns Chessington Zoo and Madame Tussauds. In 1977 it was the third biggest of the conglomerates owning British publishing houses, with a turnover of £290 million per annum. So King and Hutchings, though it is a big fish in the employment market of Uxbridge, is in reality no more than a minnow within the conglomerate that owns it.

King and Hutchings publish 11 different weekly newspapers, each of which is produced in several localised editions, and some twice weekly. They also produced (until recently) a daily evening paper and had branched out into 'free sheets'. (Local newspapers are essentially advertising media, obtaining about 80 per cent of their earning from adverts. 'Free sheets' carry this trend to a logical conclusion. They are distributed free to readers and rely wholly on advertisers to finance them.) The firm serves the area between Shepherds Bush in West London and High Wycombe. At the time of my interviews in 1980 it employed about seven hundred, 250 in production. There was a composing chapel of 115 men.

In the era of hot-metal composition and letterpress printing King and Hutchings had about ninety composing staff, working night and day shifts, producing about two hundred pages or more each week. The typesetting was done on 23 Linotype and Intertype machines. Productivity was high and hot metal might have held on there for many years more, but for a crisis in 1968 which precipitated the firm into technological change some way ahead of the field. A fire completely gutted the premises and destroyed all the hot-metal machinery. Re-equipping in the aftermath Westminster Press converted the firm to offset litho and photocomposition. They went for the current phase-one system of 'idiot' keyboards and a photosetter which produced bromides of column-width for page make-up with scissors and paste.[15] They did however introduce one or two video screens for production of display advertisements.

The rather fatherly mode of management that had survived the takeover by Westminster Press, combined with a Dunkirk spirit of loyalty produced among the men by the fire, enabled the firm to introduce the new technology for both composing and printing without even the negotiation of a new house agreement with the union. After the fire, however, the old managing director retired. Westminster Press replaced him with a relatively young man who embodied a new dynamic marketing-oriented style and an uncompromising line in industrial relations. The old paternalist relations of production had outlived their day and were quickly buried.

Throughout the seventies Westminster Press's profit ratios were healthy. It survived the 1975–76 depression with only a dip in the graph of its growth. It was among the most successful of the altogether buoyant regional newspaper industry. As turnover and profits visibly increased at Uxbridge the men began to feel that the gains from new technology were all going one way. The NGA chapel saw that photocomposition had been slipped in by the management under cover of the crisis before anyone on the union side really understood its full implications or had had time to develop a set of conditions for its acceptance. The NGA head office had been of little help, since photocomposition was new everywhere then and there was as yet no national photocomposition agreement such as later established terms for its acceptance and ensured each man a minimum of £11 per week increase in wages on conversion.

A period of conflict and disruption followed. It was damped down only in 1979 by the appointment of a new, more conciliatory managing director, which coincided with the election of a moderate FOC. Between them they negotiated a new house agreement which gave the men a considerably shorter working week for the same pay. It gained for the firm the abolition of overtime (the source of much aggravation in the past) and guaranteed productivity by a group-bonus scheme tied to output.

More importantly, however, this agreement prepared the ground for the introduction of phase two of composing technology. In 1980–81, the recession notwithstanding, the firm scrapped its phase-one equipment, spending half a million pounds on an Itek system which involved more powerful computers and visual display units (VDUs) and advanced graphics terminals and setters.[16] This investment put them among the most technologically advanced newspapers in the country. There were no threats of redundancy at the time: the firm was banking, the management told the chapel, on increased demand for newspaper advertising and growing output. However, in 1982 the FOC at King and Hutchings brought the story up to date by reporting as follows. The company, hit by contracting demand for advertising, had stopped production of its evening newspaper. It was also meeting with increased competition in the free-sheet field. Overcapacity in the modernised composing area resulted in demands for 33 redundancies and a £10-per-week wage cut for those compositors remaining (on the grounds that they were no longer entitled to the supplement customarily paid for production of an evening newspaper). It has not escaped the chapel's attention that the Itek system has given the firm the capability of going to direct entry using journalists and tele-ad women typists, who, in King and Hutchings, are only semi-unionised.

In contrast to King and Hutchings, *Croydon Advertiser Ltd.*, founded in the nineteenth century, remains a family concern even today. Among the many takeovers and mergers in the regional press it has maintained a surprising independence. In 1980, the grandson of the founder was still the president of the company and his son the active chairman. In the fifties the company dropped its general printing interests and concentrated on its chain of newspapers alone, pushing total pagination up from eight pages a week in 1950 to a current maximum of 185 per week. The 11 titles have local markets in Sutton, Beckenham, Bromley and Croydon, an area immediately south of London. In 1980, the firm employed approximately four hundred people, two hundred of them in production, of whom 84 were composing personnel or proofreaders.

The company's personnel management style, as reported to me, was relaxed and still somewhat paternal in nature. There was a deliberate policy of keeping a low profile on the industrial relations front, both unions and management avoiding entrenched positions. The firm prided itself on salaries and employment conditions 'as good as anything to be found in London outside Fleet Street'.

The first step in technological evolution at Croydon Advertiser was the introduction in 1969 of a teletypesetting (TTS) unit in the composing room. The unit was never very significant in production terms, but it appears to have served the purpose of preparing people's minds for greater changes to come. The keyboards on this TTS unit, it is worth noting here, employed the linotype 90-key lay, with which the men were familiar.

A decision to go cold was announced in 1977, following sporadic discussions between management and chapel over two or three years. It was the first newspaper group falling under the NGA London region jurisdiction to make the break. (King and Hutchings is technically within the Chiltern and Thames Valley region.) They did however benefit from the experience earlier in the seventies of some regional newspapers outside London, notably the Portsmouth and Sunderland group. The lesson they learned from other firms' mistakes, the management reported, was 'not to forget that it is about people'.

The reasons for the changeover were ostensibly the obsolescence of hot-metal equipment and difficulty in getting spare parts, growth of demand for newspaper pages and the need for more capacity. The firm had emerged from the 1975–76 recession still steadily profitable and the firm's family owners seem to have enjoyed the kudos of being among the leaders in their field with photocomposition. The decision also perhaps included an element of social engineering. A representative of management said that it was hoped that the endemic rift and mutual prejudice separating the manual workers in print production and the office workers on the editorial and advertising side would be smoothed away by the new 'white-coated technician' image of photocomposition. The office workers were not unionised at Croydon Advertiser and had no tradition of activism. Even the production areas had a history of moderation. Behind management's reasoning, then, there seems to have been a hunch that it would be preferable to risk the disruptive moment of a changeover to photocomposition in the short run in order to achieve a long-run gain: the change to office-type occupations might have a desirable side-effect in forestalling a development of union intransigence so characteristic of London, particularly Fleet Street, production workers.

A house agreement for the introduction of photocomposition was negotiated which, together with some national wage rounds, virtually doubled the men's gross earnings between 1978 and 1980. Hours were shortened and re-arranged to produce a three-day week-end. The firm assured itself the necessary productivity incentive by standardising production time per page and then allowing the men to 'cut and go' each day once the edition was achieved.

Despite the late date, the £100,000-worth of equipment introduced by Croydon Advertiser – keyboards producing 'idiot' tape, a modest computer and a simple photosetter – was primitive. As with King and Hutchings' first investment, however, Croydon also bought a handful of more advanced boards with VDUs, in this instance for correction work.[17]

No attempt was made by management to flout traditional craft demarcation lines. No threats were made concerning redundancies or the eventual introduction of direct entry. The transfer therefore appears to have been made with exceptional smoothness and goodwill on both sides, and without loss of production. The gains from increased productivity in 1980 were estimated to amount to around little more than 25 per cent after two years of operation and even that was shared fifty-fifty by the men and the firm. Two years later, however, the recession was beginning to oblige the firm to take a tougher approach to the chapels and the NGA was forced to accept redundancies.

Desperation on Fleet Street

In marked contrast to the regional press, the national newspaper industry was experiencing recurrent financial crisis throughout the sixties and early seventies. Most national dailies had been running at a loss for some years, although some were kept afloat by profitable Sunday titles. The 'qualities' have proved especially vulnerable.[18] The main concern of official opinion was not, as with the regionals, monopolisation. A succession of financial failures and closures provoked such alarm that concern over consolidation was forced into second place. When Rupert Murdoch's News International acquired *The Times* and the *Sunday Times* in 1981 it brought the market share of the three leading corporations (Reed International, Trafalgar House Investments and News International itself) to 69 per cent, compared with 46 per cent in 1948.[19] Yet the stark alternative – closure – deterred resistance.

The poor financial showing of the nationals has been the main focus of concern of a number of enquiries – both government and private. When it comes to parcelling out the blame it has become customary to accord most to the gremlin in the works: the Fleet Street printers.[20] It is in the nature of daily newspapers to tilt power towards production workers. The papers are a uniquely 'perishable' product. If an edition is even a little late, missing the evening news stands or the night trains to the provinces, it is useless. Newspapers, besides, cannot yet be produced overseas by cheap labour.[21] Indeed, the need for proximity to the main railway stations holds the firms to central London and here, of course, the compositors and machine men have constructed their fortress. It is also said that a perverse form of capitalist competition has resulted in boosting wages: Lord Beaverbrook, owner of the *Daily Express*, deliberately allowed wages to soar in order to increase the cost of entry to Fleet Street for aspirant rival press lords.

The establishment has sweated fearfully over the high earnings and restrictive practices of craft labour and the degree of chapel control which has inhibited technological innovation in Fleet

Street. Wages of craftsmen have indeed been very high in the postwar period. Those of compositors were highest of all. And almost one in five of all production employees in Fleet Street is a compositor. Production wages have become specially important to national newspapers due to the trend to increased size of each issue, combined with constant circulation. This has the effect of elevating the already-high 'first-copy' costs of a newspaper, the highest factor in which is wages, which account for more than half the cost.

Aside from their power to negotiate high official rates, the actual take-home pay achieved by chapel pressure within the separate publishing houses was often three times the formal rates. For instance, a practice had developed whereby operators had a right to charge for the advertising lineage, increasingly brought in ready-set from trade typesetters, as though they had set it themselves. The employer thus paid twice for the composition of each advert. It is not surprising perhaps that the Economist Intelligence Unit complained in 1966: 'The general level of pay in the newspaper industry is out of all proportion to the effort expended and skill employed compared with most other industries.'[22]

The compositors may not have developed the notorious money-spinning systems that prevailed in the machine rooms, such as 'ghosting' (sharing the pay of non-existent workers) and 'blow' (rest time during shifts). But nonetheless they had their own time-honoured ways of boosting their earnings. In particular, the London Scale of Prices, by which piece-workers charged line by line for their output, was capable of being manipulated to yield phenomenal earnings. The tinkle of the linotype is sometimes likened to the merry sound of a cash register.

Various official investigations have also, however, criticised management for its share in responsibility for 'the Fleet Street disaster'.[23] They have blamed the press owners for having permitted the chapels to usurp management functions. They deplored lack of employer solidarity and 'a disposition among publishers to yield easily to threats of unofficial action'.[24]

From 1973 disruption increased markedly in the national newspaper industry. With it went loss of copies. This was not, as might be thought, the effect of increased militancy among the workforce so much as among the desperate owners. As the Royal Commission put it, 'a small number of strikes is not necessarily a sign of good industrial relations, or an increase a sign of deterioriation. The latter might, for example, be the consequence of new decisions by managements to resist claims they thought unjustified.'[25] The flurry of interest in computerised photocomposition technology along Fleet Street in the mid-seventies was one sign of the increasing determination of capital in the national newspaper industry to break free of the grip of its gremlin.

Every Fleet Street proprietor dreamed of an American-style, direct entry, computerised photocomposition system. Commitment, however, remained at the level of leafing through the technical literature and the glossy brochures of the suppliers until 1975, when *Mirror Group News* (MGN) took the initiative of seeking a photocomposition agreement with the National Graphical Association. MGN did not, however, seek direct entry by journalists and advertising personnel, but settled for the least aggravational terms: the technologically-redundant 'second keystroke' would continue to be made by craft compositors.

The post-war period had brought changes to the nature of this publishing house as it had to others. Having been the personal plaything of first one, then the other, of the Harmsworth brothers (later Lord Northcliffe and Lord Rothermere), in the 1950s, under Cecil Harmsworth King, the *Daily Mirror* had become the basis of the International Publishing Corporation (IPC), soon to be the largest newspaper and magazine publishing enterprise in the world. IPC was subsequently taken over by the Reed group. Like many other British newspapers the *Mirror* had passed into the hands of a multinational, most of whose profit derived from quite different activities. No longer a family concern, it was a small component of an enormous corporation. Its management style changed in parallel, away from the eccentricity and individualism of the past to a corporate hierarchical system.

The Mirror group's London titles are the *Daily Mirror*, the *Sunday Mirror*, the *Sunday People* and *Sporting Life*. Reasons behind the company's decision to convert them to photocomposition are complex. It seems to have been felt that hot metal as a medium was doomed to disappear within a few years. Manufacturers of the equipment were losing interest in it, spares getting difficult to obtain. MGN's initial plan was to gain substantial savings at the Manchester end of the Mirror operation, where an exact duplicate of the production process of Fleet Street was carried out each night to produce the northern edition. The idea was to do all the composing in London by photocomposition and electronically transmit the pages in 'facsimile' to the north, doing away with the pre-press operation in Manchester. MGN also intended to use the same 'faxing' process to serve its southwestern and Scottish newspapers. Computerised photocomposition promised an integration of their operations, therefore, and the creation of an electronic data base might assist later developments into electronic news.

If the rationalising of production was the pull, the push was labour costs, grossly inflated, MGN believed, by high earnings and over-manning in all departments. The giant *Daily Mirror*, with its mass circulation, was declining in prestige and was weighed down by the *Sunday Mirror* and *Sunday People* which were faced with a diminishing demand. The firm was being pushed by economic circumstances into a corner where it must confront its craftsmen. In composing, the wage levels were indeed staggeringly high. In particular, linotype operators (piece-workers) had manipulated the London Scale of Prices to the point where they were 'virtually writing their own paycheque'. MGN aimed for a reduction of about twenty jobs in Manchester and 97 jobs (one-quarter) in the London composing rooms. In particular, the company intended to buy out the London Scale of Prices once and for all, putting all men on time rates. For this they were prepared to be the first national newspaper group to leave the trenches and go over the top.[26]

In 1975 Percy Roberts, chief executive of MGN, backed by Alex Jarrett, the new chairman of Reed International, took the first public initiative over photocomposition. The company had in fact been investing in research and development on its own cold-composing system and had already converted the company's Glasgow titles before announcing to the London personnel, in a management document, that 'The Future Is Here'. This initial sally was more of a declaration than a negotiation, though the details of the house agreement by which the company bought the right to convert to cold composition subsequently involved hard bargaining between the firm's management and the national officers of the NGA. It was seen by both sides as a negotiation with repercussions far beyond the walls of MGN, setting a precedent for Fleet Street as a whole.

In the outcome, the agreement was costly to both sides. The price paid by the workforce, as summarised by Les Dixon, President of the NGA, was agreement to 'the integration of the five separate titles and five Imperial Chapels, a complete change in shift patterns, a considerable loss of employment opportunities and the buying-out of the London Scale of Prices'.[27] The MGN management was, however, blamed by other Fleet Street owners for having sold out to the unions:

> The notorious London Scale of Prices for lino operators was bought out – for lump sum payments of thousands of pounds in some cases. In return, the NGA were granted exclusive rights to run the computer typesetting equipment: editorial and advertising material would be given them for keyboarding rather than being directly put into the computer. As a result, Roberts was not able to derive anything like the full savings from the conversion. Indeed many of his rivals complained bitterly that his system was so costly and wasteful of staff as to postpone the date when others could afford to try it.[28]

Nonetheless, as this commentator admitted, 'the wall of union resistance had been breached'.

The equipment purchased by MGN was a fairly advanced configuration, involving keyboards (some blind, some with video screens) on-line to the computer, and three electronic setters capable of producing bromides as wide as a whole newspaper page.[29] To make use of this full-page capacity, MGN also acquired some page-view terminals for making-up the newspaper on screen. These, however, were later abandoned. Work began on this new equipment, but the full weight of production was very slow to move across from hot metal to cold composition. Even in 1980 the process was not complete. Meanwhile even those manning gains had not been achieved in practice: on the contrary, there had been an overall increase in composing personnel to cover for loss of production due to retraining and loss of efficiency during the changeover. The chapels of the different titles had still not integrated, nor had the chapel committees and FOCs relinquished any of their traditional rights.

The house agreement embodied a very short working week, officially 32 hours but effectively reduced by 'cut' to about 24 hours on a three-shift, four-day week, together with eight weeks annual leave. The time hands also received a substantial increase in pay. Operators on piece-rates lost in earnings, but were partially compensated by a lump sum payment of several thousand pounds each. As we shall see, however, a most important factor in this agreement was that built into it was the re-integration of work in the new labour process. That is to say, all men, whether they were originally stone hands, piece case or linotype operators, would be retrained for all aspects of the new work. I will have occasion to discuss this feature of the new agreement further in the next chapter.

The trauma undergone by *Times Newspapers Ltd.* (TNL) in the course of its conversion to photocomposition a short while after MGN made national news for many months. Indeed it brought photocomposition perhaps for the first time to the awareness of the ordinary, non-printing public.

The Times has long been considered the voice of the British establishment. Founded in 1785, it gained this pre-eminence very early. It began as the personal property of the Walter family but was bought by Lord Northcliffe (as he later became) in 1908 and was sold to J.J. Astor when Northcliffe died in 1922. In the early 1960s the paper underwent a dramatic change in management policy. Gavin Astor, facing a crisis of stagnating circulation and loss of position to rival quality dailies, changed the style of the paper. It was a shift to a marketing orientation, in line with the current corporate ideology belatedly seeping into Fleet Street. The paper's image was modernised. An advertising campaign was launched, brashly proclaiming what everyone already knew – that 'top people read *The Times*'. In two years circulation did indeed go up by 50 per cent, but since top people like to be exclusive, high-class advertising revenue suffered from the change and losses increased. Astor did a U-turn. Soon after, he let it be known he was looking for a buyer for the title.

In this period a new kind of proprietor was entering Fleet Street – the businessman-owner, who applied normal commercial standards of profitability and was unsympathetic to excessive union demands. Roy Thomson, a successful Canadian businessman, who bought *The Times* from Lord Astor in 1966, was expected to be of this kind. He had already established himself in Britain with interests in Scottish independent television, the second biggest chain of regional papers in the country, a large travel organisation and investments in North Sea oil. He had acquired *The Scotsman* in 1954 and purchased the profitable *Sunday Times* from Lord Kemsley in 1959.

As it turned out, however, when Thomson bid for *The Times*, he acted less as the head of large business corporation than as an old-style, individualist social climber. The paper was not an economic asset for his business so much as a social asset for himself and his family. Through it he, in turn, acquired his seat in the House of Lords. Thomson placated the Monopolies Commission by promising to subsidise the ailing *Times* from his family fortune. This indeed he was required to do, to the tune of £8 million by 1975. By the early seventies the annual losses on *The Times* were in the order of £1½ million in spite of a trebling of advertising revenue.

The second Lord Thomson, after his father's death in 1976, made it clear that the drain on resources by *The Times* now had to stop. A new and tougher management line filtered down from the parent organisation in Canada. The introduction of photocomposition seemed only common sense to North Americans, to whom hot metal now seemed as outdated and laughable as steam railways. In 1976, without consulting the union chapels, TNL purchased new composing equipment, installed it secretly and kept it under wraps in New Printing House Square. In the following year they published a document – to say a 'discussion document' would scarcely be the truth – called 'Opportunity For Success'. It set out clearly the management's intention to obtain a direct entry system of electronic composition. More determined than the Mirror group, or more foolhardy depending on the point of view, TNL were demanding a system in which the *first* keystroke, that of the journalist, editor or advertising typist, would be 'captured' to drive the photosetter. This would, as in the USA, potentially reduce the number of compositors needed quite drastically. The proposals were promptly rejected by the NGA composing chapels at TNL. This surprised no-one, since *The Times* document followed closely the main provisions of a paper, 'Programme for Action', the product of a joint committee of national newspaper owners and unions, which had already been rejected by ballot of the NGA membership.

In 1978, after a series of disputes that cost TNL continual loss of copies, management delivered an ultimatum: the unions must negotiate agreements committing them to continuous, uninterrupted production, with punitive sanctions to deter unofficial strikes. Agreement must be made by 30 November 1978. If the deadline date were to arrive without such agreement, publication of *The Times*, the *Sunday Times* and the three weekly *Supplements* would cease.

This is not the place to detail the harrowing events of the following nine months. They have been ably recounted elsewhere.[30] It is enough to say that during the course of a lock-out that began as retribution for non-compliance over a 'no disruption' agreement, a second major issue gradually became entangled with the first. The ghostly presence of the veiled new technology was making itself felt. The management seemed to have decided to make this struggle an all-or-nothing bid for control, for 'the right to manage', taking on all chapels and all unions at once. The NGA stood firm throughout the dispute against an application of photocomposition which gave them anything less than unique hegemony of the keyboards – though they showed themselves ready to make many other concessions over manning the new technology.

The Text II system of computerised photocomposition purchased by TNL cost £3 million. The firm had studied the American experience and had gone for a 'fully integrated, interactive, accounting/advertising/editorial/production system'. It was an advanced, high technology on-line system which skipped the earlier phases of photocomposition gone through by many other papers.

Even though it was not brought into use until three years after purchase, it was even then as advanced as anything in Britain. The setter used digital techniques to generate its characters. Input was dealt with by visual display terminals grouped round mini-computers providing basic functions, including H-and-J. There were 117 such terminals, each with a detachable keyboard. These were not only installed in a new composing area, but were distributed to the other areas in which, in the best of all possible worlds, the management hoped to use them. From the outset, the system was wired up for direct entry.

The dispute was perhaps the most viciously fought in newspaper history. It involved the men in 11 months on dispute benefit, to which all Fleet Street NGA chapels and many others contributed willingly, for the future of all compositors was felt to depend on the outcome. When at last TNL titles got back into production in late 1979, the agreement turned out in fact to have settled little concerning the handling of new technology. The management were still determined on direct entry in the near future but had been forced to go back to work on the basis of compositors on the keyboards or not at all. All they had obtained was an agreement by the unions to enter 'quadripartite talks' (NGA, NATSOPA, National Union of Journalists and management) on the question of direct entry. Immediately there arose a difference of view as to the date for which such talks were committed.

A score of hot-metal comps did now begin retraining for production. As at MGN, men from all areas of speciality were retrained for integrated working. When I interviewed at TNL they were installed in the new composing area, fully competent, yet condemned to continual repetition of 'dry runs' while the papers were produced in hot metal and talks continued.

The chapels felt they had gained from the changeover to photocomposition in terms of their members' earnings, hours and fringe benefits. The London Scale of Prices was, as at MGN, bought out by lump-sum payments to the operators and piece case hands, and time hands' pay went up substantially. Whereas in MGN those comps remaining in hot metal had continued on separate pay agreements and the operators remained on the piece, at TNL the whole of the composing personnel, whether momentarily working hot or cold, converted to the new pay structure. This had the effect of increasing union solidarity by ironing out rivalries. The firm had been unable, however, even to begin to effect the 50 per cent reduction in manning it had sought. Nor did it succeed in wresting from the chapels anything of their traditional authority. In spite of attempts to reassert management control, the 15 full-time FOCs at TNL relinquished none of their rights or duties on return to work and did not change their practices in any way that they did not themselves wish.

In this long-fought struggle, therefore, the management had won little. They had conceded substantial wage increases, bringing *Times* workers from among the lower-paid in Fleet Street to among the higher. And the overall loss in profit due to 11 months' suspension is calculated variously as being between £30 million and £45 million. Other Fleet Street managements felt the settlement was bad news for them. It had recouped nothing of what had been lost in the *Mirror* agreement a year earlier. It offered a poor prognosis for other managements on the question of getting new composing technology into operation on their terms. In fact, it was 'a bloody menace', as the managing director of the *Daily Mail* put it.[31]

Finally, however, Thomson threw in his hand, putting up TNL for sale. By the time Rupert Murdoch emerged as the purchaser, his threats to close the papers unless manning of the new technology met his terms had a ring of sincerity conferred by the deepening recession. Though he had not achieved direct entry by 1982, he had converted *The Times* and the *Sunday Times* totally to photocomposition and ruthlessly farmed out the production of the *Supplements* to purpose-formed typesetting companies (among whose employees were women).

A stay of execution

In all four of these newspaper companies the owners took a risk in revolutionising their forces of production. It was a risk of at least three kinds. First they did not really understand the technology they were buying. They themselves became dependent on a few specialists within the firm. Manufacturers and suppliers of computerised photocomposition equipment are themselves capitalist firms, competing with each other, using pressure marketing techniques, making exaggerated claims for their products. It was clear that, quite aside from any question of the men's lack of enthusiasm, the firms had encountered many technical difficulties. Two considered taking action against their suppliers and one experienced the liquidation of its supplier soon after the purchase. The second risk was that in the course of negotiating for new technology the firms might incur heavy loss of production due to union disruption. The third was that, even if the craft compositors could be set to work on the equipment, either they would peg output to a low level that suited chapel interests, thus defeating any boost in output, or the recession would eat into newspaper circulation and advertising demand, reducing the expensive additional capacity to a mockery. Besides, it should be added, the new equipment is much more rapidly obsolescent than the old and must be made to pay for itself fast.

Nonetheless, technological innovation for these firms, as for much of British industry, was long overdue from an economic point of view. To replace ageing plant with anything less than the latest technology would have been foolish. Besides, Linotype themselves were phasing out their hot-metal machine in the interests of their own new electronic products. It was clear that new technology had to be taken on board sooner or later, whether for purposes of cutting labour costs while markets were scanty or in preparation for exploiting new possibilities for expansion. The recession was putting a tightening tourniquet on profitability and reducing the owners' room for manoeuvre. Peace could no longer be at any price: the press owners were forced to tackle craft control.

Newspapers are not yet dead. Indeed a degree of growth is predicted.[32] What is informative, however, is to compare the graph of expected output in printing and publishing with that showing employment and output per man. Output climbs steadily, employment declines steadily, and output per man leaps skyward. The message is clear: the manner in which the industry's prosperity will be bought is by shedding labour. The statistics show that the attrition has already begun. Productivity in the industry has risen faster, at 32 per cent, than the national average. This has been due not to investment and to increased output, but to reduction of labour.[33] Between 1973 and 1980, employment in the regional newspaper industry fell by about 2 per cent, and in the nationals by about 7 per cent. In 1979–80 the number of compositors alone fell by over 10 per cent. By mid-1982 NGA unemployment, after decades of labour shortage, was nearly 5 per cent and rising fast. The steep plunge, however, is still to come. It is estimated that by 1987 employment on the regionals will have come down another 15 per cent and on the nationals by around 20 per cent.[34]

A forecast made in 1979 by the Printing Industries Research Association (PIRA) concluded:

> The major opportunity for the printing industry to resolve its problems in the next five to ten years is to dramatically increase involvement in new technologies and achieve high productivity which in turn will lead, if properly managed, to lower unit costs, producing products which are competitive both with new media and other sources of print manufacturing.

It foresaw the rapid introduction of lasers, computers, microprocessors and digitisation techniques converging in what it termed 'informatics'. It made the future for compositors starkly clear:

> The increased use of word processors and their enhanced capability at low cost will lead to input being carried out by people other than the traditional compositor. Input will tend to move away from the printer and towards the originator of the text. Full-page make-up systems will require a range of skills different from the present manual paste-up ones . . . The keyboard will remain the main input device, albeit that it may be increasingly used outside the printing plant and the design will follow the QWERTY pattern . . . In the traditional printing industry there will be a continuous decline in the number of workers required in composition. The skills required will change significantly: in future they will be more related to word and data processing and editorial functions than to the traditional skills of the compositor . . . the implication is the need for data-processing related skills

including systems analysis, design and utilisation, file management and editorial ability.[35]

The government is doing its bit to urge technological change on the printing and indeed on all industries: 'The rate of technological innovation in UK industry will need to increase if its products and manufacturing processes are to match those of our major competitors. This is a necessary condition of our future survival as a trading nation.'[36]

Meanwhile, in the bigger world outside, technological developments continue apace. An international report of 1979 read 'phototypesetters continue to proliferate at an incredible rate. Over 40,000 phototypesetting units are in use worldwide. *About 25,000 were sold in 1978.*'[37] Prices continue to fall year by year.

The men in King and Hutchings, at Croydon, and in TNL and MGN are right to feel that what they have been engaged in can only be a holding operation. The real crisis in relations between capital and craft in the British newspaper industry is only now beginning.

Why new technology?

Just as the events in my four case studies of newspaper firms reflect the circumstances in printing more generally, so the recent history of the printing industry is a reflection of wider processes within the development of capitalism as a whole. Behind computerised photocomposition is a far-reaching new technology, *electronics* – and in particular the *microprocessor*. It is revolutionising both production (by automating some manufacturing processes and creating new ones) and circulation (by greatly increasing efficiency in banking, insurance and other commercial activities). In the same way steam power revolutionised industry in the nineteenth century, and electricity and the internal combustion engine in the early years of our own.

Technology seems to play a key role in the struggle between capital and labour, and consequently in capitalist development. Capitalist economies are subject to cycles of boom and depression.[38] Periods of profitable growth produce full employment and so strengthen the working class. Workers have a choice of jobs, unions can demand high wages and exert a confident sway over the actual process of work. It is, of course, in the interests of capital as a whole to have a wealthy working class to buy its goods and services. But each individual firm, or each nation, if it is to be competitive, needs a poor working class so that its wage bill is lower than that of its competitors. Advanced technology 'saves' on labour and increases a firm's capacity, enabling it to profit by expanding markets. But as more and more capital is drawn into use, production tends to outstrip consumption and the boom to be broken by crisis. The weakest firms go bankrupt. The economy contracts, workers are laid off, unemployment rises and the working class is weakened once more. Now capital again has the power to depress wages and to intensify its authority over the worker. The more efficient units of capital survive, but they do so by abandoning the unprofitable industries and investing in new areas where labour is cheaper (in the third world, for instance, or in country areas) or buying-in new forms of technology that enable the capitalist to bypass costly workers.[39]

Investing in new technology is not risk free, however, as the case of the newspaper industry has shown. To pay the bills for the new equipment any firm needs assured profits. It casts around, seeking new markets, trying to obtain a monopoly situation where it can be sure of manipulating the demand for its goods. But above all, if it is to prevent a deterioration of profit ratios it has to assert control over the labour process, to override the human priorities of the workers by the imperative of productivity. It may or may not succeed. Besides, even if an individual firm manages to win exceptional profits in this way, one technological revolution cannot be a lasting cure for the ills of the system as a whole. As more firms take this course, capital as a whole needs to extract more and more from its workers if it is to prevent a decline in profitability – and is seldom able for long to stave off a downturn in the economy. Crisis is in the very nature of capitalism.

Keynesian economic policies such as those which characterised the Labour government of the mid-sixties, aimed to palliate the economy's feverish peaks and troughs, but the crisis of the seventies proved too strong for the remedy. The monetarist policies of Margaret Thatcher's Conservative government offer an alternative medicine – or rather no medicine at all – allowing the sickness to run its course in the hope of a spontaneous cure and an economy eventually immune to such ills. New technology is central to the current strategy as it was to the old. The government has thrown its full weight behind a scrapping of inefficient firms and outdated machinery, a re-equipping in growth sectors and a purposeful *dis*organisation of the working class, thrown into disarray by high unemployment. In converting to computerised photocomposition, and scrapping craft compositors, printing firms have had all possible encouragement from the state.[40]

Technologies, then, are not chosen by those who purchase them only for their greater efficiency or productiveness, though this is important. They also reflect 'the need of the controlling class to choose technologies that facilitate the exercise of its power'.[41] After all, the worker has, as Andrew Ure put it, celebrating industrial capitalism in the nineteenth century, a 'refractory temper' and is subject to only 'irregular paroxysms of diligence' that fall far short of the application required by the capitalist of his workers if he is to make anything out of their employment.[42] Any worker who is in charge of tools or machinery, an expert in a particular labour process, will eventually learn ways of 'soldiering', of spinning work out. He or she may get to know better than the boss how things can be done. Compositors were as well versed as any in the tricks of ca'canny and they are quickly applying their wits to the new technology. If a Luddite is one who feels certain that new technology is not primarily a gift emanating from human progress but, rather, a weapon that will be used to wipe out the value inherent in his or her knowledge, then Luddites are correct and the compositor is a Luddite. One way of reading the history of capitalist technology is to see it as the 'dequalification' of one generation of workers after another.[43]

We tend to think of technological revolutions as being expressed only in machinery. But they are also revolutions in *management*. It is not only the formal agreement over wages and hours of work that concerns the employer, but how hard and well the employee works. The pace of work, the division of labour, who gives the orders, the quality of the product, safety, all may become subjects of struggle between the employer and the worker.[44] Capital is always busy extending and renewing its command over the labour process through conscious, scientific management, by reinforcing the hierarchical structures of responsibility and authority. Machinery is just a part of this process. A printing employee expressed this unity of machinery and management when he wrote in the *Newspaper Owner* in 1910 that the main cause of discontent was 'machinery and the soullessness thereof':

> By machinery I mean chiefly the 'modern business methods' and the 'organisation' fads with which we are harrassed at every turn . . . Some ingenious person devised the syndicate whose proud boast is that it is non-moral, impersonal, machine-like, automatic; and now we are being machined in every possible way.[45]

Photocomposition and computer technology in printing cannot be seen as standing alone; they are part of a politics of control.

The newspaper industry has frequently been blamed for its weak management. To render it more effective in increasing its markets, cutting costs and subduing its labour force has been a constant harping theme of the state. Every mention of up-dating technology has been yoked with a plea for firmer management.[46] Where managements with a new-broom mentality come up against immovable shop floor organisation as in newspaper chapels, the level at which pressure is most painfully experienced is that of lower level or 'line' management. Graham Cleverley wrote of the bottom level of managers in the national newspaper industry:

> Junior management, thanks to several factors, is itself of no great importance. Partly, it arises from the strength of the unions and their habit . . . of insisting on dealing directly with the top . . . The role of the junior manager is effectively debased to that of an intermediary message-carrier.[47]

The attempt to re-insert these hapless line managers into the practice of top-down control is one of the features of the management reform accompanying new technology in the press. Like Christian gladiators, they have been thrown anew to the FOCs of the shop-floor arena and, if reports from these case-study firms may be believed, they have once again hit the sand.

At Times Newspapers, the management style since the Thomson Organisation took over ownership had already, in the men's view, noticeably changed from that practised at either *The Times* or the *Sunday Times* under previous management. The men said they felt there were more managers and that it had been made more hierarchical, with greater numbers of industrial relations experts, development teams, accountancy and legal experts and other features characteristic of large corporations. The management atmosphere had become one more typical of business and less of publishing. When the compositors of both papers came back to work after the 11-month lock-out they met with a clear attempt to diminish the role of the FOC. The management stopped recognising the FOCs in certain ways, not formally, but *de facto*. In the new agreement as it applied to the composing area the role of the FOCs was not written in, as they might have expected it to be, and as was the case with other chapels. Meanwhile, also, some of the staff men were now retermed 'managers' on both newspapers and it was felt by FOCs that staff were expected by higher management to exert more control over the shop floor than heretofore, and to *manage* production more directly. For instance, FOCs were told that if they had a grievance they were to take it first to the lower levels of line management rather than going direct to a higher level, as had been their practice in the past. For some weeks there ensued a silent struggle over the imposition of a correct and effective hierarchy of control. The already heavy pressure on lower-line management was increased by this pincer movement.

Likewise, at Mirror Group News, the men experienced at the time of changeover to computerised photocomposition an attempt to restructure management and reinsert it more forcefully into the control of production. Management roles were relabelled. The old terms Head Printer and Chief Printer, for instance, (it is said that some confused newcomer in senior management complained, 'they all sound like Red Indians'), were renamed Controllers. The managers' pay was increased as part of the photocomposition agreement. Their rates were formally established according to a set differential above production workers, to symbolise their authority. The FOCs felt clearly that the introduction of new composing technology was part and parcel of an assertion of management rights and powers. But by 1980 the men felt they had defeated this intention:

> The Controller of the new composing area, he and some other line managers got an introductory course on the new technology. But once we moved in it was us who got all the working experience, because the chapel doesn't allow the Controllers to touch the machines. Not in the course of production. So they became wholly reliant on us.
> Management never had control here, really, and they still don't.

An anecdote from King and Hutchings may clinch the point. Above the new paste-up area management had erected a clock face. There are hands that can be moved by the manager to point to the time the next newspaper edition is due to go to press, the compositors' next deadline. This management toy is never used and its wooden hands have become a symbol of chapel power. The men laugh, 'We know better than him when edition time is due.'

However, the computer and its peripherals, the photosetter among them, are perhaps more than any preceding technology visibly about control as well as productivity. Computers and linked systems of telecommunication can enable the far-flung parts of giant multinational firms to operate as one. They can enable managers themselves to be better managed by higher managers. They can enable junior managers better to control production workers and clerical workers. It has become almost impossible, in this phase of technological innovation, to separate the twin weapons of organisation and machinery.

Most of the men I talked to feared that the firms, in the long run, would all get what the owners want out of new technology. They feel that capital has time on its side. The men's lives may be wearing out, but 'they are talking to infinity as far as they are concerned. The system is going now, it can only get more and more effective.'

The above account of economic trends, the business-behaviour of certain newspaper firms and the meaning of technological innovation, has been told only in class terms. It is a comment on the greater sophistication of class analysis than of sex/gender theory that the latter can as yet play no greater role than to be tagged on as a tail-piece. There are a number of points to note, however. First, when we talk of firms, corporations, or an employing class, we are talking about entities in which women play little part. Second, when we speak of managers and of technicians we are also talking, overwhelmingly, about men. More than that, we are talking about institutions in and through which men operate in their interests *as men* as well as in their interests as capitalists or as managers. We do not know yet how to disentangle the two motives or their effects. It is clear that the connection between the patriarchal family and the business firm has waned with the rise of the multinational corporation. Male power, however, is expressed no less cogently through the latter than through the former. When firms scrap old plant and invest in new technology they make calculations concerning the relative value of male and female labour power. The workings of the sex/gender system play a part in determining those relative values and on that system, in turn, capital's actions have an effect. We will see, too, in subsequent chapters, that the relation between men and women is mediated in part through their respective proximity to, and distance from, industrial technologies. First, however, we have to step inside the very masculine world of the newspaper firm and look in closer detail at the impact of technological innovation on its male target: the craft compositor.

4. Cold composition: change in the labour process

New technology involved a rupture in the relations of production within each of the four companies I studied. The rupture was precipitated by the employers' marshalling of their new force of production, and this itself was an expression of external movements in society and economy. But its timing and form were determined by tensions within the firm itself. It was a severing of the old ways of doing things, old ways of relating. As the linotypes and Ludlows, the galleys and steel chases were turfed out and production began again on the new equipment there was struggle over the form the new relations of work would take.

Often a new labour process implies a new labour force. A company sacks one lot of workers and engages others. It may set up manufacturing in the third world, for instance, or accept state aid to relocate in some region where labour is cheaper and more malleable. In the case of London's newspapers, however, because of the combination of union strength and the impossibility of 'exporting' production, capital was obliged to convert its existing craftsmen. This is an unusual situation, then, in which we can see what happens to individuals when they are retrained rather than replaced, and the meaning they make of the changes.

When the men first learned that their firm was to 'go cold' in the near future, most were far-sighted enough to feel profoundly ambivalent. Only those who lacked imagination (and they later came to realise this) were totally resistant or purely enthusiastic. It should be remembered, though, that a number of men left at this point, to compete for the dwindling number of hot-metal jobs elsewhere. Those I met were the ones who had felt it was worth a try at least, or who had reasoned that, given the way the world was going, there was really little choice: 'better now than later'.

The men were given confidence by their chapel strength. There was no likelihood in any of these four firms that men could simply be 'dissed off' by the company. There would perhaps be early voluntary retirement, with redundancy cheques, for some elderly chapel members. But for anyone who wanted to stay, a job of some kind would be there. Of course the way the firm went about the changeover affected the way the men felt. At Croydon Advertiser, where reasonable and courteous discussions between FOC and management had preceded the changeover, the men were less resentful and embittered than at TNL, where the ownership had presented an ultimatum backed by threats. As a whole the men were cool, a little sceptical. Photocomposition was a fact of technological innovation and that in turn is a fact of life: 'you can't stop progress'. Beneath this surface acceptance, however, lay a complex web of stresses – excitement tinged with fear, stimulation and resentment, and anger competing with hope.

The transition to computerised photocomposition in the two 'regional' firms differed from that in the two Fleet Street companies. At Croydon and at King and Hutchings all the men were retrained and the whole production force went cold at one and the same moment. At MGN and TNL, by contrast, the papers transferred from hot to cold a few pages at a time. There was thus a politics of selection: which men would transfer first? At TNL the men were chosen by seniority, with the result that many were elderly. At MGN most chapels pulled names from a hat. In neither case was it necessarily those men who were most enthusiastic about the change who went first, (and thus whom I came to interview). There also remained in these Fleet Street papers a continuing hot-metal composing operation alongside the new, to which the newly trained photocompositors could look back – with scorn or envy as the case might be. There was therefore more scope for regret and annoyance. This arose especially at MGN where piece-work remained the practice for linotype operators. Their earnings, by liberal interpretation of the London Scale of Prices, shot upwards in the years after the *photo*comps had become stuck on the new flat rate. The experience of new technology was also coloured in the nationals by differences in the conditions the men had had in hot metal. Notably these were differences in hours, shift

patterns, pay and other practices in the various title companionships comprising the one firm. Thus to work on *Sporting Life*
had been very much more onerous, skilled and relatively less-well
paid than to work on the *Daily Mirror* or *Sunday Mirror*.

The practical differences between the old hot metal and the new
photocomposition labour processes will by now be familiar from
preceding chapters. Here I want to single out three aspects of the
men's new situation and examine them in the round, so to speak, as
free-standing questions. Each throws some light on the complicated question of 'skill' and 'de-skilling'.

One of these aspects is *text input*. This raises the problems of
discarding one keyboard lay and learning another, the politics of
keyboard design and selection, the question of quality of craftsmanship, and the relationship of man to machine. The second is the
transfer from *metal to paper*, analogous to the shift from factory to
office. It is a problematic in which class and gender relations clearly
interact. The third is *integrated working*. In the two regional
newspaper groups, employing phase-one technology, the men
merely shifted from a hot-metal specialism to a cold-composition
specialism, stone hands normally (though not always) becoming
the new paste-up hands and linotype operators becoming the new
keyboard tappers. In the Fleet Street papers, by contrast, going
straight to phase-two technology, the men, whatever their origin,
were taught about the whole system and took turns in all the
production tasks involved.

Text input: 'a glorified typist'

Of the 50 men I interviewed, 28 had been linotype operators in hot
metal. The current photocomposition tappers were not necessarily
ex-lino operators, but most were. Eleven men were now working
on the new keyboards continuously and 22 were taking turns
intermittently. Twenty-five normally worked on boards with no
screen. Most of these had a 'marching display', in which the last
few characters tapped are shown to the operator in an electronic
window above the keyboard. Of these, 11 were producing punched
paper tape ('idiot' tape, for conversion by the computer) and 14
were tapping direct into a computer memory, in which case they

saw no product at all. The eight *Times* compositors, however, were using video screens for all work. Most of the men tapping on blind boards took occasional stints at more advanced units with screens when inputting advertisements or making corrections. All the machines had the QWERTY, or typewriter-style, lay.

The lay of the linotype keyboard, from which the men had come, differs greatly from QWERTY. Not only does it have 90 keys in contrast to 44, it also, in the case of the more elaborate models, has optional side magazines. Each of these has its own set of keys which enable the production of occasional type in different faces and sizes. The relative positioning of the letters of the alphabet also differs from that of a typewriter. Vowels are clustered together, for instance. The keys are larger and spaced further apart and the touch is very light. The use now of one set of characters, now of another, means that the operator's hands travel more distance than those of a typist. He taps with his elbows out, more actively. 'With the linotype you use a flatter hand, it's far more relaxing. The rake is different, the whole feel of the thing. It has more of a flow to it somehow.' In contrast, the typewriter keyboard seems cramped to ex-lino operators. The men feel it is fiddly. To our eyes, used to seeing women and girls sitting at typewriters, the men in their shirtsleeves, often quite heavily-built men used to more strenuous manual work, do indeed seem out of scale with the new equipment.

Apart from such observable differences between the linotype keyboard and the typewriter keyboard of photocomposition there is the separate problem of *learning a new lay*. Here, those readers who are competent typists on the QWERTY board will understand better what the men experienced than those readers who are not. The operation of a keyboard becomes, after a few years' practice, as natural and unreflective as riding a bicycle or driving a car. The men can talk or sing, even listen to the radio, while still processing words via eyes and fingers onto the board. A similar deftness characterises other phases of hot-metal work such as assembling matter on the stone or hand setting. Such a manual capability is *part* of what the men mean when they talk of skill. It is experienced as very pleasurable.

It is consequently a painful experience for linotype operators to be asked to relinquish it and start anew on another keyboard. It may be that the second time of learning is harder than the first, because the fingers have positively to *un*learn what they know. Besides, there is an emotional aspect. When learning the keyboard the first time, even a moderately capable performance causes pride and satisfaction because it is an improvement. Learning the second keyboard you compare your performance unfavourably with that of which you know yourself capable on the familiar board. It is like stumbling along in a foreign language, knowing that you will never again need or be able to use your own native idiom.

The men had been taught the new keyboard by typing instructors, unconnected with the printing industry. In some cases the teacher was a young woman. 'They weren't ever operators, they didn't understand things', the men said. 'They were *typists*.' 'She gave us tests, which I hated, to be quite honest.' The job of these instructors was to inculcate the correct fingering and the practice of touch-typing. This is to say the typist is required to keep his or her eyes always on the manuscript copy and to operate the keys without looking at the hands. Linotype operators did not touch-type. 'On linotype we had our own way of doing it. I would take in so many words and then turn to the keyboard, watching my hands as I tapped them in. Then, just before I reached the last word I would look up and take in another phrase or two. And I still do that on QWERTY. It isn't touch-typing, not to be honest.' The manner of teaching touch-typing ability is a kind of brainwashing, using earphones. You are taught to forget the meaning of words. 'You learn to tap key for letter, key for letter, like a robot. They try to turn you into an optical character recognition machine.' So the training was felt by the men to be insulting, even frightening. It abused all they felt about cognition and skill, yet their livelihood depended on obedience to the instruction.

Of course some men had learned the QWERTY board before, on the Monotype perhaps, or in the armed forces. They were as adept on the new equipment as on the old. Inevitably, however, because the men had not been really free to choose whether to change to photocomposition (and the employers had no more been free to say which men they wanted retrained first), some of the new operators were the slower or more resistant learners. Many of the men felt afraid of failing. 'I think, God, when will it come? They all say it comes eventually – but to me? I wonder, sometimes.' There were a handful of casualties during the training period in each firm, men who had heart attacks or nervous breakdowns. In a situation where management is not particularly awe-inspiring there is still the opinion of your workmates to goad you. There was tension between competition and mutual assistance: 'Some people will never get it. Never. But we just have to help them along as best we can.'

The outcome of such a change is a sharp drop in individual input-efficiency in the early months following changeover, which is only gradually recouped over a period of years. Some men, even after eight or nine years on the new boards, still felt slower on QWERTY than they had been on lino. At Mirror Group News, where new technology had been in operation for two years, the men's average typing speed, from what I was told, was around thirty words per minute. A good typist is at least twice this fast. Of course there is a good bit of soldiering. 'I'm not at all fast, no,' said one man happily enough. 'Of course we have to keep ourselves in work. Can't get too good, can we?' But some of the ineptness is far from purposeful. Many of the men, once training was over and the instructor out of sight, lapsed to the wrong fingering. One comp said, 'Most of the men are still typing with two fingers. I stood and watched the line of input men only an hour ago while I was waiting for this interview and there must have been six or seven in my view then and only one of them was using the proper fingering.' Many too have abandoned any pretence of touch-typing, which alone can produce the high speeds which the QWERTY board allows.

It is ironic that, given the enormous effectiveness of the electronic system as a whole, though the individual worker is slower at text input than he was previously, the throughput of pages is probably greater from the word go. The workforce *as a whole* has gained in productivity, and the advantage to the employer increases with each year of operation. The men however hate what they see as their own *individual* deterioriation. They become frustrated. 'I get all bottled up inside.' 'You get so wild with yourself.' Some men came fresh to the QWERTY board, having been stone hands. Some of them took to keyboarding, while others felt they had opted out of it during apprenticeship days for reasons that still obtained. The predominant feeling among ex-operators however was clearly one of resentment: at the loss of the stimulus of piece-work payment, at the scrapping of the lino. Since they continued to belong to a craftsman's union and to be paid craftsman's rates, some of the men, reduced to what they saw as fumbling incompetence in a job that thousands of teenage girls could do better, felt fraudulent and ashamed. 'I am going in there, playing at things, it seems to me. Compared with what I used to do. I have once or twice been a bit disillusioned with myself. If somebody came to me and said, what have you done this week for the amount of money you've been paid, I would be the first to admit – fair enough, I quite agree with you, it is abysmal.'

Electronic circuitry is in fact perfectly capable of producing a linotype lay on the new-style board. Linotype Paul have manufactured one. It is even possible (since in the more advanced systems the boards plug in and out of the VDUs at will) for each operator to select his preferred board at the beginning of the shift. However there appears to be a consensus among most manufacturers and most employers, that getting the linotype lay out of use is economically and politically important. It is the only way that the linotype operator, the highest paid of all the craftsmen, can be reduced in status or, better still, by-passed altogether. Even short-run loss of productivity is tolerable if it promises such a long-term gain in control. Some *chapels* too, notably that of Mirror Group News, see an advantage in banning the lino lay once and for all. At MGN the management did in fact purchase a number of the lino-lay boards. But the majority of the chapel and its officers saw the introduction of photocomposition as a chance to achieve at last a healing of the divisions and jealousies between lino operators and other chapel members. All, operators and stone hands alike, would be reduced to the lowest common denominator of competence; novices on the new board. The lino boards were therefore put away in a corner of the room, where they remained an aggravating reminder of what might have been.[1] One operator even considered taking legal action against his union for depriving him of the right to exercise his skill. The question remains however – why QWERTY? The original design of the typewriter board was a compromise between mechanical possibility and fingering efficiency.[2] The new electronic boards, having no moving parts, could have introduced an entirely new and speedier lay. This would have rendered typists (mainly women) and linotype operators (men) equal competitors for the new machines. As it is, it is clear that the continued use of QWERTY has been to enable the integration of office and printing technologies and to enable the use of relatively cheap female typists on both.

Another important difference in the labour processes is the manner in which corrections are handled. Under the linotype system, because each machine had its special characteristics, it was quite common for each man to get his own proofs back for correction. He thus knew how and in what way he was erring and could measure his performance. One might think it would be in the firm's interest as well that work should be cleanly set. The fact is, though, that the corrections can be so quickly and easily made on the correcting screens that the management prefer the men to take a somewhat mindless approach to the initial setting, to scramble it in fast, and leave all the corrections to be done at one time by someone else. If the men's individual standards fall a bit, therefore, management will neither notice nor care. 'The only pride you have is doing a job well, for someone to tell you – you made a good job of that. *And now they are not even looking.*' It is impossible not to sympathise with the men's sense of having lost their product to the system. 'Some people take a crafty look for their own proofs, others have given up bothering.' There is something fundamental about this matter of corrections. It is absolutely contrary to the function of human skill to divorce quality control and correction from the craftsman. It is, however, equally contrary to management imperatives of accumulation and profit, given this technology, to allow the craftsman to take the extra time needed to perfect his work. There were precisely two criteria by which a linotype operator judged himself and acquired his self-respect: the speed and the cleanness of his output. Neither is meaningful without the other. 'The only pride you can get out of keyboarding – apart from being fast – is being thorough with it, so that it comes out quick and clean.' Now most of the men are reduced in speed and none have control over quality. As a result the scope for self-respect in this job is greatly reduced.

Standards of work are felt to be falling. Some men feel they are ploughing a little uphill furrow, trying to maintain the standards to which they are accustomed in the face of indifference all round. 'I get the feeling that I'm not supposed to be concerned with quality any more, but with quantity.' An instance of this is that end-of-line decisions produced by the computer's limited programmes are inferior to those devised by the judgment of an experienced operator. The advantage to management of using the computer, however, outweighs any residual concern with quality. Bad word-breaks are something newspaper publishers (and their readership) can learn to live with. The men feel that quality is now out of their control, in the hands of the computer programmer. 'There is a limit to how much you can change, how much you can put right. You can't help but be sad. There is nothing as such that you can do.'

Other factors enter the equation in which the keyboard operators weigh their present and their past labour process and compare them. In hot metal you have a tangible product. You hear the slug fall onto the galley, it is solid and you can burn your fingers on it. In the electronic system, 'you are not kind of seeing the product as such, it's all kind of invisible to you'. You *feel* less productive (irrationally perhaps) because the product is so ephemeral, either a sliver of punched paper tape you can only with difficulty decipher, or an invisible impression on a magnetic disc in some distant computer room you never visit.

Another factor the men feel is a deterioration in the delicate balance and interplay of hand intelligence and cognition in the job. Electronic composition, as we have seen, provides for hyphenation and justification to be carried out by the computer. As linotype operator the comp knew, remembered and observed a set of rules for splitting words. He had to be ready to decide when to 'turn the line over', how to deal with word breaks, how much white space was tolerable between words. This decision-making influenced his setting from the first character of the line till the last. Apart from engaging his intelligence, this method of setting afforded rhythmic breaks, made a pattern, allowed the operator a 'breather'. By contrast, 'new technology now, it's relentless. It is like one of those endless bands that goes on and on and on . . . and you see nothing of value at the end.' The loss of the line-rest speeds up the setting process, but it makes for a subtle deterioration in the experience of work.

The men also report a striking change in their relationship to the equipment on which they work. The linotype was large, its parts were visible and moved. As we've seen, the men knew the function of each component. They listened for changes in the sounds made by the machine and would respond to them, for instance, by moving round to the back of the machine to unblock the disser. They kept an eye on the supply of lead to the melting pot, the cleanness of the type face, the sharpness of the blade that cut off the slugs. The new electronic keyboards however are small, smooth, encased and unrevealing. 'We used to clean the linotype – the spacebands, all the parts. With this – what's cleaning? A squirt of Pledge on the case and wipe it over.' Most of the men had had a glimpse inside the input unit. They saw an enigma. 'There's nothing moving in the damn thing. It's all chips and solder.' Men brought up in a mechanical era, used to cars as well as to linotype, feel helpless before computer technology. No-one would dare touch the circuitry or offer an opinion if it went wrong. They sit as passively as a woman machinist in a garment factory while the male technician attends to a repair. In such ways the men have moved from an active and interactive relationship to a technology to a passive and subordinated one.

The result of all these changes is of course that people (many, not all) are fed up with the 'battery hen' keyboarding job. People describe themselves as 'brassed off' or 'bored stiff', find it 'extremely tedious' and 'wouldn't mind if [they] never saw a keyboard again'. Even for those who are very proficient on the new boards, 'setting blind, the interest has gone'. But – and let it be said right away – the men also said how much they appreciated the quiet, the cleanliness. 'It was a real clamour. You'd have 15 or 16 linotypes clattering away. People on the stone – bang, bang, bang, with a mallet on the planer. You'd have the press going, the sound of the ventilation system, saws operating. You had to shout to make yourself heard. Now you can talk as quietly as I'm talking to you here. It aids the concentration for doing the job we do.' Though of course there are health hazards to the new keyboarding job – backache, eye strain, headaches – less is known about them than about lead poisoning, burns and cuts. So the men also see the work as less unhealthy.[3] And they voiced these gains in the same breath as they enumerated their losses.

The input practice of newspapers today is an uneasy compromise, a midway stage in technology development. Input of text is still the major bottleneck for employers in the newspaper industry. The word is a stubborn material for an industrial process. It is difficult to capture accurately and quickly. Optical character recognition offers few gains. One day, speech-recognition systems may become commercially viable. In the meantime, each character, each word must be tapped into the computer by someone. The capitalist's ideal is that it should be tapped only once, preferably by someone who is semi-skilled and cheap or by someone who already has to do it once anyway, such as the journalist (making his rough manuscript into the final copy). In the meantime, they must make do with compositors, who have far too much understanding and ability in typography and, many of them, too little ability on the QWERTY board. As modern technology eases the process, removing mechanical elements and actions, so that the machine becomes the merest, barest of interfaces interposed between operator and word, the word-handler comes to feel that he is just a pair of eyes and a pair of hands harnessed to the page. One comp said, 'I feel like a sausage machine, taking words in and spewing them out all day long'.

The increasing use of the computer is said to be making it a necessity for more men, even senior executives and managers, to learn to use the keyboard. There is a considerable difference, though, between two-fingered dabbing at the board which is all that is necessary for such a purpose, and real efficiency at sustained input. Certainly there has not as yet been much upgrading of the popular image of the typewriter. And the compositor must now, for all or part of his working week, settle for being a typist . . . even though he may prefer to call himself a tapper or an operator. One compositor cautiously thought round the experience like this: 'You might find some psychologists would say that men feel they have lost a bit of *manhood* from it or something. Although other people might say that that was going too far.' Everything about the work, the keyboard lay, the styled plastic machine, the closeness of the keys, the smallness of the installation, the posture of the operator and the history of typing, all of these things make him feel that he is doing 'a woman's job'. He feel emasculated. Work that has been done by women, because women are relatively low-paid and low-status, is seen as unprestigious. Because women are seen primarily as domestic creatures, their paid jobs are not seen as real work. The compositor, therefore, in this typing phase of his new labour process, feels reduced in sexual authority as well as in that initiative and control in work that had secured his class standing.

Rex Winsbury, in a recent article in *Print*, the NGA journal, argued that it would be in the interests of the men and of the union to relinquish the keyboard to others: the very argument of the employers. 'I personally do not believe that the NGA, as a skilled group of printing experts, is in the least superfluous. But as keyboarders its members are superfluous.'[4] The distaste for 'typing' would lead many compositors (and perhaps the union too) happily to abandon the board to the women – were it not that the comps on the 'call book' would by far outnumber the 'printing-expert' jobs optimistically designated for them by Winsbury.

From metal to paper: 'lick and stick'

Input apart, photocomposition comprises a cluster of tasks. The job requiring the most application and the most commitment of hours, with the exception of input, is *paste-up*: assembling the bromide prints, slicing them, waxing the reverse side, and arranging them on card according to layout instructions governing the newspaper page. In this section I shall refer to the compositor (meaning the comp who is *not* spending any time on the input function) as 'the paste-up hand'.

The paste-up hand often takes a turn at mark-up, inserting instructions on the manuscript to guide the keyboard tapper in setting. In the photocomposition system this means knowing and using format codes: the instructions are converted into a sequence of digits or characters for the tapper to follow, so instructing the photosetter to vary its output. They also operate the small photographic appliances that produce headlines. They do the job that used to be random hand, now carrying paper to and fro in place of heavy galleys of metal type. They do an occasional stint on the photosetter, which involves little more than positioning cassettes of film or tearing off strips of bromide. 'Executive desk, that's the name they give one of these jobs. Sounds grand, doesn't it? But I could give that job to my seven-year-old daughter. As for putting bromides through the waxer, a toddler could do it. Nothing could be more soul-destroying.' While retraining for the QWERTY board took six weeks or more of hammering the keys, followed by months of practice, the retraining needed for the remainder of the comp room jobs was negligible – not because the skills required were the same as those the men had, but because anybody could get the hang of the jobs fast. 'Retraining for me was what, a morning? That's all it took. They just said, here's the paper, do it.' No doubt, were the craftsman replaced by cheaper and less self-conscious labour, these little processes would all be separate and routinised tasks. The compositor, at least, has kept them united.

The shift from metal to paper as a production material has a complex significance. It appears to be a metaphor for larger matters, some of which the men feel positive about, some negative. The cleanness and lightness of the work is appreciated by everybody. That is, it is appreciated with one part of themselves. Yet most also complain, 'there's no *feel* to paper, is there, do you know what I mean? Well, it's a positive thing, picking up a piece of metal. Pick up a bromide and look at it, you think, so what? There's no permanence to it.'

It seems that, working with paper, it is impossible to think of yourself as a craftsman. The material simply doesn't draw that effort or ability out of you. It is too easy. 'When you are putting a "box" round an advert for instance, a fancy rule . . . in hot metal you would have to go to a rack to find a particular rule, walk to a saw, cut the rule to length, go to a mitring machine and mitre the corners, walk back to the stone with it and fit it into the page. You may well have to put some little "leads" down the side to get it to fit correctly. Compare that with paper make-up: you have a box full of rolls of Chartpak plastic strip beside you. You peel some off, stick it on the page and knife off the spare. About 15 seconds, I should think, compared with two minutes.' (Note, too, the physical movement made possible by the hot-metal version of this task. The men hate static work.)

Paradoxically, though it is so easy to apply, it is more difficult, using paper, to be sure that lines are straight and at right angles. The pieces of metal themselves fitted together, imposing their rectilinear standard on the compositor. To position small pieces of paper or film by hand, exactly straight and square, requires judgement and diligence. This is something the comp feels he could offer, over and above an amateur. But time is not available for perfection. They fear that an unskilled paste-up hand, a newcomer to print, doing a slapdash job, would satisfy the boss just as well, while being cheaper.

Paper paste-up is much quicker, more productive, than hot-metal composition. Production of a newspaper page in paper is between two and four times as fast as production of its equivalent in hot metal. Ancillary jobs are relatively faster still. The chapels have resisted demanning relative to number of pages produced (to a greater extent in some firms than others). For many of the men therefore the work is now done under less pressure than it was. This is unlikely to last – employers often build up the productivity gains from new technologies a little at a time. But meanwhile, the apparent pace of newspaper production has wound down. 'There is the silence. In hot metal there was always something going on somewhere and it used to build up over the course of the night and then there would be sudden quiet. Now it only winds up to a certain pitch, no further,' said a comp working on a daily title. For the men who were naturally competitive (and that includes many linotype operators) a lot of the kick has gone out of the work. 'I like to squeeze 12 hours of work out of a nine-hour shift. It's my temperament. I have got to finish mine first. Now you have all the time in the world. It's not the same. I'm *playing* with this equipment.' 'It's nice if you are under pressure and you get something away. You feel you have achieved something.' Now, curiously, they feel less productive although they know, intellectually, that 'they have speeded up the work. You don't realise it perhaps, But you just sit there and you have done that much more.' They have struggled to share the employer's gain in productivity but, now they have succeeded in winning a slacker day, they feel flat. Not all the men who like to work hard and fast are piece-workers. Many time hands do too. These same people realise that they are exploiting themselves on the employers' behalf if they press themselves. But they are tempted to continue to do for pleasure what their political acuity tells them is foolish. It is the contradiction of any craftsman caught up in capitalist production.

A further question arises for the men. Whose is this labour process? A change in the material from metal to paper has led to a shift in power. Lead alloy and the machinery used to process type may have literally belonged to the capitalist, but in effect they belonged to the compositor, who alone knew how to put them to work. Paper and glue – these are the materials of the kindergarten. They are everyone's thing. The journalists and editors who come down to the stone to see their stories being made up used to be unable to read the lead type except with difficulty, back to front as it was. Now they look over the comp's shoulder and can read the bromides as well as he. Composing has lost its mystique and the compositor much of his authority. He no longer has to interpret or explain, he can no longer blind the editors with technical know-how. 'It was always a useful psychological barrier between you and the editor, that piece of metal. He says he wants this or that done. You could tell him – that will cost you another hour's work. Whereas now, *they* start making suggestions. It does tend to rile you a bit.'

A similar set of contradictions exists in the change of working environment brought about by photocomposition. Nearly all the men remarked on their pleasure in the physical characteristics of the new composing area. 'Oh, it's very good, very nice. Well decorated, air conditioned. Perfect working conditions really.' 'It's nice to be able to come in to work with a suit on. Not to be going home each shift filthy dirty, smelling of ink.' 'I always think if you live in muck, you know, your mind can't sort of get on much further. It holds you back.' It has been a shift from factory to office.

The work is physically less tiring as well. 'There are more seats. In hot metal you always used to stand by the case or the stone. Varicose veins were common among the older men.' 'Lifting, carrying, a lot of the men had back problems.' 'Whenever we go back there, now, any of us, we see the noise and the dirtiness and, everyone says, yuck! how did we stand it? The secret is, you wanted to do that work so you were prepared to accept the noise and the heat as one of the conditions. But we wouldn't want to go back.' And yet many of the men evoked the old atmosphere with nostalgia. 'It's not the same without that mixture of smells, the ink, the grease, paraffin. It was like a dose of everything that was good for you, you know.' And, 'What does a little dirt matter after all? People have to work and get their hands dirty, you get more satisfaction out of it than those people that sit there, you know, like a tailor's dummy at an office desk.'

Besides, the physical cleanliness of the new environment is impossible to separate from the social transformation that took place as the old companionships were torn apart and reorganised. 'You see, in hot metal, along with the noise you can also have a laugh with your chums. Someone will pass a comment and you get a bonhomie among many of the lads. Now in the new composing area you feel you are more under the eye, eyes looking across the room. It may be all very nice having a carpet on the floor but . . . ' He meant to say, I think, it's not *our* place any more.

The paper industry and paper-handling aspects of print, as well as clerical work, have long employed a large number of women. Paper therefore is a material attributed to women and to intellectual workers. (That double association is of course itself contradictory.) Thinking of his new working material a comp said to me, thoughtfully, 'I don't know. It just isn't masculine enough to satisfy me. I think that's what it is.' An office, because of its association with women on the one hand and mental labour on the other, is seen as a less virile environment than a factory. 'I think it may make softies of us – I feel it may make us, I don't know if this is the word, "effete". Less manly, somehow,' said another comp of his new composing room. It is sometimes hard for men, the world that men have constructed. They would often like to be able to allow themselves to evade the labour and discomfort that they believe are necessary concomitants of manhood.

Integrated working: 'all singing, all dancing'

The new labour process in the two Fleet Street firms included in my study differed from that in the two regionals in at least three respects. The chapels were historically very strong and thus able to resist the *diktat* of management to greater effect than was the case outside Fleet Street. The technology introduced was, from the outset, more advanced in these firms: they were on-line systems. And all hot-metal composing personnel, regardless of their former role in the composing room, were retrained for the integrated practice of all photocomposition tasks, organised by rota. These three differences are not unrelated.

The integrated job in computerised composition in both Fleet Street firms involved a rota which took the men in the course of several weeks through mark-up, input, corrections, photosetting, random and paste-up. There were small differences: at TNL the rota also included proof-reading; at MGN waxing the pieces of paper was a separate job on the rota. A comp at MGN described waxing and some other tasks as 'mickey mouse jobs'. 'Really in a sense these are manufactured jobs in order to keep our own little empire. To establish our position. Like inching our way into the computer room.' The aim of the NGA chapels must be continually to secure their flanks against the possible encroachment of other unions and where possible to push control outwards.

At TNL, eight of the 12 men I interviewed were former linotype operators, retrained and installed in new technology as all-purpose workers. Two were current linotype operators anticipating transfer, and two were readers in hot metal also waiting to go across. At MGN I interviewed a very mixed group. Of 15 men, seven had been hot-metal comps (stone hands), one had been on piece-case (Ludlow) and six had been lino operators. All were now on integrated photocomposition. The 15th man was a reader in hot metal who had remained a specialist reader in the new technology.[5]

Integrated working, of course, is not as new a theme to comps as it is to operators, since stone hands in any case used to rotate during their working week, doing short stints on copy desk and random. It is true they now have to learn the keyboard, for input and correction: an important new factor in their lives. But it is the linotype operators, used to a specialism, who are the ones to feel most the impact of integrated working.

To integrate work was essentially the *chapels'* decision in both firms and they were strong enough to impose it on management.[6] There were several good reasons. It would alleviate the boredom produced by an overall trivialising of the component tasks. It might forestall any long-term fragmentation of the comps' political domain. And it would enhance chapel unity by levelling out operators and comps in both performance and earnings, giving everyone a shared interest. The high pay and elite attitudes of the operators had produced jealousy, dislike and division in the chapels, especially at MGN. Now, 'the object is to say we are all equal, we can all change over jobs, there are no specialised jobs and no extra money.' 'There'll be no more *prima donnas*.'

Most of the men welcomed the variety and felt that it made for a better team. 'You see everyone's problem if you move around.' 'Using the VDUs you have a whole composing room at your finger tips. You don't have to move, hardly, you can do the whole operation from this very keyboard. And that makes me a more complete person than I was before.' There were individual problems of course. Some ex-operators found the change in the labour process exasperating. And some ex-stone hands hated input. Besides, swopping from job to job slows down the process of getting to feel confident once more. But chapel strategy inevitably had to come before individual choice in this matter.

As it happened, management too detected certain advantages in integrated working. Strong chapels are a fact of life. The knack of managing national newspapers is getting the best out of a hand short in trumps. Management foresaw that the proportional demand for specialisations in the new technology might differ from that in the old. Perhaps fewer tappers might be needed, perhaps more, for instance. If men were retrained rigidly, passing direct from one specialism to its equivalent in new technology, it might lead to a costly situation where some men had to be given redundancy pay-offs while new men had to be taken on to fill different gaps. If all men were retrained for all jobs this would be avoided. Besides, health factors limit the length of time a worker can continuously operate a video display screen.

The men were under no illusion that the acceptance of integrated working had been motivated by management altruism:

> What the company is saying is, we've got 40 bodies, we'll have 38 setting at first and when the bulk of the setting's done we'll

shift 30 of them over to paste-up. The company will score because the overall manning levels can be that much lower. The flow of work in newspapers is governed by the rate that the news and adverts come in. It makes for a lot of dead time. The news industry is the opposite of the car industry. A robot makes sense on the motor conveyor belt perhaps. But in printing it works the other way round. Yeah, if you put someone in and throw him onto every different job in turn as the paper is produced you get the same high productivity you get in another place by having a moving conveyor belt and a robot.

At TNL one of the big gains management sought in the new system was that all titles, instead of being produced by separate companionships, with different shifts and hours, would be produced by a united work force working a three-shift day, seven-day week. A similar tendency was observable at MGN. Management saw that the flexibility thus acquired could potentially be greatly enhanced by integrated working. The struggle thus moves, once integrated working is established, to flexibility in the deployment of living labour. The issue of flexibility is contradictory: it cuts both ways. Some of the men cannot tolerate certain tasks and prefer to swop their place on the rota. Management too would prefer 'horses for courses' (a favoured phrase among comps), to the extent that they would get the most productive tappers, for instance, spending more time on the keyboards. On the other hand, as noted above, the union wants a formally integrated chapel for the sake of solidarity and equality, and management wants everyone notionally able to do every job. The balance of power is reflected in a rota organised by the FOC to whom both management and men can appeal for occasional alterations. The balance is tipped towards the men by virtue of the fact that the rota is organised and managed by the *chapel* in these two firms.

The contest then advances to the question of how frequently, and for how short or long a stint a man may be deployed on a task for which he is not listed. An MGN comp said:

> In the early days we were a *little* bit unco-operative over the question of flexibility. The management wanted it and we

didn't initially. We still don't want it on a
management-controlled basis. We don't mind it on a
chapel-controlled basis whereby when *we* see that they are in
the muck and the mire in a particular area then *we* would see
that someone is sent across to sort it out.

Resisting flexibility they use the argument, 'Most people when they
come in to do a job like to be left on it for a day . . . or at least not
to do four or five different jobs in a single shift.' The management
at MGN pays a premium for each alteration agreed and the chapel
pools the proceeds of this 'fine' among the men. When it suits the
chapel, however, they actually arrange flexibility autonomously.
For instance, towards the end of a shift, if a lot of the men are to be
given the chance to 'cut and go', it is impossible to leave the
photosetter unmanned. In their own interests, therefore, the
chapel throw in a man for an hour or two to cover the absence.

Skill and 'deskilling'

It is interesting to consider Harry Braverman's account of change
in capitalist labour processes more generally, in the light of this
experience in the printing industry.[7] He took up and developed
Marx's proposition that the more and more effective control of
production by the capitalist class must lead to an ever-increasing
division of labour and 'degradation' of work.[8] Braverman defined
as the first principle of scientific management, 'the dissociation of
the labour process from the skills of the workers. The labour
process is to be rendered independent of craft, tradition and the
workers' knowledge. Henceforth it is to depend not at all upon the
abilities of workers but entirely upon the practices of
management'.[9] This same prospect was expressed equally starkly
by the Brighton Labour Process Group:

> Deskilling is inherent in the capitalist labour process because
> capital must aim at having labour functions that are calculable,
> standardisable routines; because this labour must be
> performed at the maximum speed and with minimum of
> 'porosity'; and because capital wants labour which is cheap
> and easily replaceable.[10]

The account I have just given of the recent experience of compositors points to a greater complexity than these theories allow. If what the men say is true we have, first of all, to distinguish several meanings of the word 'skill'. Then we have to distinguish loss of skill from 'degradation of work'. We should be cautious too, about supposing that deskilling for one group implies an overall deskilling in the enterprise. And finally we need to separate out loss of skill from loss of control. Unless we are prepared to unravel this complexity in the notions of skill and deskilling it will be impossible to understand the individual man's ambivalence or his trade union's current strategy.

To begin this unpacking process: *skill* itself (if we read the men's experience in hot metal aright) consists in at least three things. There is the skill that resides in the man himself, accumulated over time, each new experience adding something to a total ability. There is the skill demanded by the job – which may or may not match the skill in the worker. And there is the political definition of skill: that which a group of workers or a trade union can successfully defend against the challenge of employers and of other groups of workers.

In the nineteenth century (and even perhaps until after the second world war) the three definitions of skill were, for the compositor, more or less co-terminous. In his apprenticeship and working life he acquired abilities that were fully demanded by his job; his unique right to practise the skill was more or less defensible through the union's pre-entry closed shop. For the capitalist employer, existence of a viable skill does not necessarily spell unprofitable production. The stability of craft production can, within certain tolerances, serve accumulation well. As Tony Elger has said in his discussion of Braverman: 'Forms of specialised expertise and craft competence may be embedded within a complex structure of collective labour effectively subordinated to capital accumulation.'[11] Nonetheless, craft skill represents a constraint on managerial initiative which may become intolerable in certain economic conditions. The employer then turns to shake off these fetters, increasing the division of labour, intensifying work and introducing new technologies. Increasingly in newspaper production the three definitions of skill came out of synchrony.

Computerised photocomposition throws them wildly awry.

The skill the men possessed has been made redundant by the scrapping of hot-metal plant. The new tasks can be learned all too quickly. (They would of course not be able to take up the new work if that were not the case.) Thus, 'It took me six years, perhaps eight, to learn how to be a good comp and operator. You could take any competent typist from out on the street and I would maintain that within two months she could be doing my job.' Nonetheless, some skill is required by the new work. Some of the men's old knowledge – spelling, for instance, or an aesthetic understanding of how a newspaper page should look – is still useful. Secondly, as the men have found to their cost, typing is quite hard to learn. All of the men found that retraining for the new processes demanded something of them. And if we take 'skill' to designate the accumulated abilities of a person, then learning the new technology has enhanced their skill. It was, as many of them said, 'another string to my bow'. But what is a man's skill if, say, 80 per cent of it cannot be practised? All that is demanded in the new job is perhaps 10 per cent of the old knowledge and the 10 per cent increment recently acquired. In such a situation it is more comfortable to dwell, as many of the men do, on their 'internal', though unsaleable, skill, the acquisition of a lifetime, and continue to claim '*I* am skilled', even if the *job* is not.

Many of the men I talked to were ambitious and keen workers. This applies particularly to linotype operators who, at the end of their apprenticeships, went on ahead of the other comps to learn their 'extra skill' and so to acquire their greater earning power. Many of these climbers were also among the early enthusiasts for photocomposition. 'I thought to myself, I want to be one of the first ones to retrain, to go over. If there is anything going on up there I want to get a look at it.' In a sense they have gone on up a ladder of learning, alluringly set before them, and dropped off the top. For instance, a man said, 'I've gained really. I mean if I can't do anything else I can type, I suppose, now. I could always be a typist in the last resort.' Then, realising where his train of thought had led him, he made a grimace of alarm.

So the men are deskilled in the sense of bring deprived of the power to use their original skill. But they have been offered a new knowledge. It is nothing very remarkable but, in the case of the more advanced systems, using VDUs and graphic-display terminals, in an integrated operation in which the men know something of the computer and photosetter, there is a knowledge worth having. (And it seems that this style of working is, if anything, under-represented in the news trade. There are fewer 'idiot' boards, more VDUs, in general printing.) But here the political definition of skill enters, to play a contradictory role. First as tangible skill is hollowed out, the strength of the political shell becomes critical. If the union cannot lay effective political claim to the whole of this new field of work, to the 'second keystroke', (as the NGA have so far done) the compositor as a *distinct skill group* can kiss goodbye to work altogether. Second, however, political exigencies ironically *prevent* the full development of the new skill, in the man and the job. The full potential of computerised photocomposition is only released when operated as a direct-entry system. It would be a relatively skilled and satisfying job to be one of the few remaining compositors who – as the 'text processor' or 'typographic expert' on the new-style newspaper, assembling complex advertisements or whole newspaper pages on the large video screens of the page-view terminals – works alongside the new-style journalist, editor, accountant, administrator or telephone-advertising clerk to produce a computerised newspaper effortlessly, speedily and cheaply. But that is precisely the situation that the compositors, collectively, must resist. For only a few would get such jobs, the great majority being doomed to redundancy. They are therefore obliged to stay the torrent of productivity, rather than being permitted to revel in it.

Thus the men had felt during the training period, while being shown the full potential of the new systems, that for the first and last time they were treated as intelligent, interested and competent people – which indeed they are. Reflecting on that time, they now felt it had been a tease, a come-on. Even in 'integrated working' situations the compositor does not personally produce as large a part of the whole product as the remaining compositor would in a direct-entry system.[12] The employer/union bargain has produced a compromise role for comps. From the present perspective, 'Well, it is an idiot system, once you know it. The brainpower aspect goes clean out the window. I feel they are paying me to sit on my backside. All the activity is occurring now inside the computer – and that is pretty quiet!'

As a result of all this, many men were very disillusioned with their work. They would have understood Marx when he wrote, 'The lightening of the labour, even, becomes a sort of torture, since the machine does not free the labourer from work but deprives the work of all interest.'[13] As one compositor put it, 'There was a hell of a lot of pride in the old work. With the new system, it's taken the soul out of the job. I don't buck against it. It's secured [sic] my livelihood. But if there is one thing I absolutely dislike about it, that's it, the soullessness of it.' Others said, 'All the skill has gone, basically,' 'It's one big *nothing*.' Many of the men consequently take a more instrumental attitude to the job than they did as craftsmen. 'New technology, great. I'll be mercenary shall I? It gives us more money, more time away from the firm. In other words, we've got a job where we get in, do it, go home and forget it.'

The men, then, feel that in one way they *have* been deskilled. And in one way they are right, since in capitalism the means of production are not owned by the worker and in these four newspaper firms the owner had simply scrapped the old plant and scrapped the old skill with it. *Skill in the man* was now out of kilter with *skill in the job*, and the union was only with great difficulty ensuring that *skill as a class political concept* held the line in the turmoil of this employer-inspired revolution.

'Skill' is, however, not only a class political weapon. It is also a sex/gender weapon. Skill as a political concept is more far-reaching than the class relations of capitalism – it plays an important part in the power relations between men and women. The sexual division of labour in society is of great antiquity: men and women tend to do different work. Over very long periods of patriarchal time women's particular abilities and work processes have been arbitrarily valued lower than those of men.[14] It has been a two-way process: women's inferiority has rubbed off on their activities and the imputed mindlessness of the activities has reflected on women. Anne Phillips and Barbara Taylor have pointed out that the skill attributed to a job has much more to do with the sex of the person who does it than the real demands of the work.[15] Other studies have shown how, even in the rare circumstances where men and women do comparable work, the man's work is usually graded higher and rewarded more generously than the woman's.[16] It is of course not difficult to see that men had much to gain, materially and ideologically, from such an overestimate of the skill of men's work and an underestimate of the skill of women's work. In the instance of photocomposition, the sexual character of skill is clear enough. Hot metal was undeniably male. The comps undervalue the typing and paper-handling skills they are now being taught because they see them as female. The men are caught in a contradiction: they must either acknowledge themselves totally deskilled, or acknowledge that many women are as skilled as men. The dilemma accounts for much of the bitterness they feel.

To continue the unpacking of skill: is the loss of skill equivalent to the 'degradation of work'? Degradation can be measured along numerous scales: earnings, hours, conditions, the extent of the division of labour. In all these respects newspaper workers, while being deskilled, have improved their lot throughout the fifties, sixties and seventies. For most, the change to new technology has brought a marked increase in earnings, a reduction in working hours, and a relaxation of pressure. Besides, it has not further subdivided the work but has in some cases reintegrated detailed tasks. It has produced a more pleasurable working environment. Advances in production are to some extent and in some ways advances for society and some of the gain accrues even to the deskilled worker. If these things are not recognised, it is difficult to understand why, in spite of all their negative feelings, recounted in detail above, very few indeed of the men were prepared to say that they would want to go back to the old processes. Though they like to glorify craft (social historians do, too), there was in reality little that was glorious in the practice of such a craft in the recent phase of capitalist production: it was hard, tiring work. So if, capitalism replaces work that is rewarding but exhausting with work that is boring but easy, you may heave a sigh of relief . . . while continuing to mourn the loss.

There is, however, one way in which the men *have* experienced degradation and this accounts in part for their bitterness. Degradation can also be measured *socially*. Does the new work reduce the standing of the old worker relative to others in the working class? Because the work is more generalised and easier, the men feel they are slipping perilously down the worker scale toward the general 'hand' or labourer. 'I think I have gone from skilled to semi-skilled, that's what it is. And I feel a bit let down. It has been a worry in my mind all the time.' 'What should I call myself? What am I now? We haven't even got a job title.' 'It's just a kind of clerical job really. You couldn't call it print.' Compositors, used to holding their head up among other working men, now feel loss of self-respect. 'I daren't think about it, much, but sometimes I do think — perhaps this is a little bit bumptious — I think what if some of my friends outside of print could see me now, what would they think?'

Besides this descent to the common *man*, we have seen how the men feel reduced to the level of women. 'If *girls* can do it, you know, then you are sort of deskilled you know, really.' The men are sensitive to this. 'If some knowing person down the local says, oh that's right, you've all become bloody typists haven't you, he's liable to get his head filled in.' I will return to these social effects in Chapters 5 and 6. Meanwhile it is enough to note that many compositors talk as though they feel the pull of gravity, levelling them down to what they see (and have always feared) as the undifferentiated mass of the working class: unskilled men, unemployed men, old men . . . and women.

A further consideration is this. It is clear from the instance of photocomposition that the deskilling of one group of workers, and an overall weakening of the position of labour in society as a whole, may be achieved by capital without actually deskilling the overall production process within the enterprise. A newspaper house is a social system of co-operating work groups. Marx called this 'the collective labourer':

> The various kinds of collective labour that combine to form an overall collective productive machine participate in quite different ways in the direct process of production of commodities, one mainly with his hands, another mainly with his head, one as a manager or engineer or technician etc.,

another as a supervisor, yet another as a direct manual worker or perhaps just as an assistant.[17]

The totality of workers, each possessing labour-power of different kinds and different values, comprise a 'living production machine'. Capital's thrust, in revolutionising newspaper production technology, may be directed mainly to removing the block represented by the composing room, but the owners also hope to make more productive and profitable the activities of journalists, advertising personnel, managers and many others in the firm. If capital gets its way, the composing group as a whole will be destroyed, and unemployment and loss of job opportunities will occur at the societal level. Yet, for those who remain in the slimmed-down newspaper operation, overall skill levels in production may not fall. For example, the massive routine copy-typing or 'input tapping' job, characteristic of phase one of the new technology, will no longer exist as such. 'Typing' on the new keyboards will be a smaller (and more interesting) part of what are essentially other jobs – a part of the work-time of the journalist, editor, graphics person or telephone-answerer. Routine paper paste-up will give way in phase two and subsequent technologies to text manipulation on screen. Small comfort for the majority of compositors discarded from the labour force, but satisfactory enough for those left within the charmed circle. Phase-one technology did indeed bring the expected polarisation of work into routine unskilled occupations and enhanced technological occupations. Phase two, on the contrary, appears to be producing a cluster of semi-skilled, semi-responsible linked occupations.

This effect is not, of course, limited to the newspaper industry. Bryn Jones, in his work on the effect of numerical control on engineering skills, has concluded that degradation of work or overall deskilling does not result from new technology in every kind of enterprise. Contrary to Braverman, he has found that the divisibility of task-skills may be related to such factors as the kind of product being manufactured, the kind of technology on offer and the strength of trade-union organisation.[18] The 'integrated working' we have seen at Times Newspapers and Mirror Group News, curiously flying in the face of 'the capitalist division of labour', may be an indication that such factors will produce, in the newspaper industry of the future, a production process that is characterised by less rather than more division of labour. However, this is not to say that labour will have, in some sense, 'won the battle'. The battle is not only won or lost within one work place, or through the quality of one labour process: it also takes place at a societal level. And skill is not its only trophy.

The question we are led to ask, then, is 'Is deskilling commensurate with loss of control?' A high degree of control over the hot-metal labour process had been built by comps on the possession of a skill. Now that skill is eroded. But the political organisation, the trade union and its chapels, have by no means had their control swept irreparably away. The men have fought back and influenced the way the technology is applied and managed. The worker's closeness to the new technology can be used to rebuild knowledge. Andrew Friedman and other critics of Braverman have pointed out that this possibility is scarcely allowed for in the scenario that predicts the relentless division of labour and degradation of work in capitalism.[19] In that scenario, relentless deskilling dooms us to ever-diminishing control of work. But compositors have bought time in which some of them at least may build up their competence and know-how on the new equipment in order to re-establish a degree of control based, not merely on political assertion of skill, but on real ability. Of course, there are pressures pushing the other way. Electronic information technology is essentially a generalised technology applicable in all industries and throughout society. The comps' protected corner in the labour market is gone. As one told me, pointing up the contrast with the old days, 'I might tell a mate in the pub – we've got this hitch with the line printer. And he'll say to me, yes, we had the same problem at the Express Dairy.' Computerisation of work is happening to every Tom, Dick and Harry. Any one of them therefore might be able to challenge the compositor for his new job. Production processes that can be manned from a large undifferentiated labour market of polyvalent, interchangeable workers is a capitalist's dream. It is in recognition of this that trade unions (the NGA among them) are abandoning the direct equation of 'skill' with 'control', and are reorganising and redefining trade unionism so as to use other (and less divisive) ploys with which to challenge capital's power over production than the apprentice-based pre-entry closed shop.

A more worrying factor enters here however. Electronic information technology, as noted at the end of Chapter 3, is precisely *about* control from above. The men are aware of this. 'It's their tool, you know,' said a proof-reader, gesturing towards the new hardware. 'And it tends to have more command over you than your pen did.' Computerised photocomposition is not only used to contest craft control; its very introduction was a gesture of capitalist authority. Though the owners used the persuasive theme of progress, the men for their part made it clear that they felt acted upon: 'We are *victims* of progress,' they said, 'we are *victims* of change.'

Skill, already such a complex concept, has yet another facet. It has a different meaning for the individual from the meaning it has for working-class organisation. The individual producer dates back to a period long before the advent of capitalism. He or she has purely human interests in transformative labour, in production. He or she may very reasonably struggle to retain the pleasurable 'use-value' aspects of skill in the face of changing technologies. The trade union however was born in the same cradle as capitalism; it is a product of capitalist class relations – it has no other *raison d'être*. Skill for the collective employee of capital, manifest in the trade union, is, sadly, no more than a means to an organisational end. (In the same way, for the capitalist employer, it is no more than a means to the end of producing 'exchange values', the end of capital accumulation.) There may be collective struggle *over* skill, but it is not necessarily *about* skill. It is about the value of labour-power and control over production. If the weapon of skill, for the union, becomes blunted, others must be sought. And these, indeed, the NGA is seeking. This is why a union may find itself sometimes required to trample, as capital does, on the individual worker's pleasure in the practice of a skill.

There is always a danger, however, that trade unions, locked in the capital/labour struggle, will adopt the instrumental view of 'skill' in its entirety, forgetting that skill cannot, in the last resort, be evaluated without also evaluating its product. In referring to a 'use-value' aspect of skill I pointed to the pleasure that may be taken in the capability of producing useful things. But it is not only pleasure in the labour process itself that capitalist production destroys by its management disciplines. It perverts the product too. The political pamphleteers of the English Revolution of the seventeenth century, putting printing techniques to work for the first time in a popular movement against overlords and monarchy, could take pleasure in a skill used to produce something useful and purposeful for themselves and their comrades. What pleasure or pride can be taken by the comp in producing the destructive and abusive inanities of the *Daily Star* or *The Sun* – however clever the hot-metal techniques still used to produce those two papers today? Applying skills to bad ends is also a kind of deskilling.

5. A man among men

In 1980–81, when this study was made, four important unions, held together in a symbiotic web of fraternal co-operation and internecine strife, structured the industrial relations of print. The National Graphical Association (NGA) represented compositors and pressmen, together with a few numerically smaller categories, predominantly skilled. The Society of Lithographic Artists and Designers (SLADE) had members on the graphic design and camera side of the industry. Again, it was in the main skilled and male and had been energetic in its pursuit of a closed shop. The National Society of Operative Printers, Graphical and Media Personnel (NATSOPA) was a union mainly of unskilled and semi-skilled. It represented those among the non-craft workers with whom the NGA member was most often in contact: clerical workers, cleaners, maintenance engineers, proof-readers' copy holders and machine managers' assistants. The fourth union, the giant Society of Graphical and Allied Trades (SOGAT) was predominantly semi- and unskilled and many of its members were in the finishing operations of print, as well as in the paper manufacturing industry. SOGAT did, however, have a small craft section, and in Scotland it represented compositors. A fifth union had a kind of 'honorary membership' in print, alongside the four principals: the National Union of Journalists (NUJ), representing mainly 'mental' as opposed to 'manual' workers: editors, photographers and writers.

All the four printing unions were the outcome of amalgamations between the smaller, specialised, sometimes local unions or trade societies of former times. Sectional strife and tensions within them are vestigial forms of the old separate identities. As mentioned in Chapter 2 the NGA was formed in 1964 by the unification of the London Typographical Society (LTS) and the provincial Typographical Association. The LTS had itself only gelled a decade previously out of separate societies representing the London compositors and the London machine men, previously hostile factions. Since 1964 the NGA has been joined by 'correctors of the press', press telegraphists, stereotypers, litho printers and employees of the wallpaper printing industry. The unions have continued to circle round each other in cautious reconnaissance with a view to further consolidation. NATSOPA and SOGAT's memberships were for a time united, then split asunder again, and now plan to renew their alliance in SOGAT 82. In mid-1982, the NGA and SLADE have also joined forces. And the enlarged NGA and the NUJ continue to discuss further amalgamation.

The most vexatious issue within the overall drive to which all unions are now committed, for a single union for the printing industry, is the relationship between skilled and less-skilled workers. Although the NGA dallied with NATSOPA for some years, the unification of skilled and unskilled has always been the most difficult task. The recent developments have, if anything, hardened the split along skill lines – with SOGAT 82 uniting most of the non-craft workers and the NGA/SLADE/NUJ proximity further reinforcing the idea of a higher echelon of print employees. The question of pay differentials continues to excite dissension as the less skilled creep upwards and the skilled express outrage. The 'official' gap is now as narrow as it has ever been, with the semi-skilled getting 92.5 per cent of the skilled person's rate and the unskilled receiving 87.5 per cent.

Within the NGA there is now a noticeable divide between those who, whether for tactical or for genuinely egalitarian reasons, want to see an industrial union for printing, and those who see no reason for craft identity to be swept away. A majority are now voting for 'one union for the print'. But that idea is not altogether incompatible with craft distinction, since it is interpreted by many members as meaning a union with internal sections and differentials and a continuance of demarcation at work. The politics of *skill* thus continue to preoccupy the membership of the NGA: within the debates in the union's journal and in reports of meetings and conferences it is possible to see all the strands of meaning traced in the previous chapter. For instance, the threat members feel to their status through loss of skill is closely entangled with distress about the deprivation of pleasurable work. The internal division within the union reflects the old conviction that skill is the proper basis of control of work and the new conviction that it can no longer be depended upon to serve this purpose.

The rivalries and mutual fears, which we saw emerging in the early days of industrialisation and continuing into our own times, still run very deep. I want to explore two aspects of this disunity in greater detail. In this chapter I will look at what the men say about the rivalry of the *skilled man and the unskilled man*, and in the following at the dissension between *men and women*.

It is tempting to theorise the relations between skilled and less-skilled men as relations occurring 'within the class', as essentially class-fractional relations, identifying those between men and women as essentially sex/gender relations. In reality, both sets of relations demand analysis in terms of both systems. The dissension of men and women springs partly from the processes of patriarchy, reflecting the interests of men in subordinating women, and partly from those of capitalism: capital has super-exploited women's labour power and has repeatedly used women to weaken male workers. Likewise, relations between men, even though these are enacted in this instance within the sphere of capitalist production, nonetheless reflect the structure of patriarchy. Patriarchy is as much about relations between man and man as it is about relations between men and women. Think, for instance, of the principle of inheritance from father to eldest son, of the taboo on male homosexuality, of the relations between master, artisan and apprentice in the early days of printing. As Heidi Hartmann puts it, 'Patriarchy is a set of social relations which has a material base and in which there are hierarchical relations between men, and solidarity among them, which enable them to control women.'[1] The male hierarchical structures of skill and the rivalries between the grades of labour-power require explanation in terms of both sex and class. Nor is solidarity across this divide altogether absent: we will see in Chapter 6 an instance in which an alliance between skilled and unskilled men over-rode their rivalry on a matter concerning women.

A number of the topics on which I questioned compositors,

including union amalgamation and the pay differential, elicited views and feelings about men less skilled than themselves. The discussion of new technology also raised comments on the changing relations of compositors with those such as journalists and editors, whose status manual production workers have been used to according respect (albeit somewhat ambivalent). I will describe these relations as the men express them, and then look, first, at the sex/gender dynamic in them and, second, at their class signficance. The scrapping of skill by new technology means a shake-up in the occupational hierarchy of the newspaper. It has been carried out by capital for its own class purposes and represents a moment of peril for the working class in print. Nonetheless, the dislodging of skill is seen by some within the unions as an opportunity as well as a threat, opening up new political perspectives and possibilities.

The compositor and the Natty

In the wish to be courteous and fair to the compositors I find myself shrinking from giving a full account of the derogatory terms many of them used in telling me about their less-skilled colleagues. But nothing is to be gained from ducking this issue. In fact, much could be lost, politically, by failing to recognise the unpleasant distinctions that have survived to the present day between man and man in the printing workforce.

Let's be clear at the start, however. There were in my study, and probably always have been in printing, a handful of individuals who are wholeheartedly egalitarian – who express a very different ideology from the one expressed by the majority. Such people would say, 'As far as I'm concerned we are all workers.' 'Some people in the NGA class themselves above members of NATSOPA and that. I personally don't. I don't look at it like that.' 'I see working people as brothers. Justice is important. I think it is progressive.' 'I suppose I'm awkward, but I have always felt that it was just good fortune that my parents happened to have the contacts to help me become apprenticed in print. And because the man I work alongside didn't have anyone to push *him* forward, that doesn't mean that he is less intelligent than me. Quite probably he is more so.' Many would like to see one union in print, bringing together workers of all categories in genuine equality of opportunity, and not so as to lock up the lesser grades in regulated sections.

However, a high proportion of the comps I talked with showed a cool contempt for men less skilled than themselves and wished to be sharply distinguished from them. The 'dustman', the 'milkman', the 'general hand', 'the chappie who sweeps the floor', these are characters that frequently enter into the skilled man's account of his work and world. The semi-skilled and unskilled in the life of the comp take shape as a particular group: the members of NATSOPA and SOGAT. They are often represented (and dismissed) by comps in the term 'bloody Nats'. 'Messenger boys, wipers-up, you know, all this sort of people. You can't really identify with them, can you?' 'I suppose it's how you regard yourself, really.' 'Labourers, they are *labourers*, really. Not talking about individuals, of course, I'm generalising. But a man pushes a reel along on a barrow: he can't equate with me, producing something where I have to use my brain power.' Thomas Wright, the engineer, writing in 1873, put it no clearer when he said, 'Between the artisan and the labourer a gulf is fixed'.[2]

You still hear echoes of the past when, in the printing trade and to a still greater extent in other craft occupations, the unskilled worked directly for the individual artisan and was sometimes paid out of the craftsman's own wage. 'Snobbishly, yes, I suppose. But they've been the skivvies. All right, we can't do without them. But they have been the skivvies of the talented, you know, the *trained* men.'

The expressions the craftsmen use to describe the less-skilled and their own relations to them often take the same form as expressions of racial prejudice. You even hear, 'Some of my best friends are unskilled.' In actual fact, of course, racism and anti-catholicism are also present in these expressions because the skilled in printing, taken as a whole, have a higher proportion of white Anglo-Saxon protestants among them than the semi- and unskilled. The scathing reference to 'Brady on the shop floor' reflects the presence of many Irish, for instance.

In one of the Fleet Street titles a momentary shortage of linotype operators has led to the appointment in the residual hot-metal area of some operators whom the comps perceive as 'immigrants'.

These men, several complained, are trainees, who have taken only short courses on the linotype and are not full craftsmen. 'You have these chaps from abroad coming over here, chappies from Cyprus, the West Indies, Asia. Jolly good luck to them. But it causes a lot of resentment with the other guys.' 'You could teach a Nigerian chap the keyboard. But there is no way you could suddenly say to him, however *nice* he was, here is a page, make it up. He just couldn't do it.' There is a resonance here with the compositors' old usage of the term 'foreigner' for any kind of non-apprenticed intruder on the craft. A generalised chauvinism finds its keenest expression when other races are involved. However, though a proportion of the broom-pushers and toilet cleaners in the demonology of the craftsman may well be Irish, black or Asian, it would be wrong to ascribe all the craftsman's disrespect to racism.

Along with uncharitable feelings towards unskilled and semi-skilled men in an individual sense, the comps harbour many ill-feelings towards NATSOPA and SOGAT as *unions*. 'Quite frankly, they are out to destroy our union, the bosses and the non-craft unions between them.' 'It is just ever a shame that they managed to get such a bloody great foothold in print as a whole.' The NGA men suspect NATSOPA, particularly, of ambitions to penetrate (and degrade) skilled occupations.

It is a commonplace to a comp that NATSOPAs, both individually and as a union, have been trying to encroach on skilled areas of work. They are portrayed as watching for every opening to get a foot in the door, to gain a right to a new occupation. One man reported a 'shocking' incident in which a NATSOPA man had had the effrontery to 'insist on getting up there and having a hand in work on the stone.' The narrator himself had been an NGA Father of Chapel at the time and had 'had a constant battle with this fellow to keep his hands off the stuff. Because immediately you allow one of them to do a job for any length of time they claim it as a practice of the house. And our rule has always been, must always be, while the type is up on the stone it belongs to the NGA. Once it's gone on the floor or in the bucket, then it is Natty's, to take to the melting pot.'

The craftsmen scorn and resent the lower ranks for 'climbing on the skilled man's back' in pay negotiations. And they mistrust the industrial volatility they ascribe to the less skilled. They feel they are 'here in print today, gone tomorrow.' Because they have no house feeling or loyalty they are liable to start disputes for the least little thing. They don't even identify with print itself. 'You get people in the SOGAT and NATSOPA ranks (and once again it isn't their fault) who have probably been milkmen, postmen, you name it. They haven't got the pride in the job. It's just another job to them, they couldn't care less. And I object to that.' 'You have a different type of animal down there, I regret to say.'

The result of this thrust to put the other man down and hold him there has naturally enough led to bad feeling among the less skilled. Apprenticeship, entered as a teenager, has been the only gateway to the better jobs. As the Arbitration Service reported to the Royal Commission on the Press in 1977, 'A high level of craft-consciousness among skilled workers has led to resentment among other workers who find promotion paths blocked to them on what they feel are unreasonable grounds.'[3] In the machine room where NATSOPAs are assistants to NGA machine managers, yet unable to advance to the senior job, the bitterness is even more acute than in the composing area. Given the rigid work-demarcation lines imposed by the craft unions it is not surprising that some of the unskilled chapels elbow around for more room. And though it is sad, it is nonetheless understandable, if at times the less-skilled men elevate the craftsman to the status of the main enemy and overlook the greater foe they share.

Death throes of craft identity

The same men who differentiate themselves so sharply from 'the other fellow' also tend to be cautious about any future amalgamation with other unions. Not a few of those to whom I put the question would clearly prefer, other things being equal, that the NGA stay as it is. Many, indeed, would prefer it to have stayed as it was in the 1950s, the London Society of Compositors. As Londoners, they felt they had been swamped by the provinces. 'The chap in Wales who goes to work in his coracle, you know, what relation has he to London print?' As comps they felt they were in danger of losing their identity, even among the other skilled crafts. 'We've become a blob, a cipher.'

A preference for belonging to a small elite band within the larger working class of print can be as easily rationalised, politically, by reference to militancy as to passivity. Some of these men who wanted to be in a small union wanted it because it could be more tough and effective, could 'use guerrilla tactics'. Besides, chapel autonomy and the swift recourse to unofficial action, so important to the print worker, might with a larger organisation recede one step further into the past. Others wanted it for precisely the opposite reason. If you were in with the big unskilled unions it would be a matter of 'the tail wagging the dog'. The comp might be drawn willy-nilly into industrial disputes that were none of his making.

Whatever the men wished, however, they had no doubt that further amalgamations were on the way. That is why I wrote that the men would prefer autonomy, 'all other things being equal'. They know full well that things are not equal: union consolidation is as much part of an irreversible trend as is concentration of capital in the newspaper industry. Because they are realists, this fact colours their preference. For the great majority, then, the question arises, with which unions would it be preferable to amalgamate? When pressed further, all but a few of the men I talked with, even among those who accepted and welcomed the idea of a single industrial union in the long run, were more enthusiastic about joining with SLADE and expressed doubts about linking up with the less skilled. All the old fears crept out. 'Quite frankly, deep down, no. I wouldn't want to join with them. It's prejudice you see. I would freely admit this. I have seen so much of NATSOPAs and SOGATs, the *type* of people they have recruited, that I think' (with a diffident laugh) ' . . . I think I shouldn't like to be associated with them.'

The men feel that if they were to link up with unskilled and semi-skilled men in a general union they would be lost to view. Association with the lower ranks brings you down to their level. 'Look. There are some highly skilled men in the ranks of SOGAT, even in NATSOPA. But who remembers that? They have lost people's regard. People just think of them all as Natties.'

If amalgamation is seen by the men as the relentless tug of gravity, razing to common ground the social artefact of craft, any suggestion of a levelling of pay is even more sharply contested. The higher pay of the skilled man is justified by him by recourse to a belt-and-braces ideology in which one strap may hold fast should the other be sundered. On the one hand it is represented as the recognition of inborn, natural superiority. The men say, 'Mother Nature didn't make us equal,' or, 'I think intelligence has a lot to do with whether a person is skilled or unskilled. It is the intellectual make-up of a person to start with.' 'Even the unskilled man, he is not kicking against the pay differential, because he knows deep in his heart that he couldn't *do* what I can do.'

On the other hand, higher pay is represented as the prize for endeavour, for unremitting effort. 'Supposing you get a NATSO-PA coming in off the street, pushing a broom about the place. No way would I like to think he's getting the same money as me. *He's not given up what I've given up.*' The men hark back to the long years of apprenticeship, doing menial jobs at low pay. 'My friends, when I left school, were always on a lot better money than I was, able to do more things than me. But I felt I was doing the right thing, because I would earn better in the long run. Now, if I find myself working alongside people who got the ready cash when they were younger, *and* now get as much as me, well . . . ' One is reminded of the scribes, the pen-pushers put out of work by the printing press, who in the fourteenth century 'claimed frankly that as they had spent time and money in learning their craft they should be given preference in the exercise of it'.[4]

In the general trade where many of these men started, it was the apprenticed lads who did much of the work that would have been done, in different circumstances, by the unskilled men of another union. Since the older men 'wouldn't have been seen dead with a broom in their hands', it was partly on the skivvying of the apprentices that the differentiation of skilled and unskilled was able to stand up at all. Skill once acquired, the compositor then felt entitled to his pound of flesh. 'A road sweeper may come in here and take a job as a messenger boy. All he has to do is to carry this folder from here to there. Not like a skilled man who has to think all the shift through about his job.' 'It's a joke that they get 87 per cent of our money.' 'Half of them can't read.'

There is a fundamental flaw, of course, in the logic of the pay differential. It is this: the men say, 'I could do the unskilled fellow's job, but he could not do mine.' One comp, giving this very reason, said, 'I think the levelling-out of the differential between skilled and unskilled is a terrible mistake.' When prompted as to whether he would *like* to do the unskilled man's job, however, he answered unhesitatingly, 'I would be bored to death. All he does is sit in a chair and push tubes up a spout. I couldn't do it. I wasn't saying I *would* do it', and he laughed uneasily. The fact is that many men try to have it both ways. They say that their job is harder and deserves more pay, yet they wouldn't take the unskilled job *even at the same pay*. Unskilled jobs are less pleasant and above all carry less status. This flaw in the logic is, interestingly, revealed by phase-one photocomposition. At King and Hutchings the photocomposition tappers, who are said to have the most boring and monotonous job, are permitted a small differential over the other craftsmen. It was reported to me that scarcely a man on the paste-up boards would resent this. But can the premium be both: a payment for boredom *and* for skill?

Many of the men seem to hold onto the pay differential as a basic motive force in society. It is a metaphor for competition, reward, achievement and self-development. 'It's a carrot, isn't it.' 'It's an incentive to learn new techniques, to progress.' It seems to be the law of the jungle, but in reality this struggle within the working class doesn't have the graceful impartiality of nature, red in tooth and claw, since the skilled men have actively organised the subordination of their inferiors and continue to do so. 'They've got to be *kept* under us.' Worse than nature, it is the hierarchical principle of patriarchy and of capitalism as it is manifest in the sphere of work. The political definition of skill, like class and gender, is always dynamic and relative. For every person or job that is defined as skilled, another must be defined as less skilled. It is not surprising that craft ideology has coexisted in most uneasy tension with socialist ideas.

The politics of masculinity

In all that the men are saying about skill and status they are saying something, too, about sex and gender. There are large-scale tensions and power struggles among and between men *as men*. Men identify work itself, the fact of waged work outside the home and family, with masculinity. Second only to warfare, work is the arena in which men wrestle with each other for status and survival. Andrew Tolson, in *The Limits of Masculinity*, writes:

> For men, definitions of masculinity enter into the way work is personally experienced, as a life-long commitment and responsibility. In some respects work itself is made palatable only through the kinds of compensations masculinity can provide – the physical effort, the comradeship, the rewards of promotion. When work is unpalatable, it is often only his masculinity (his identification with the wage; 'providing for the wife and kids') that keeps a man at work day after day.[5]

It is curious how many lively and detailed portrayals of men at work – studies of dockers, coal miners, shipbuilders, car workers – hear what the men are saying about class but fail to analyse or comment upon what they are saying equally clearly about sex and gender, about their self-definition as *men*.[6] We saw in Chapter 1 how the print apprentice follows his father out of the childhood home and takes up his role as a young man in a world of work, a world structured not only by capital but most importantly by older men in the printing craft, and how apprenticeship itself appears to be a rite of passage into manhood.

To be threatened with loss of work, therefore, means more than mere loss of livelihood. The men I talked with who had been through the 11-month lock-out at Times Newspapers, experiencing both idleness and the prospect of losing their jobs altogether due to new technology, voiced feelings that showed that they had felt their masculine identity threatened. Some of them had been fearful and resentful of the idea that now they were not working outside the home they should, perhaps, do more housework. 'At union meetings the men would complain to each other, "I'm fed up stuck at home with nothing to do". And someone would shout across the hall, "What about the washing?" There'd be laughs. It became a standard joke. But you know, it wasn't a joke. It wasn't a joke at all.' They found themselves 'under the wife's feet'. 'I had become a permanent part of the scenery at home. Which she didn't like to start with. And voiced it. That screwed me up.' A man's position in the household is one of power. But that power is contingent on his absence at work all day. *Being* at home does not enhance the power – it tarnishes it.

One man felt that this pressure was part of the industrial strategy of the employers. 'It's all very well to talk about the job up here, but it was putting pressure on the wives, on the family. And I believe this was the idea in the company's mind. It was a deliberate attack to cause a man . . . because if you take away a man's livelihood, you sack him, you know . . . the idea is to say, "We are bigger than you because we have the money."And they *do*.' Most would not ascribe such a conspiratorial intention to the employers, but would agree that the firm is able to exploit the fact that a man depends for his self-respect on the idea that, though he is small in relation to capital he is big in relation to his home and wife. A part of the process by which the owners can smash him is by undermining his position at home and in society, where his stature depends on being in a high-status job, earning good pay. So, 'I found those months during the lock-out very degrading, *very* degrading. I felt ashamed of myself. It put strains on our marriage.'

Masculinity also enters into the class struggle that resists such disasters. The solidarity forged between men as a group of males is part of the organised craft's defence against the employer.[7] Many women who have had reason to work with compositors will confirm my experience that they make a big show of apologising for 'bad language', explaining that in the normal way, as men with men, they are accustomed to 'use language' that would offend a woman's ears. By this they don't mean the odd 'damn' or 'bloody'. The social currency of the composing room is women and woman-objectifying talk, from sexual expletives and innuendo through to narrations of exploits and fantasies. The wall is graced with four-colour litho 'tits and bums'. Even the computer is used to produce life-size print-outs of naked women.

In this, compositors are no different from garage mechanics or any other group of men working in the absence of real, as opposed to fantasised, women. It says something about their relationship with women (a theme which is explored further in Chapter 6). But it perhaps says as much about their relationship with each other.

The rapid apology, often tendered far sooner than need be, to a visiting woman is a way of saying, 'You are different. You are out of place.' It is directly descended from the ritual payment of money on the visit of a woman to the chapel in the nineteenth century as recounted in Chapter 1. Women are the subject of a traffic among men[8] that serves the purpose of forging solidarity within the workshop and giving meaning and strength to the chapel, which needs all the strength it can get in its struggle against the employer.

Work is a daily reminder of the working man's relative powerlessness in the face of capital. Even craft can do no more than modify this powerlessness. Just look at Emile Zola's description of a moment when the balance of power is tilted. It is from the novel *L'Assomoir* published in 1870.[9] In it, an employer had recently introduced into his hand workshop a new invention, a machine that forged rivets at tremendous speed 'with the quiet ease of a giant'. Goujot, the skilled hand rivet-maker, contemplated with rage and despair this monster that 'possessed arms more powerful than his own'. If he could, he would destroy the machine with his hammer (which he affectionately called 'Fifine'), both for its threat to the working man's livelihood but also because he feared that his girlfriend, Gervaise, 'would despise him after seeing the machines. For though he was stronger than [other men] yet the machines were stronger than he was.' There is always a fragility in men's reliance on work as a prop for their masculine identity: work can be fragmented, skill flouted, and a man's tool made to look impotent beside the employer's new machinery.

Listening to the skilled man's account of his relation to the less skilled, it is impossible not to sense a competitiveness and fear that has a sexual basis. And once this is brought into a conscious analysis of compositors' circumstances, it becomes clear that it is effects stemming from the sex/gender system that introduce the contradiction into otherwise relatively simple class situations. For instance, a class analysis alone would suggest that the skilled man's supremacy over the unskilled is assured. Seen in sexual terms, however, it is problematic. Skill, technological knowledge and high earnings are positively correlated with masculine stature, but so too (and perhaps more fundamentally) are physical strength and endurance. These latter qualities accrue much more to manual labouring than to skilled craftwork, and within the crafts, to some more than to others. Paul Willis, for instance, suggests:

> The conjunction of elements of manual labour-power with certain kinds of masculine gender definitions in the culture of the shop floor is one of the truly essential features of [its] social organisation . . . Manual labour is suffused with masculine qualities and given certain sensual overtones. The toughness and awkwardness of physical work and effort – for itself and in the division of labour, and for its strictly capitalist logic, quite without intrinsic heroism or grandeur – takes on masculine lights and depths and assumes a significance beyond itself. Whatever the specific problems of the difficult task, they are always essentially masculine problems, requiring masculine capacities to deal with them. We may say that where the principle of general abstract labour has emptied work of significance from inside, a transformed patriarchy has filled it with significance from the outside. Discontent with work is turned away from a political discontent and confused in its logic by a huge detour into the symbolic sexual realm.[10]

A compositor's work has always been less physically demanding than some crafts, especially those associated with engineering. He is no 'coal-black smith' of the sexual ballad. Quite the contrary, he has wished to be considered an intellectual among working men and has been proud to recount the fact, for instance, that Henry II of France dubbed compositors 'gentlemen' and exempted them from the tax levied on 'mechanics'.[11] For men there is a contradiction between the scale of class standing and of masculine standing. In adopting semi-intellectual status through mental or sedentary work, a man, within the patriarchal value system, forfeits a little masculine toughness.

This may be one way of making sense of the energy committed to maintaining and increasing the pay differential over unskilled labourers – it has a compensatory importance for the craftsman. If an artisan's masculinity is overshadowed by the physicality of the 'uncultured, rough' labourer he may seek to reassert it by winning more rounds in the struggle against the employer, carrying home a higher wage. Calling this 'the fetishism of the wage packet', Paul Willis suggests:

> The male wage packet is held to be central, not simply because of its size but because it is won in a masculine mode in confrontation with the 'real' world which is too tough for women. Thus the man in the domestic household is held to be the breadwinner, 'the worker', while the wife works for the extras . . . The wage packet as a kind of symbol of machismo dictates the domestic culture and economy and tyrannises both men and women.[12]

None of this is to under-estimate the vital economic importance for the worker (whether man or woman) of the wage bargain struck with the employer within the power relations of class. It is to situate it *additionally* within the second context of the power relations of patriarchy, where it can be seen to have quite different resonances.

A compositor reading the above passage in draft commented, 'She is saying we are homosexuals.' An objective reading will show that that is not the import of the above few paragraphs. But this response to them bears out my point: to these men it matters crucially that their 'masculinity', as they have defined it themselves, is never in doubt. It is often felt to be challenged, and it is just as often reasserted. One form taken by this reassertion has been the preservation, until recently, of the craft trade unions as all-male institutions, clubs from which women are excluded. That the less skilled were 'obliged' to include women among the membership of their general unions could be represented as a kind of political impotence.

The Cain-and-Abel rivalry between the skilled and the unskilled is only one face of a more general and fundamental fear in which men hold each other. As women, the source of our fear is always *men*. When we visualise danger – rape, murder, tyranny – it is (and quite realistically) men whom we fear. This sometimes leads us to forget that, for men, too, other men are a source of fear: men who are rivals in the rat-race for success, men who may throw a punch in a pub brawl, or draw a knife in a back alley.[13] At a societal level it is characteristically men who militarise other men, imprison them, establish tyrannies or dictatorships over them. It is predominantly men, too, who flesh out the ruling class of capitalists that so determines the chances of working men. Male solidarity is not only a way of excluding women, it is a way of assuring a more secure presence within the dangerous world of other men.

If 'craft v. labour' is one dimension of men's relationship to men in work, there are others too. One is proximity to *technology*; and the other is the distinction between *'mental' and manual work*.

Like the physical strength and skill it replaces, technology is a source of power. As I shall argue in more detail in ensuing chapters, men have acquired, in the course of their history, a close and inter-active relationship with technology that has tended to exclude women. Technology also confers power on those groups of men that are close to it, relative to those other *men* who work with their bare hands or as mere slave operators of the machinery. Comps built their old craft strength on the foundation of their control of a specific technology. Their right over the tools, the lead and the linotypes, was one of the things that set them apart from the unskilled manual labourers. The technology was, almost literally, a lever to status and pay. Now the old wizardry of hot metal has vanished before the new wizardry of electronics. A new set of men (and it *is* men) have inherited the mantle of technological power. It is not just in composing for print that the technician has risen in ascendance over the craftsman. Dennis Gleeson points to the increasing divergence of craft and technician apprentices in technical education: 'Conferring upon the technician a recognisable status has become one of the prime objectives of technical education.' Educational policy 'actively reinforces social (rather than technical) hierarchies, distinguishing the two types of worker.' As a result, technician students and teachers tend to look down on craft apprentices, ascribing to them a 'rough and moronic mentality', lumping them in with those other despised groups 'blacks, illiterates, the unemployed and so forth'.[14] These phrases echo the craft compositor's scorn of the Natty. Now he in his turn is being socially constructed as inferior.

The technological dimension of power within the male sex, however, is also contradictory. Though proximity to technology wields relative power within the field of manual workers and is high in the masculine scale of values, in class terms it is nonetheless subordinate to mental work. Even the electronic technician may have less status than the administrator, the accountant and the journalist. Journalists (editors and reporters) have high prestige in the newspaper as people who handle ideas, important personalities, the world outside. As I suggested above, mental work has two conflicting values for men and both are reflected in the above attitude of compositors to journalists. On the one hand their work is seen as having higher status because it is active in influencing and controlling the labour process of manual workers, and because it is given prestige and rewards by capital in recognition of a governing role in production. Comps frequently express respect for the editor and senior journalists on their paper. They are often proud to say they are on first-name terms with this one and that one, some of them famous personalities whose names are by-lined in the newspaper. They describe 'what he said to me and what I said to him' on those occasions when the journalist comes down to the composing room to check the progress of an article. When comps express scorn for the journalist's lack of practical knowledge of type-production it often seems to be an expression of defiant self-defence against the imagined class superiority of the intellectual. On the other hand, equally convincingly, mental work can be seen as the occupation of sedentary, pale-faced weeds of fellows: 'no work for a man, that'. This both reflects and is reflected in the fact that a higher proportion of the incumbents of *these* occupations, than of craft and technological occupations, are women. (A parallel observation: I was told in interview by a NATSOPA officer that men in the all-male machine branch often write off men in the clerical branch of the union, a mixed branch with women members, as 'a bunch of poufters'.)

The cross-valorisation of masculinity and manual labour – an effect arising in the sex/gender system – has been shown to have its uses for capital. If 'mental' work was highly valued on both class and masculinity scales, who would want to fill the mass of labouring jobs? In a study of teenage lads, Paul Willis has found that it is a social imperative for them to differentiate themselves, sharply and clearly, from girls.[15] Manual work is identified as hefty, masculine and desirable; mental work as effeminate and despicable. In their eyes, only a boy whose masculinity was suspect would opt for white-collar work.

The revolutionising of technology, then, has a disordering and restructuring effect within the hierarchies of patriarchy as well as those of class. It threatens with illogicality the meanings we are used to making of our experience; it demands reassessments. Nor does it bear only on relations between men and women – it disrupts relations between men and men.

Class in turmoil

The compositors' uneasy relations with their fellows may seem to lend credence to the idea that comps don't think of themselves as belonging to the working class, as print *workers*. But that is not the case. They see quite clearly a structure that binds the various parts of the print workforce into a whole. It is a hierarchised whole, certainly, but the very detailing of the hierarchy, the unrelenting necessity to maintain or improve that patterning from one's own sectional point of view, as well as the shared battle with the employer, give it some sort of unity. It is a unity in which the skilled man sees himself included as much as the unskilled.

The impressions I gained from this study in many ways bore out those of I. C. Cannon in a study of London compositors made 20 years earlier.[16] He set out to enquire whether, by virtue of his material position and the social ranking he is given, the compositor's class and political affiliations were at that time breaking down. He concluded on the contrary that class consciousness was stronger among comps than among skilled workers in general. 'Despite their material prosperity there is still a considerable amount of feeling of belonging to the working class.' He believed the forces maintaining the comps' allegiance to the working class resided in the pressures of the occupation itself, in an occupational ethos. 'The good comp is a good trade unionist, a member of the working class and a supporter of the Labour Party.'

Of course, many of the printers I talked to, and they are not alone in this, preferred not to *use* class terms if at all possible. In everyday life an egalitarian person feels distaste for the idea of 'class distinctions'. 'I've got no truck with the class system. People are people.' 'I'd like to see a classless society.' Class ideas in current usage are a double bind: to hold them is either to be a snob or to have a pointless inferiority complex. Thus a man would say, 'I am what I am, I don't care about who I meet. If I like people I like them. If I don't I leave them alone. I like people for what they really *are*, not for their station or class in life.'

This representation of 'class' is not dissimilar from the usage of mainstream sociology in which classes are seen as strata, like the sediments in the earth's crust laid down by prehistoric oceans. 'An arrangement of society into layers', Ivan Reid called the concept of social stratification in his primer on class in Britain.[17] It is a categorisation that relies on factors such as income distribution, house ownership, occupation, patterns of consumption, even the accent you talk with. In this meaning of the word, an important factor is how much money you earn and how you spend it. 'You are measured by where you live.' 'One will go and get a nice house for himself, spend his money on books. Another will go over to the pub at the end of the day and piddle it against the wall.'

There is no dynamic in such classes – one does not take part in creating or destroying another. They are inert. The individual, however, by choice and willpower, can crawl up from one to the next. Through fecklessness or mischance he may slip a stratum or two. It is not surprising then that the more open-minded, fair and generous people mistrust the idea of class altogether, if this is what it means. Even within this account of class, however, the great majority of the 50 compositors I interviewed saw comps as a whole, and themselves in particular, as working-class. Only four (three of whom were in Fleet Street) preferred to see themselves as middle-class.

Such a representation of class, however, exists alongside another alternative meaning, apparently without contradiction. Among the men I spoke to, even those who would not call themselves socialists, let alone marxists, held a clear working understanding of class as a question of the relationship to the means of production – though they would not have used that term. They saw it as making a fundamental difference whether you owned or did not own the resources that determined the work-chances and life-chances of the rest. Thus a man who expressed right-wing views in other respects, when considering his own class position said, 'There are capitalists. Yes. But to be capitalists they have to employ someone. At least, at the moment they do. Does that imply a working class? Yes. *You can't have one without the other.*'

When talking about the firm, their position in production, the great majority of the men described it as a terrain of latent, sometimes active, conflict. With few exceptions they were conscious of the exploitation of labour by capital, of an imbalance of initiative and power. It is impossible now to know what their consciousness of these things was before the changes in the pattern of ownership and management in the industry that has occurred in the last twenty years, and before the disruption and alarm caused by the introduction of new technology. But there were few who did not have an awareness of working in a large corporation where little love is lost or loyalty given on either side.

This was especially the case at Times Newspapers where the men still felt raw from the lock-out. Many were convinced that the Canadian-based Thomson Organisation wanted to 'grind the unions into the dust'. (The advent of Murdoch, of course, had left them in even less doubt.) The awareness was, as might be expected, least in evidence at Croydon Advertiser, the family firm where the changeover had been least traumatic. A man at the *Mirror* said 'IPC, they would do away with us tomorrow if they could. They have turned London into a desert as far as print is concerned. Because they have closed down every print firm, Southwark Offset, all the big places. They are gangsters, really.'

If the men were clear enough that the scrapping of hot-metal technology was a class measure, it did however give rise to a new confusion about the relative status and identity of individuals and groups *within* the working class. What had happened with the advent of new technology was that the hierarchisation, the internal patterning of class as well as of sex, seemed to be melting away and reforming, into some as yet unforeseen pattern. Computerised photocomposition had taken up this age-old set of relations, the structure the skilled men saw themselves as inhabiting and had done so much to create, and tossed it about like a playing-card house in a high wind. They were no longer precisely sure what the structure looked like or of their place in it.

One reality of course is that new technology in printing, and elsewhere, entails higher levels of unemployment. Joblessness itself is a great leveller. Besides, during the lock-out at *The Times*, for instance, some men had found themselves *glad* of work as milkmen or window cleaners. Painful as they are, such experiences can lead to a reconsideration of social distinctions. But it is not only the harsh democracy of the dole queue that the compositor tries to envisage. He is trying to discern, too, what will happen to him if he is lucky enough to stay on in work, as computerised photocomposition proceeds to exert its own logic on the labour process. As we have seen, the distinction between men's work and women's work, apparently a natural distinction but in fact one that was historically constructed, loses its clarity. The ambiguity of the new keyboard is a symbol of this: is it 'his' or 'hers'? The line between mental and manual work gets retraced. The ordinary compositor working on the electronic system seems less 'manual'; conversely, the journalist working on it seems to be no longer a pure conceptualiser, but closer to production. The sharp divide between production hands and clerical or administrative staff is also softened. The technological forecast of the Printing Industries Research Association and the Printing and Publishing Industry Training Board foresaw that skills in the compositor's general area of concern 'will need to be more aligned to data processing and editorial functions'.[18] The new work team may well be a semi-mental, semi-manual editorial/ typographic interface between the origination of written material and the printing press. Several of the men I talked with, momentarily suspending their commitment to resisting a direct-entry system at all, mused on the possibility of acquiring some editorial skills, or filling out their role to become a new kind of 'typographic expert'. Such changes are not just characteristic of new technology in print. Ernest Mandel notes, 'The decline of traditional skills is accompanied by a greater mobility and plasticity of labour-power within the plant.' In automated factories, 'the distinction between workers and office employees largely loses its meaning.'[19]

This scenario of class restructuring is as yet no more than a hunch about the future. In newspapers the shake-out has as yet barely begun. Many of the compositors however already seemed to be experiencing a kind of crisis of class identity, as well as of gender identity. They felt unsure as to whether the changes they were living through implied an 'upgrading' or a 'downgrading' of their occupation in social terms. Most felt pretty sure that the new technology had made *some* difference to the job, but they were divided between each other and in their own minds, as to whether it had raised it or lowered it. The upward theme in part reflected the idea that advances in the forces of production are societal advances from which the worker is not altogether barred. 'When other people hear you are working with a computer they tend to feel that you have been upgraded.' And if you ranked white-collar work high, then 'It has pushed us *up* to the office-type class of worker more.' One compositor had already detected a change at Times Newspapers. 'One or two of them now are coming to work in suits, used to be an old pair of slacks before. They have a little air about them, acting unpaid lance corporals', he said, bitterly.

Equally strongly, though, some felt themselves reduced in social standing. 'I think we are being declassed. It has brought us down a peg or two'. 'We are downgraded, definitely. Taken it right out. Yes.' In part this reflected the historically lower status of clerical work. But it also responded to a realisation that even jobs such as journalism, computer programming and the lower levels of management, were now subject to more routinisation and control and no longer carried the status they had done in the past.[20]

Most people however were confused in their own minds about it, so that they produced circular arguments. 'I'm not sure. If photocomposition has done anything it has pulled us up. But then again, printers, compared to the rest of the workers, now compared with then, we have gone down in prestige, down in the world.' The men are used to believing that a working man is one who 'has black hands to earn white money'.[21] 'If you have clean hands you are seen as a professional. But I don't know. An electronics engineer, he is a very, very clever person, yet he gets his hands dirty. And someone in an office may only be filling in forms. I'm not too sure about this one.' 'I'd say the job has been upgraded through the cleanliness of photocomposition, the office type of environment. But as regards skill, it's been downgraded. I don't know if you can make anything of it? I can't understand the thing myself. To me, it's a paradox.'

No wonder comps say they no longer know whether they are blue-collar or white-collar workers, and that some of the men were readier than they had been to see the contradictions and illogicalities in their hardened attitudes to others. Some of the men were ready to see the humanity and sense in the NGA's new ideas on abandoning a fixed term of apprenticeship and developing an open, flexible modular system of training for the industry. 'That's right, it's quite wrong for the NATSOPA lad to be stuck there, so's he can't progress. It's frustrating and completely wrong.' 'The differential used to be important to me because I felt it was a skilled job I had learned to do. Perhaps now I don't commit myself so wholeheartedly to maintaining it, because there *is* no difference in the jobs now.' 'People stand on their dignity about this skill lark. But I think all that is finished with. Anyone can be trained, anyone of average intelligence, for this job. All this crafts, profession, nonsense, it is only for job protection and that applies whether it is doctors, lawyers or printers.'

So the men were feeling, as a result of the disordering and restructuring of their world by capital, newly adrift in the class structure, or rather they felt the structure was melting around them. In no doubt what their class position had been, they were less sure of what it was becoming. It was not that they felt simply reduced to the unskilled man they had once so despised, but that they felt he and they had perhaps both shed their old garments and put on the same characterless guise. And this habit, too, was not very different from that worn by people of whose class standing they were even less certain than their own: journalists, computer operators, programmers, technologists, office workers and women workers.

Given this disturbance of old patterns, it makes sense to look anew for the most politically productive manner of locating individuals within class politics. So much theorising about the proper boundaries of 'the proletariat' or 'the working class' has been sterile and academicist, leading to no new thoughts on political strategy or working-class potential.[22] It helps very little to affirm that 'we are all the employees of capital'. As many compositors pointed out, by that criterion their managers are workers too. It seems less than useful to assert that 'the journalist's labour power is exploited just like that of the manual worker', or 'the computer technician's labour too is a source of profit to the newspaper capitalist'. It is more important to know *what their relationship is to each other.*

Considering the class status of industrial, scientific and technical workers, André Gorz has suggested that, even though it seems legitimate to consider them as falling within the category of productive, exploited and alienated workers, it does not seem correct to consider them purely and simply an integral part of the working class:

> Although it is certainly true that the science and technology they produce are alienated from them, are at the service of capital and confront *them* as an alien power over which they have no control, it is also true . . . that, from the point of view of the working class, science and technology are means of exploitation and of extraction of surplus value.[23]

This is a train of thought that it is useful to pursue into the world of the newspaper. Let's think of the technicians and technologists there, the workers closest to the new computerised system. They are the ones responsible for the development, testing and introduction (and in due course also the servicing) of the very technology that so threatens the compositor and other manual workers. As we have seen, there is nothing neutral in class terms about that technology. Craftsmen have no reason to see the technologist as their class ally. As Gorz puts it, these categories of employee participate in 'the dequalification of the direct producer'.[24] In quite a direct sense, the person concerned, for instance, with computer programmes, can make choices, or be required to implement decisions that increase or decrease the control of workers' performance by management. Mike Hales makes the more general point that the work of some workers, these among them, is to design the labour processes of other workers.[25] There is an imbalance between the mutual impact of the two groups:

> Technical and scientific workers produce the means by which other workers are exploited and oppressed . . . manual workers, on the other hand, do not produce the means whereby technical and scientific workers are exploited. At the

point where the relationship is direct it is not a reciprocal one, but a hierarchical one.[26]

Once we begin to apply this principle in the now familiar world of the newspaper, it raises questions, for instance, also about the journalist. Much of what is written for the press and more of what is eventually published is of an objectively anti-working-class character. Even the Royal Commission on the Press, reporting in 1977, was obliged to make one of its major themes the complaints of the labour movement concerning the overwhelming support for the Conservative Party in the press as a whole and the destructive interpretation habitually published of trade unions and strikes.[27] Many independent critics have made the same point.[28] Women writers and women's organisations complain of the continual exploitation of women as sexual commodities in the press itself and in the advertisements carried by newspapers, and of a universal trivialising of women's problems and the women's movement.[29] I discuss these aspects of the press further in Chapter 7.

Taken overall, the product of journalists (reporters and editors alike) plays an important part in establishing and maintaining in popular currency ideas that inhibit fundamental social, sexual and economic change. And if many of the basic flaws in newspapers, seen from an egalitarian and progressive point of view, stem from their capitalist ownership and operation, there is no denying that ultimately it is 'the practice of journalism which defines news'.[30] The stories are selected and given priority, the phrasing chosen and amended, by reporters, editors and 'subs'.

Finally, then, to return to the compositor. As a 'mere' manual worker, are his hands clean of the exploitation of others? It appears not. We've already seen how craftsmen organised, within the labour process and without, in such a way as to disadvantage other groups – the less skilled or women. The historical reasons, even justifications, for this are clear, but the fact remains. Just as the technician stratum today is, under capital's tutelage, playing a part in constructing the old craft stratum as an inferior fraction of the working class, so, through the very definition of skilled labour processes, craftsmen have, in part, created 'unskilled' labour processes.

Besides, do compositors not share with journalists some of the responsibility for the disastrous role that their product plays in society, for newspaper content? Compositors have a curious detachment from the text they handle. The union has a long-standing agreement with the employers' organisations to abstain from 'interference' in press content. When on the very rare occasions that individual comps or stereotypers 'batter the type', it is usually only to obliterate the figures that reveal their own high earnings, in reports of disputes or pay deals. The chapels seldom protest about newspaper content, and when they do it is almost without exception to demand the right of reply to a report bearing on their own union. None of the compositors I interviewed felt that it would be proper or practical for themselves, the chapel or the union in any way to 'censor' (as they put it) newspaper articles they are called upon to typeset or paste up.[31] To render the press more serviceable to the working class and less exploitative of women has not been a major theme in union strategies. Whatever the objective class status of newspaper workers then, not excluding manual workers, working-class solidarity has not, in observable practice, been very strong.

The current shake-up within 'the collective labourer' of the press of course offers advantages to capital. It temporarily upsets the structure in which the workers have organised themselves and have developed a degree of control of work. Groups that were strongly unionised, like the compositors, lose their power base. The groups that emerge as economically important may, in the first instance, be the less strongly organised and least militant (computer programmers, for instance, or tele-ad typists). Besides, interchangeability or polyvalence in a workforce affords the employers the freedom of selecting workers from within a more numerous and potentially cheaper labour market. It tends to break down union-imposed demarcation lines and to enable a more flexible use of labour in production. So it is a moment of peril for working-class interests.

On the other hand, such a crisis could open up new possibilities. At worst, the turmoil could be resolved by a renewed split – privileged and secure workers reconciled to 'progress' and to their role in capitalist production at the expense of the peripheral workers, unemployed people on the margins of the economy, and the rest of the working class who have the misfortune to feature both as the raw material and the consumers of their newspaper product. But if the structure of the working class, partly as a result of skilled workers' strategies, has in the past meant division, rivalry and strife, a restructuring cannot be all bad. It could open the way to a more embracingly class-conscious movement of solidarity within the industry.

In this respect a hopeful and positive glimmer within the newspaper workforce to date is the Campaign for Press and Broadcasting Freedom, formed in 1979. It is supported by all the printing trade unions, including the NGA, by the NUJ and by many individuals and groups involved with the radical and left-wing press. The Campaign lays the blame for the quality of the press primarily on its capitalist ownership and its dependence on advertising, and on state-imposed restrictions on reporting. But it offers a critique of the content of newspapers, pointing to their anti-working-class and anti-union bias and their endemic racism and has devised a code of practice concerning press content, including clauses on racism, that should bind the members of all the unions involved in newspaper production. Some members are seeking a code on sexism too. The Campaign's main demand is for a 'right of reply' for those groups or individuals misrepresented in the press. The role of printing production workers could be to monitor press content as it is prepared, to alert potentially wronged groups, and when a right of reply is demanded, to give chapel support to it. At present the Campaign is little more than rhetorical, but it symbolises a potential socialist responsibility among workers in the industry. In a way that print unions individually have seldom done, the Campaign gives a central importance to the disastrous social and political significance of the press in Britain and recognises that, collectively, labour is not altogether guiltless nor powerless.

In fact, an initiative recently organised by the Campaign has resulted in an unprecedentedly altruistic action by print unions. In the summer of 1982 the Campaign put representatives of nurses and hospital auxiliaries, who were in dispute over low pay, into direct contact with Fleet Street chapels. The chapels espoused the hospital workers' cause and demanded of their editors the inclusion of statements in support of the strike as the price of their own continued co-operation in production of the newspapers. It is not coincidental, I think, that the Campaign for Press and Broadcasting Freedom, a united organisation of many different labour interests in printing, and this kind of class-conscious action, have arisen at a time when new technology is giving all groups in the newspaper workforce a shared problem.

It is a long throw from a 'class-as-against-capital' to a 'class-for-itself'. Notional alignments by labour with or in opposition to capital, acquiescence or militancy, are an insufficient measure of working-class consciousness. 'The working class' is never likely to become a historic force by virtue of its relation to capital alone. Its revolutionary potential lies in the relationships it could embody within itself and carry into material practice.

6. Women: stepping out of role

It may seem curious that the foregoing discussion of class and class dissensions has at times had a rather masculist tone, with not only the skilled but also the *unskilled* characterised as male. It is a fact, however, that the craftsmen I talked with seemed to represent women as a distinct kind of problem. Women were never merely lumped in with 'the Natties'.[1] It is as though the old pay-grade structure in which there was a craftsman (Grade 1), semi-skilled and unskilled men (Grades 2 and 3), and a final category appended below the rest and labelled 'Women', continued to be not merely a negotiating tool but a social reality.

Among the many divisions and tensions within the working class in printing, the rift between men and women has been one of the most deep and destructive. The aggressiveness of craftsmen and their unions towards women as potential rivals for work is often represented in union history (and even today) as an unfortunate but inevitable by-product of the men's class struggle with the employer. 'They were only defending themselves against the employer's exploitation of women as cheap labour.' The conflict cannot be reduced to this single dimension of class, however. Had nothing but class interest been at stake, the men would have found women acceptable as apprentices, would have fought whole-heartedly for equal pay for women *and* for the right of women to keep their jobs at equal pay. As it was, the men and their unions sought to have the women removed from the trade. The arguments used by men against women differed from those used against male rivals. They expressed the interests of men in the social and sexual subordination of women.

In this chapter I want first to recount the story of one particular three-sided struggle between employers, women and men which will serve to illustrate some of the sex and class interests at stake. Then I will analyse the position of women in the printing industry and the NGA today, and finally, delve deeper into the meanings men ascribe to their relations with women as workers, comparing their attitudes in the late nineteenth and early twentieth century with those of today. The ideologies men have invoked and the union strategies they have adopted make sense only if a sex/gender analysis is combined with that of class.

A crusade against women

There is no doubt that, in the last resort, the craft work of composition for print was men's work *because men said it was*. In the report of the proceedings of the Fair Wages Committee of 1907, Mr. Naylor, General Secretary of the London Society of Compositors, said in the opening remarks of his evidence, 'We regard the work of a compositor as work to be done by a man and not by a woman.' 'May I interrupt you for one moment?' asked one of his interlocutors. 'On what ground do you contend that composing work is work for men and not for women?' 'By the fact', replied Naylor, 'that it has always been regarded as men's work . . . a large number of men are attracted to the trade because it is a man's employment.' The committee examiner did not let him off the hook so easily. 'You do not suggest that there is anything unsuitable in the work for women, do you?' he pursued. 'No', said Naylor, 'I do not.' 'It is merely on the ground that there are men already in it and that it is unfair to prejudice them by the introduction of women, is that it?' 'Yes.' Nor was it merely a problem of women getting lower pay: Naylor's Scottish colleague pointed out to the Committee that 'when a lady passed for the Bar, although she did not want to work for under-pay at all, she was not admitted, and the result is that she cannot practise. That is what happened in the legal profession and we say that what is good in one case is good in another. Self-protection is the first law of nature.'[2] Since, with equal pay, no undercutting could occur, we must suppose he meant 'protection' from a flouting of patriarchal order.

The typographical associations did not stop at rhetoric: they organised to exclude women and were not ashamed to say so. 'If it were not for the union in London I venture to think that women would be all over the London trade,' said Naylor. 'Fortunately, the London Union has been strong enough to keep them entirely out.' It was in very similar vein that men said to me only last year, 'It has been the policy of our union: keep them out.' 'Women will only come into the news trade if the union loses its grip.'

The 'woman question' has not existed only at the level of a tension-ridden fellowship between the sexes. At times it has broken out into bitter conflict between men and women.[3] One such incident occurred in Scotland early in this century. In the course of a strike among compositors in Edinburgh in 1872, a number of women had been introduced by employers and trained to replace the men. In this way women had gained a foothold in the city, while the local typographical association was in disarray. By the end of the century there were 750 women in Edinburgh in direct competition with the journeymen. Other Scottish cities had also become 'plagued' by the use of women typesetters. During the depression, women were bitterly blamed for the numbers of unemployed men. Despite many resolutions on 'The Female Question', however, the compositors' craft organisation had been too weak to deal with the scandal.[4]

The situation in Scotland was irritating and alarming not only to Scottish compositors but also to the trade south of the border. It was an instance of what might happen in southern cities if the societies let up their firm position on women. It also enabled Edinburgh employers to undercut southern prices, so putting London jobs at risk.

In December 1886 a national conference of delegates from the Scottish Typographical Association (STA), the Typographical Association of England and the London Society of Compositors discussed as an urgent matter: should women compositors be enrolled into the unions? The men faced a dilemma. From the point of view of working-class interests of course all the advantage lay in enrolling the women. But for many of the men it was unthinkable that women should be allowed to join the all-male trade society from which they drew so much of their self-respect as artisans and as men. It was their club, as sacrosanct as the gentleman's dining club in Pall Mall. The ambivalence felt by the delegates gave rise to the curiously worded resolution mentioned in Chapter 1, by which women were technically admitted to membership, but on a condition which, in practice, they would be unable to fulfil.

The associations could rest assured that an employer would be very unlikely to employ a woman at the male craft rate. And so it proved. Though some hardy employers continued to use women at cheap rates and the societies to resist it, no women were admitted to the Typographical Association of England,[5] and only one (a Mrs. Jane Payne) to the London Society of Compositors – and she resigned in 1898.[6] The resolution likewise had little effect on the attitudes of men to women in Scotland. In towns other than Edinburgh the STA withdrew its labour from firms using women comps. But the Edinburgh branch, still on its knees, protested that it was unable to put such a decision into practice.

In ensuing years two attempts were made by feminists to organise women compositors in Edinburgh. The STA was reluctant, however, 'on the grounds that, if the females were organised, their position would be improved as an industry for females [sic], which would result in a great accession to their numbers in the printing trade in Edinburgh.' The men were happier to see the girls starved out than to see them inside their own union.[7]

Male activism began once more when, in 1904, a dispute in Glasgow stirred up an acute bout of hatred for women in the trade. The men had approached the employers for an increase in wages. The Arbitrator refused to award a wage increase on the grounds that, by excluding women, Glasgow compositors were tying the hands of their employers in their competition with Edinburgh firms. The comps responded sharply:

> What the average printer in Glasgow would do with the ladies I cannot fathom, for while they may be taught to sling plain dig [i.e. book setting], I am not aware that the lady jobber has yet come along. The very nature of commercial work, which constitutes the general run of Glasgow work, precludes her employment.[8]

Association branches in other cities in Scotland now began to move against women. In Aberdeen after a 15-week strike the local branch succeeded in obtaining a pledge that no further women would be introduced either at case or on machines. In Dundee the branch achieved a reduction of its 'compesses' to two in number. And Perth reported complete abolition of women members after a strike on the issue.

In Edinburgh, however, the rot continued. It was not until 1909 that the Edinburgh comps launched the big crusade against women for which the trade had been waiting. In the meantime, the monotype machine method of typesetting was spreading fast in the book trade. It separated the processes of setting and casting, making the typesetting occupation, on a typewriter-style of keyboard, highly compatible with contemporary views of women's employment. The Edinburgh men were now in competition with women for both hand and machine composing.

Towards the end of 1909 a 'memorial' was sent to the masters by the Edinburgh branch of the STA: get rid of the women. The members were determined to back it with action. 'What course that action will take is today the agitating thought in Edinburgh printing circles.' There was considerable support for the energetic pursuit of demands. 'The fight, if fight it must be, should be a solid, out and out, all along the line movement. A short, sharp battle is better than months of disheartening and harrassing guerrilla warfare.'[9]

The employers at first replied with 'vague promises to reduce the number of girls at case' (i.e. hand typesetting). This the men well understood to be a useless gesture, since the current threat both to themselves and the hand-compesses alike was the use of women on the keyboards. The Edinburgh comps now sought the backing of the local Federation of Printing and Kindred trades. 'This force is . . . not only new, but untried and is being slowly and surely welded into shape and homogeneity by the present movement.' The compositors were receiving particular support from the unskilled men of the Warehousemen and Cutters' Union and the National Society of Operative Printers' Assistants to whom they offered thanks 'for invaluable services rendered'.[10] Jonathan Zeitlin has pointed out how the craftsmen gained the allegiance of the unskilled men by promising to lend their own muscle to the struggle of the unskilled for recognition by employers.[11]

Public opinion on the issue was sharply divided. The men had support from the labour movement. But, 'throughout the length and breadth of the land the Edinburgh compositors' action and attitude has been criticised and reviewed and, often, unfortunately, with such an apparent bias and ignorance as to entirely falsify the real position,' they complained.[12]

A curious memorial was received by the masters individually and the Master Printers' Association, their trade body. A copy also reached the STA. It became known as the 'We Women' memorial and was signed by 300 women. It read:

> That we, as representing a large number of the women compositors of Edinburgh, feel that a question affecting a considerable body of women should not be settled without these women having an opportunity of giving expression to their views.
>
> That while recognising that the men have had a real grievance in that some firms have employed an unfair proportion of young girls at apprentice wages, or nearly so, *we women* regard it as a great injustice that one of the main skilled industries open to Edinburgh women should be closed against them.
>
> That *we women* feel that the fact that women have been employed in Edinburgh as compositors for nearly forty years gives women a claim on the business.
>
> That up to the time in Edinburgh the Monotype machines have been largely, if not chiefly, operated by women, and that women have proved themselves entirely competent to work these machines, so that it seems a great hardship that women should be debarred from working at them in future.
>
> That since we have realised the position of women in the printing trade is seriously threatened, *we women* have been trying to organise ourselves with a view to securing justice for ourselves and for the women who may in future desire to practice the business of compositors or monotypists.
>
> That in view of the foregoing considerations we ask you . . . to urge the Masters' Association to delay any decision hurtful to the interests of women compositors until the women's case has been given full consideration.[13]

The STA hit back energetically. 'The vast majority of girls', it contended, 'knew absolutely nothing either of the memorial or its authors'. It was certainly the product of a small coterie of outside feminists 'engaged in political warfare'. Those women comps involved were certain to be the better paid ones. 'The bitterest opponents to this funny little game . . . are to be found in the ranks of the girls themselves,' they claimed, who had no wish for 'the sympathetic help of a class political body, or My Lady's tea-parties'.[14] The 'suffragette-assisted' association responsible for the memorial was accused of collaboration with the masters.[15]

In fact, of course, the women at work in Edinburgh printing firms were terribly torn. It seemed that they were being asked to choose. They could not be both independent wage-earners *and* responsible members of the working class. They would have liked, none more, equal pay with the men. But they knew that on such terms, and without the STA's genuine support, there was no likelihood that the employers would have them. Some abandoned the 'working-class' principle, as the men were defining it, and insisted on women's right to work – for less pay if need be. The STA claimed, however, that the vast majority of the girls were at one with the men in their struggle – and no doubt they were right. To prove it, these women were 'at last taking their place in the ranks of trade unionism and are quickly finding a place and protection even within the ranks of the Printing and Kindred Trades Federation'.[16] This was to say: they were withdrawing their challenge to the craft and were accepting their subordinate position as semi-skilled workers by entering general unions.

The remainder, however, still had to be dealt with. The men were warming to their sense of 'conscious righteousness', secure in the 'knowledge that they will have the moral backing and financial support of the entire trade of the UK'. 'We are going into battle. Let us stand together like comrades and brothers,' they (very appositely) cried.[17] 'Stand fast, Craigellachie!', was their battle-cry.[18]

A well-meaning member of parliament intervened, to be attacked in his turn. He protested:

> Men, in seeking to close the composing-room altogether to
> women are doing a thing which cannot be defended on moral

grounds. The men have no right to impose a barred door between a woman and that kind of work . . . The printing trade is one in many respects suitable for women, and it would be a piece of intolerable tyranny to say that this work shall be the sole monopoly of men . . . The modern women's movement is up in revolt against the very restrictions which the Edinburgh male compositors are trying to impose . . . A hundred other professions and trades are now open to women which were closed to them in years gone by. The women will force their entrance into the composing trade.[19]

He was wrong.

The employers responded. Their proposals were submitted to a packed meeting of the men on 18 May 1910.[20] It is worth noting that 'The Woman Question' pulled out unprecedented numbers of men into active union participation. The meetings in Edinburgh at this time 'for size and solidarity of feeling . . . beat all records within the personal knowledge of its members'.[21]

The employers now agreed that 'no firm should take on any fresh female learners in the composing department for a period of seven years and that all upmaking and corrections of machine-set matter shall be done by men'. They left a loophole for themselves however: women might still be moved up from the case to mono. The men were quick to spot it, and rejected the proposals.

Eventually, however, the employers conceded: no new female learners would be taken into composing departments for a period of six years, i.e. up to 30 June 1916. All keyboards of composing machines installed in future would be operated by male labour.[22] The men were unhappy with this compromise but settlement was made. They need not have worried. The temporary stop became a permanent ban on female apprentices in Scotland. The ban was still in effect in 1953, by which time the few female compositors remaining in the city were all elderly, having been apprenticed before the agreement of 1910. They continued at that date only in Aberdeen and Edinburgh, where they received 70 per cent of the male rate. Elsewhere in Scotland women were completely banned except at the craft rate of pay: consequently there were none.

The craft societies had survived as male power bases. The cost had been paid by women – and perhaps we may say, therefore, it had been paid by the working class, properly conceived. A progressive voice was raised in the *Scottish Typographical Journal* appealing for comradeship with the now diminishing number of women in their defeat. Referring to the unskilled union the author wrote:

> It is not to become members of the same that these girls want. To put it bluntly, a female branch of the Edinburgh Typographical Society would be far more acceptable, and it is what those who threw in their lot with the men really desire. They were educated up to this during the last movement by the 'leaders' and as they (the girls) responded in such a splendid manner, it is surely bad policy to delay matters further . . . You have taken the girls under your wing . . . weld this good material into a staunch sister union.[23]

But his appeal fell on deaf ears. Though the printing industry now grew by leaps and bounds and the roll within the unions affiliated to the Printing and Kindred Trades Federation more than doubled between 1914 and 1920, leaping from 75,000 to 190,000, women with very few exceptions were to be found only among the semi-skilled and unskilled and not in the craft unions. In printing, as in work generally, the twentieth century saw skilled work opportunities pushed further and further out of the reach of women, who filled up the categories of unskilled work instead. In 1911 women performed 24 per cent of skilled jobs in Britain and about 15 per cent of unskilled. By 1971 they performed only 13½ per cent of skilled work and just over 37 per cent of unskilled.[24]

Women's disadvantage in print

Women's status in printing can be measured in various ways. We can compare their actual numbers with those of men; the kind of work they do and the kind that men do; and women's relative earnings.

Women's *participation* in employment in the industry group known as 'paper, printing and publishing', in this century as in the last, has been out of step with trends in employment in the industry as a whole and in employment more generally. Total employment in paper, printing and publishing rose steadily from the 1920s to the mid-sixties, when it reached a peak of two-thirds of a million. The industry had maintained a fairly constant proportion of all manufacturing employment (at around 6 per cent) until this time when, in spite of its own absolute decline, it nonetheless began to represent a growing share of a more rapidly diminishing manufacturing workforce. Women held a steady but low proportion of employment (around 38 per cent) throughout the twenties, thirties and forties.[25] A court of inquiry soon after the second world war complained of the small contribution that female recruitment was making to overcoming the labour shortage of which employers were complaining.[26] Rather than increasing, however, women's participation now declined steadily. Between 1975 and 1980 it fell by a further 1.7 per cent to 30.6 per cent of the industry's labour force.[27] This downward trend has been quite contrary to that in other industries and occupations. The percentage of women 'economically active' in Great Britain rose from 32 per cent in 1921 to more than 50 per cent in 1980.[28] From 1975 to 1980, the proportion of women in the industrial labour force rose by 3.2 per cent to 39.4 per cent.[29] It is clear then that women have been losing presence in the printing, publishing and paper industries while gaining ground elsewhere. Within that industry group, women have always been a smaller proportion in printing itself than in the other two categories. If we see the industry as producing a fat 'wage packet' for the working class, women have by no means received their fair share of it.

It was not, of course, a matter of mere choice for women. Job markets get segmented by the actions of employers and unions in such a way that occupations tend to become 'men's work' or 'women's work', with little overlap. Throughout the working world, women tend to be clustered into certain occupations and industries rather than spread evenly among them. This *occupational segregation* has a horizontal aspect, in which women cluster into certain types of work, and a vertical aspect, in which they cluster into the lower ranks in terms of seniority and pay. There has been surprisingly little change in the degree of sexual segregation of either kind in Britain between 1901 and 1971.[30]

In particular, women are 'segmented out' of the more rewarding jobs. This general picture is reflected in print where, as the Printing and Publishing Industry Training Board point out, 'The occupations of women mirror those followed by women in the economy overall . . . There is a tendency for them to cluster in what are perceived to be traditionally female jobs.'[31] The Board shows that women predominate in clerical and secretarial work (80 per cent of such workers are female). In managerial jobs there are relatively few women holding positions at senior level. Most of those who are in management categories are to be found in the lower levels of supervisory grades overseeing women's work. Whereas women represent 11 per cent of the workforce of national newspapers and 28 per cent of that of local and provincial newspapers, they fill no more than 5 per cent of the management occupations in those industries. As to the manual occupations, the Board confirms that 'the male-dominated craft areas lead to women occupying semi- and unskilled jobs, occupations which are relatively low paid'.

The newspaper industry, which is our special concern, has always had a worse record with regard to women's participation and segregation than other parts of the printing industry. In 1976 the Arbitration Service demonstrated the confinement of women to clerical, canteen and cleaning jobs in the national newspaper industry, with a small proportion finding work as journalists, publicity artists and in the administration. In four large Fleet Street houses the proportion of women employed, expressed as a percentage of their total workforces, was between 6 and 11 per cent. The ratio in the better-paid areas of production was much worse than this.[32] The night shift has always represented a problem in the news trade, in that employers require dispensation from the Factory Acts in order to engage women on it. Nonetheless, the Royal Commission on the Press, reporting in 1977, felt it necessary to draw attention to the fact that no national newspaper employed women in its main production areas. At this time there was not a single woman among the more than five thousand compositors on national newspapers. (In the regional press there were something over three hundred, compared with more than eleven thousand men.)[33] The Royal Commission wrote, 'While there are historical reasons . . . we hope that managements and union leaders will do more than merely comply with the laws governing opportunities for employment for women . . . and make positive efforts to increase the proportion.'[34] They recommended that the Equal Opportunities Commission, the new watchdog created by the equal pay and opportunities legislation which became effective in 1975, should look into the newspaper industry's practices with regard to women. It has not done so. Today, women are still only 11 per cent of the newspaper labour force, as against 32 per cent in the industry as a whole.[35] In the traditional crafts within the national and regional newspaper industry in 1976 (the most recent year for which reliable returns were received from firms), women comprised a mere 0.6 per cent of letterpress printers, 0.9 per cent of litho printers, 2.1 per cent of compositors, 4.0 per cent of other pre-print employees and 3.2 per cent of photographic personnel.[36]

If the legislation is effective in breaking down segregation, it should be most evident at the level of new entrants, of learners. Vocational-training figures are a useful indicator of trends in skilled and semi-skilled work. In 1978 some 24 per cent of students on day-release schemes from industry generally were women and girls; of those studying printing and publishing subjects only 13 per cent were female.[37] Between 1978 and 1980 only 1.4 per cent of all printing apprenticeships went to women, yet 5 per cent of the applicants were girls.[38] While the upward scope offered by administrative, journalistic and managerial work is gradually opening to women, the parallel technical and technological route still seems to be little frequented.

Partly as a result of the degree of occupational segregation by sex, with women situated in the least rewarding jobs, women's *earnings* relative to those of men in the industry have been low. In 1947 the Printing and Kindred Trades Federation resolved to try to bring the adult woman's rate up to 75 per cent of the male rate. In 1956 a wage round succeeded in narrowing the official sex differential to 58 per cent of the male rate on completion of training, rising to 63 per cent after four years' experience. By 1959 however the unions had abandoned the policy of pressing for 75 per cent and were ready to settle on women's behalf for 66 per cent of the men's rate. It should be remembered also that this was, in general, 66 per cent of the lowest grade of men's work.[39]

Because women work fewer overtime hours and tend to be

excluded also from various bonus payments, actual earnings are invariably a smaller proportion of men's earnings than the official wage is. Throughout this century men in printing have been higher earners relative to other manufacturing workers, but they have neglected to bring their female colleagues along in their wake.[40] Nor did the economic boom of the postwar period improve things. Between 1948 and 1968 the percentage that women's earnings represented of men's earnings in the printing, publishing and paper industries shifted steadily downwards from 50 to 43 per cent, while in manufacturing industry generally the trend was marginally upward.

An encouraging change occurred in the early 1970s. Between 1969 and 1974 women in printing and publishing pulled themselves up a notch: they advanced from 43 to 55 per cent of men's average weekly earnings, and from 51 to 58 per cent if hourly earnings are compared. (Note that we are here considering only full-time manual workers of both sexes, so that the greater proportion of women in part-time employment does not affect the percentage.)[41] This was the encouraging position when the Equal Pay and Sex Discrimination Acts became operational in 1975. Since then, women's earnings relative to those of men generally have stubbornly failed to rise.[42] Those of women manual workers in printing and publishing have actually fallen backwards by two percentage points so that by 1979 they were once more worse, relative to men's, than in manufacturing as a whole.[43]

It seems clear, then, that women have been disadvantaged in regard to employment in printing. They have been relatively few in number, particularly in printing proper and, within print, in newspapers. They have seldom escaped from 'ghettoes' of low-status women's occupations. And they have earned less for their efforts than men have earned. Capital, in the shape of the printing employers, has not been the only force acting to produce this effect. Men in the working class have also had a hand in it.

Women in the NGA: stirrings of change

How have women fared within the National Graphical Association, in among the hot-metal craftsmen? In 1971 there were 778 female working members – less than 1 per cent of total membership. Of these, 520 were 'registered card holders', with less than full rights and benefits, many of them former war-time dilutees. New techniques for originating the printing image were, by the mid-seventies, leading to composing work being done in many advertising studios and agencies rather than in the newspaper offices and trade typesetting houses over which the NGA had control. The union began a recruitment drive in the advertising world. By 1978 the number of women in the NGA had grown to 2,579. Most of the newcomers were graphic designers, paste-up artists and QWERTY typists. Then, in 1980, there occurred an amalgamation between the NGA and NUWDAT, a small union of wallpaper printers. NUWDAT was an industrial union, with a high proportion of women clerical and secretarial members. The female membership of the NGA thereby nearly doubled, so that in 1981 it was 4,783, or around 4 per cent of the total.[44] Only 121 girls, however, compared with 4,394 boys (2.7 per cent) were apprenticed to the NGA's skilled crafts in 1982.

To regularise their position in the wake of the Sex Discrimination Act, the NGA abolished the 'registered card holder' category. To accommodate the new clerical members it created a new trade group for Art, Technical, Clerical and Administrative members (ATCA), within which many of the women members are now to be found. By the merger with NUWDAT, the NGA also acquired (without voting for her) a woman as a national officer. She was given responsibility for organisation in the white-collar field.

I met a compositor in 1980 who was by no means sure that there were women in the NGA, or even that women would be permitted to join. Few craftsmen remain in this ignorance today however. And the NGA leadership, obliged to be in continual touch with the industry as a whole, have been able to see the trends more sharply perhaps than the bulk of the membership. The union's membership and revenue were declining at the same time as high unemployment benefits were eating into the bank balance. It was evident to the strategy-makers that unless the union shifted fast from its exclusive male craft character it would become a rump of pensioned-off grand-dads and unemployed letterpress artisans supported by a dwindling number of younger men in litho and photocomposition.

It was specially important to the compositors to secure the unionisation of clerical workers (mainly women) in newspaper offices. Newspaper clerical departments are not strongly unionised, except in Fleet Street where they are organised by NATSOPA. If these workers were not under union discipline they might be used by belligerent employers, to operate direct-entry systems or to type the newspaper in time of industrial dispute. The General Secretary therefore announced a 'massive recruitment and organisation campaign' among white-collar workers in the industry.[45] This brought the union near to conflict with NATSOPA. It was felt, however, that having a substantial group of white-collar members might actually prove a useful bargaining counter in future amalgamation talks. The drive took off slowly, but by 1981 it had built up to about 35 a month. The existence of ATCA was a rationale for the new recruitment drive, but the spur was the refusal of the Trades Union Congress (TUC) to give the NGA the prescriptive rights it was demanding for printing jobs outside printing proper (in-house printing in the business and government world, in particular) so as to protect itself from the recent incursions of the general white-collar unions, such as the Association of Scientific, Technical and Managerial Staffs (ASTMS) and the Association of Professional, Executive, Clerical and Computer Staff (APEX). The NGA was being forced to shift from an occupation-based craft union to a general industrial union.

Though none of the national officers, when announcing the new policy to members in the pages of *Print*, the NGA journal, actually mentioned the word *woman*, what was meant by white-collar workers was clear enough. A full-page photograph illustrated the kind of person that the leadership meant when it captioned the announcement 'let's work together'. It showed four women, one at a video screen and keyboard, another mixing ink, a third wiping down a small offset cylinder and a fourth at a draughting board. Photos of three men in varied occupations accompanied but by no means dominated these images. Since one of the girls was Asian, it seemed that the NGA was trying to kill two kinds of chauvinism with one stone.

A second revolutionary strategy currently being canvassed within the NGA is a training scheme that would end apprenticeship once and for all. In 1975 an apprenticeship agreement had already reduced the period from five to four years. The employers have been bargaining hard for a further reduction. In its consultation document and ensuing white paper on the 'New Training Initiative', the government is pressuring craft unions to replace time-serving and age-restricted apprenticeship by 1985 with recognised standards of achievement.[46]

In response, the NGA officers have devised a completely novel system of modular training involving an 'induction module', a 'basic skills module' and a number of specialised 'skill-development modules'. The individual would be able to qualify at his or her own pace, but would normally reach the agreed standard in two years. As the Assistant General Secretary put it, the new combination of formal and on-the-job training would have 'more in common with video display terminals and laser platemaking than with Gutenburg and Caxton'.[47] The wage-for-age apprentice scale would be replaced by a trainee rate, 60 per cent for under-18s, 80 per cent for 18-plus. The union hope to be able to insist that trainees get positions in firms before taking training. Colleges, in contrast, are pressing for courses that would be open to students without an initial commitment to the industry. The aim of the NGA is that training agreements, replacing the old indentures, will be signed by the trainee, chapel and firm, and all will supervise the recording of the trainee's progress in a personal log book. The nationally-agreed apprentice quotas and ratios that have imposed restraint on the employers in the past will have to be abandoned. Instead the NGA propose (optimistically perhaps) to limit intake by voluntary agreement between chapel and firm.

There are many dangers in such measures. The new training principles could aid capital's thrust towards a half-educated, semi-skilled workforce. The union is going to be caught mid-way between a pre-entry and a post-entry closed shop, at a moment when an anti-working-class government is attempting in its Employment Bill to curtail the freedom of unions to organise closed shops at all. For these reasons and for reasons of male craft self-interest, the new policies are controversial to the membership of the NGA. Many will or would vote against them. Many more would only vote for them, reluctantly, in the interests of survival:

'better diluted than dead'. All three measures, however, offer new opportunities for women. The open-door policy increases women's unionisation in the industry. The new education policy could create a skills ladder reaching down to the lowest levels. It could also ease horizontal movement. The NGA is structured into a number of trade groups (letterpress, litho, ATCA etc.) between which movement is minimal. The new training scheme might help women members, for instance, to move across from the clerical jobs of ATCA to the more rewarding jobs of the production trade groups. Amalgamation with other unions, too, is bound to help the women members of the NGA, particularly if a union is achieved with the NUJ, with its strong female membership, Equality Working Party and proposed Equality Council.

The changes are already apparent in the union. The faces of young women workers have begun to turn up among the photos in the union journal, where before there had been nothing but ranks of men (flanked by the occasional 'lady wife' at a union social). The year 1980 was a turning point in the history of women in the NGA. They now had sufficient presence to send a delegation for the first time ever to the national TUC Women's Conference. At the subsequent Biennial Delegate Meeting the Rule Book was changed to make provision for attendance at this conference every year. 'It was the first reference to women in the Rule Book of the NGA.' Some active women in the union gained agreement to the setting-up of a Women's Advisory Committee, to consider equality of opportunity for women along the lines of the TUC's Charter for Women. Such developments were beginning to add up to something. At the Biennial Delegate Meeting of the union in 1980 a young woman climbed to the platform and handed Les Dixon, the President, a fluffy bouquet of sweetpeas. The bouquet responded to the moment two years before when the first-ever woman delegate to a biennial was herself presented by the male members with a bouquet. Things had changed in the intervening months. This second bouquet said, on behalf of the women who had by now penetrated this governing conference of the union, 'You are very kind. But we are tired of being treated as something different, as people who have strayed into the wrong conference, the wrong trade union and the wrong job.'

In addition to the 50 male compositors, I interviewed a number of women members of the NGA and other women in NATSOPA, working alongside male NGA members. They recount many difficulties: the transition into the male sphere of work can be painful for women. Working in all-male areas they find they are an object of embarrassing curiosity. 'The first day there, every man in the place made some excuse to come and have a look. "Have you heard, there's a woman in the reading area." ' 'The trouble is, partly, that the men believe us women are unskilled, not having a craft background like them. They think our work is not *worth* what a man's work is worth. And that makes women feel unconfident. You get to think of yourself as a 'dilutee' because that is how they think of you.'

The traditions on Fleet Street and in the newspaper industry more generally, combined with the effects of the recession which is causing redundancies among men, make it impossible for women to progress out of the fringe jobs in print, where they earn little more than the basic rate. A compositor must have done a four-year apprenticeship and two years practice in the trade before applying to the 'Soc' for a Fleet Street opening. 'It's everyone's ambition to work on The Street. But for a woman, it's madness to think of it.' Characteristically, women in the London membership of the NGA are on keyboard or paste-up work in the many trade typesetting houses that serve the industry and the press. (Murdoch, after buying TNL, took the composing of the three *Times* supplements away from the traditional composing room and farmed it out to just such a typesetting house where women workers are employed.) A woman told me, 'Some of these houses advertise for typists, rather than compositors. They recruit women using the columns of periodicals like *Girl About Town*. When women are taken on that way, they apply to the NGA for a Temporary Working Card. This provisional membership is withdrawn if the individual leaves that particular job before two years is up. In this way, many women go back to being ordinary non-unionised typists after a while. It is a clever way of seeing that the numbers of people on the unemployed 'call book' don't get out of hand. And meanwhile, the job left by the TWC holder remains an NGA job – which can then be filled from the call book.' Though this mechanism affects both men and women alike, in practice a much higher proportion of women than of men fall into the category of TWC holder.

Becoming actively involved in the union is sometimes not easy for a woman. Much depends on the chapel. One woman clerical worker said, 'They've always made every effort to help me to feel at ease, and now it is as if I'd always been there.' But a woman typesetter felt, on the contrary, 'The overwhelming male domination makes women feel awkward about going to meetings, speaking at them and standing for chapel offices. I'm sure a lot of men feel intimidated too, but it's much worse for women.' In spite of this, some women have become elected chapel representatives. But they find themselves caught in conflicting expectations. On the one hand you need to be 'one of the lads', to booze along with the best in the pub, where so much chapel business is done. On the other hand, the men operate a double standard. 'They aren't very keen on you drinking, certainly not if you get the worse for it, though a lot of them do themselves. And they don't like it when you swear, even though they swear all the time.' Though, as one woman told me, 'women bring to trade unionism all the vigour and originality the men lost years ago', some men don't take at all kindly to being represented by a woman. And some simply disbelieve that a woman *could* be representing men. 'When they hear that I am the Mother of Chapel they assume that means I represent the women. They ask, who's the *FOC* in your chapel then?'

The NGA Rule Book in some ways impedes women organising. It forbids caucusing (Rule 5, Section 3) so that women may not meet together as women to discuss their particular problems. There is a rule that you must be two years in the union before you can be a delegate to the Biennial Delegate Meeting, the most important moment in union policy-making. It is five years before you may hold national office. 'The point is that since women are relative newcomers, these rules combine with everything else we experience to prevent us playing much part.' If women are not to leave the industry altogether when they become responsible for children, they need part-time work opportunities. But, 'The chapel wouldn't allow the firm to employ a part-time worker. The NGA office wouldn't put the job on the call book for a start. It's against union policy.'

On the other hand, there are many advantages to being in the NGA. Women now, though they must pay the NGA subscriptions which are higher than those of many other unions, do at least receive full benefits, which are traditionally generous too. The NGA has more pulling-power over wages than the unskilled unions. 'My company offered us a 23 per cent wage rise when they knew that we had joined the NGA,' said one woman newspaper clerical worker. 'And this was in 1980, when the average rise was only about 6 per cent. They constantly kept saying to us, why didn't you join NATSOPA? But I think that speaks for itself.' Again, being a handful of women in a profoundly masculine union is perhaps little more disadvantaging than being women in a mixed unskilled union. Even in NATSOPA, which has had a sizeable women membership since the early days (it is now 30 per cent), women are heavily segregated into the lowest paid and least-skilled occupations, mainly in the clerical section. Accordingly to one sympathetic male officer of NATSOPA, 'The union structure is there for male objectives, and by and large it gets results for men.' In SOGAT, the London membership has long been segregated into a London Central Branch (male) and a Women's Branch. The men, by dint of diligent grading and regrading of occupations, have succeeded, in spite of 'equal pay', in keeping women members as a group in inferior and lower-paid jobs. It has been against the resistance of male members that a handful of women have recently entered semi-skilled jobs and joined the men's branch. The situation is currently subject to a formal investigation by the Equal Opportunities Commission. On the other hand, 'Because the NGA have never had a notable number of women members before, they are having to think seriously now about what to do with the new intake, and that can be very beneficial to women, coming as it has at a time when women are pushing for equality in every field.'

In spite of the many difficulties in their way, then, many women are glad to be in the NGA and some feel sympathy for the plight of the men today. When men insult the capability of women, 'what they really seem to be saying to you is "we are irreplaceable – please don't replace us". And I think it is very sad.' Many women feel troubled by the anti-union attitude that some women workers have shown in the past, and which continues to show up as resistance to organisation. 'We have to come to terms with the fact that many women have a long way to go before they join "the progressive forces" . . . Besides, white-collar people are encouraged to see themselves as almost managers, and employers play on that. Therefore a union seems of course totally inappropriate to them. After several years of that type of propaganda, which is constant and insidious, many women are lost causes to a trade union.' 'One of the major problems is the fact that white-collar workers, particularly women, see themselves as superior to the printers, despite the fact that they are less well-paid and work in conditions of unnecessary discipline and petty line-toeing.' 'The number of advertising people I have heard saying that "printers are thick"!'

Conversely, of course, it remains to be proved that the NGA can adequately serve the new kind of member, particularly the clerical worker. The experience of SLADE in the seventies showed that mass recruitment campaigns can backfire on the union by bringing in large numbers of reluctant joiners who need persuading that there is something in it for them. A woman correspondent to *Print*[48] pointed out that if recruitment were to continue, and white-collar membership to be maintained by the NGA, the union would have to prove the value for money it could offer, for instance, to women advertising workers on relatively low wages, unprotected by any closed-shop agreement. Many women are aware, too, that joining a craft union, or even entering an eventual single union for the printing industry would mean little gain if the idea is to keep women buttoned up in sections of relatively low-paid and uninteresting work. That, it must be admitted, is the expectation on which many men are pinning their hopes and basing their acceptance of the new policies.

The case against women: then and now

The steps forward may be hesitant still, but the change in the NGA is not illusory, nor is it reversible. What is happening under the impact of new technology and developments within capital in the printing industry, is the break-up of old structures within the working class, and the dissolution of some of the patriarchal forms of relationship that governed the craft tradition. The authority of old men, the subservience of the 'lads', the manhood rituals of chapel life and, above all, the exclusion of women, are melting away.

The traditional compositor, however, takes these things hard. This disquiet of skilled men who have long been sheltered by their organisation from the competition of women at work and long accustomed to possessing an unquestioned, if often benign, authority over a woman in the home, echoes in some ways the disquiet of men as they saw their women and children drawn into industrial work for the first time in the early years of the Industrial Revolution. Many of the men I interviewed in the London news trade in 1980 represented women *as a problem*. Computerised composition meant 'more women will come in, yes, and to me this is a bad thing'. 'I think there is a resentment about girls coming into the industry. It is a threat, a definite threat in that sense.'

Why do men feel as they do? What do they stand to lose and what meanings are they making, what ideologies are they constructing and deploying, to stave off their loss? It is interesting to compare the case that men were making out against women at the turn of the century and the case they make today. The similarities are striking. But what is more striking than the similarities revealed in the men's consciousness is the contrast in their circumstances and prospects, then and now. Their arguments were threadbare then, they are in tatters today. The men are continuing to handle contradiction by recourse to the same ideological formula. But mechanisation of typesetting was one thing and computerised photocomposition quite another. Its introduction coincides with a collapse of national competitiveness – there are no easy pickings of empire this time. It arrives at a time when the printing industry is fighting for survival against do-it-yourself print, cheap foreign print, electronic media and alternative forms of advertising. It is occurring in mid-recession, when unemployment is very high and working-class organisations are under threat. Computerised photo-compositon offers productivity gains of a different order of magnitude to those of mechanical typesetting. It implies a revolution in the organisation of print on an altogether different scale to that of the 1890s and 1900s. It has, besides, more striking gender connotations, both ideological and practical. The social and political contexts, too, differ markedly. Cracks have begun to appear in the structure of patriarchal rights, as embodied in law and state policy. The change is being experienced by men in the context of an upsurge of self-expression among women which has charged, if not changed, the climate of opinion since 1970. It is not surprising, then, to find that the men's practised, time-honoured arguments about women and their place in men's world have lost something of their ring of confidence.

There were in the past, of course, and there are today, some egalitarian men who speak up for women, who see their own and their class interests as lying in a restructuring of sex/gender relations. They were not then, nor are they today, men who can be accused of collaboration with the employing class; they are good trade unionists. An Oxford compositor in 1893 addressed a delegate meeting of the Typographical Association. He said that the spirit of the times was in favour of trade unionism and of extending trade unionism to women – of women advancing all along the line and being given equal rights with men. He contended that

> they had no right to prohibit these girls from the trade. If they could earn money fairly and be paid fairly they ought to be allowed to do so. The true principle of unionism would say, 'We who are strong will see you, who are weak, properly treated and properly paid. We will build you up to the same position that we have gained.' One gentleman had said that girl labour threatened the ruin of the branches. Might he not retaliate by saying that their action was threatening the ruin of the girls?[49]

In a similar vein, a compositor said to to me in 1980, 'The last decade has seen such a radical overturning of attitudes towards women workers. Girls have been told at school, why don't you become an engineer? I think that's great. So, yes, I think women will definitely come into the industry and, as for me, I welcome it.' 'I never used to like the masculine superiority aspect,' another said. 'The biggest discrimination of all was not between middle class, working class, whatever. It was between men and women. It's a good thing it's going. I'm sure society as a whole is fairer for it.'

There is no doubt, however, that this is today, as it was a century ago, a minority view among craft compositors. Perhaps it would be more correct to say, not that a minority of men adhere to it, but that within the problematic in which men argue and from which they draw their expressions, it is a minority strand. It is a golden thread that a man may now and then light upon and toy with, but which is normally smothered in the dreary fabric of male self-interest. The warp of this fabric has been a set of essentialist arguments demonstrating that women *could not* be craft compositors – because of natural physical, intellectual and temperamental inadequacies. The cross-woven theme of the weft has been that women *should not*, for both economic and moral reasons, compete with men for skilled work.

'She couldn't do it'

Why were women unsuitable for the skilled work of composition for print? *Physical* reasons are often cited first. The work of hot-metal composition was said to have been too heavy for women. Women are supposed to have weaker spines than men. 'There was too much standing involved for them,' (1980) 'When a girl is made to stand one day, she cannot the next. Her back gives way and she cannot do it. Nature revolts against it herself.' (1907)[50] There was, however, no comparable concern shown by men over women doing other (less remunerative) standing jobs, such as shop work, to which men laid no claim.

Again, women are said to be insufficiently strong to lift the formes. 'Twenty inches square of solid metal . . . a woman compositor wouldn't take too kindly to that. She'd have a couple of blokes doing it for her!' (1980) Even the machines were too demanding. 'Linotype, too, it takes a degree of heft or knack – to change the magazines for instance.' (1980) 'In brute strength the male sex will reign superior until an army of Amazons again arises. And so it happens that the machines are too heavy for the girls to work.' (1891)[51] As a result, composing, 'Well, it's been one of those jobs, like navvying, if you like, where women never attempted to do it.' (1980)

It should be noted at once that women *were* capable of the

complete range of craft skills. At the Women's Printing Society shop in the late nineteenth century the women did imposition and make-up as well as typesetting. There have also been a number of competent women linotype operators.

There is, however, something more than a mere libel involved here. Women *are* physically less strong than men on average. When it comes to 'men's tasks' they are often lacking in the necessary knack or strength. Men, however, have contributed to this outcome, in a historical process, in two ways. First, they have been influential in excluding women from the kinds of experience (including work) that develops physical strength and confidence. Second, they have been influential in designing labour processes. Small and old men also find hot-metal composing work uncomfortably heavy. In fact, 'a system of trolleys made of dexion is used', a compositor told me, 'to save you breaking your back'. It has to be supposed, I believe, that men use their political muscle in the trade union to fight against excessively heavy tasks and so save their physical muscle, only when and to the degree that this suits them. They may find it advantageous to leave within the political definition of their 'craft' certain tasks too heavy for the average woman. Today, of course, new technology has completely undermined men's arguments surrounding women's physical incompetence: the work is now light, immobile and unstrenuous.

A further physical reason put forward by men against women's employment as compositors is the health hazard. Lead is indeed a poisonous material, dangerous for anyone to work with. It can damage the brain, if ingested in any quantity. Comps are also prone to pthisis and printer's colic. The men, however, then and today, somewhat irrationally express more worry for women than for themselves. At the height of the raw feelings of 1886 a notice was slipped into the Scottish Typographical Circular, '**Warning to female compositors:** an eminent French physician says that the handling of types has a tendency to destroy the powers of maternity in women.'[52] Lead poisoning may indeed cause irregular menstrual periods and miscarriages. But was any comparable study made of dangers for male fertility? Another compositor feared that women would come into the trade for a few years, contract some industrial illness and then 'leave with the germs of the disease in their system' to 'spread all over' and 'lead to the degeneracy of the race'.(1907)[53]

The second reason the men put forward why women 'couldn't' do a comp's work is that they just don't have the *mental ability*. 'They are, basically, rather stupid.' One told me that the managing director of his firm had intended to use the typists to break a strike, but the plan had foundered due to the girls' inadequacy. 'You can't expect a *girl* to sit down and remember all the format codes.' Specifically, girls are represented as illiterate. The men like to think of literacy as part of their own exclusive stock-in-trade, something in which they can feel superior even to journalists: 'These so-called intellectuals can produce some diabolical manuscripts.' A woman with pretensions to literacy is good for a laugh. 'We have a list at work of all the howlers set by the front-office typists. And some of the spellings, you would never believe it. Just for a joke every so often we print some of them out and hand them around.' (1980) A male correspondent to *Print* recently deplored the decline in composing standards and English usage, suggesting that the culprits were 'gals straight from college with their scarlet fingernails and high heels'.[54] Nothing unusual in that attitude. But it is interesting that this time many women members hit back. The journal's editorial policy, governed by the union, is changing too: this time three angry replies from women were published in the next issue.

The supposed inequality between the male and female intellect underlies some of the arguments in the nineteenth century too. An early typesetting invention was the Hattersley machine, which had a separate mechanism for the tedious job of distributing used type. A Sheffield typographer proposed that the occupation of dissing *must* be seen as women's work because, 'a man's brain would greatly deteriorate until he became very low indeed in the scale if he was stuck at *that*, day after day. He could not understand how any intelligent printer could advocate that any intelligent man should stand playing with a thing like that all day' (1893).[55]

The intellectual argument today is, of course, on shakier ground as men see women all around them taking on demanding jobs. 'I heard on the news tonight that the first British woman has become a ship's master. I mean to say!' Closer at hand, compositors have seen more women entering journalism, and a handful in administration, jobs that are generally conceded to be 'more intellectual' than their own. At Mirror Group News the men told me of a young woman working on the technical aspects of the electronic composing system. Such women were represented to me as being 'very clever' or 'exceptionally bright'. It is difficult for a man to accept that a merely average woman could compete with men in this way. Nonetheless, they were there, a fact of life, weakening the men's grip on intellectual superiority.

The third essentialism called into play by the men is '*natural temperament*'. One form of this is the portrayal of women as having an innate aversion to machinery. 'Machinery – that's anathema to a woman. They build up a complex about it.' (1980) 'Women are too temperamental to work with machinery. They aren't happy with machinery like a man is.' (1980) It is true that fewer women than men are at home with technology – printing technology or any other mechanical technology. The history recounted in Chapter 1, however, should have been sufficient to demonstrate that men as a sex have *apppropriated* the technology – tools, machinery and know-how – of composing for print. The same thing has happened in every other industrially applied technology. Men have been the designers, developers and maintenance engineers and often, also, the operators, of machines. Besides, a male-dominated society has resulted in an education system, as well as an occupational structure, that forms boys as scientific and technological and dequalifies girls in these respects. Though capital employs women on some machines, and indeed has often displaced men to do so, nonetheless women are characteristically situated in a routine, operational relationship to the equipment. When it needs attention it is a man who is called to fix it. There is a sense in which women are only 'lent' machinery by men.[56] Given their reliance on arguments concerning women's natural technological passivity, it is particularly embittering for compositors today to find themselves in an inert relationship to computerised photocomposition systems, not dissimilar from that of most women to machinery and a far cry from the total technological grasp of the craft tradition.

Another temperamental ploy is 'women are too emotional' to cope with the rough and tumble, give and take, of the male working environment. If reprimanded by a supervisor they would not stand up to him but 'blush and burst into tears and run away'. Again, women are naturally 'unreliable'. This is seen both as an annoyance to male colleagues and a deterrent to the employer. (The contradiction here with the fact that it is the employer who is portrayed as wanting to replace men with women goes unremarked.) 'It costs £5,000 for the boss to train a woman up and what if she then toddles off and has a baby?' (1980) Several of the men alluded to menstruation as a cause of unreliability, without wishing to speak the dread word. 'Now I don't want you to take this wrong, because being a woman you might go nasty on me. But the problem is, with girls, that once a month they have a problem. So they have two days off. They have nothing but problems from the women telephone-typists here. You couldn't produce a newspaper on that basis.' (1980)

Quite apart from pre-menstrual tension, and 'period pains', though, women are represented as having a temporary and instrumental attitude to work that is incompatible with the craft tradition. 'They pick it up and drop it, go temping for agencies.' (1980) 'Girls fluctuate. The difficulty with them is that if they get an indifferent job, or if they get tired of it, they go away for a spell into something else or get employment at one of the other firms.' (1907)[57] 'However anxious a girl may be for the first three or four years of an apprenticeship . . . when marriageable age arrives, when much of her mind and time will be employed in thinking of bonnets, veils, rings, brooches etc., . . . in examining her pearly teeth in the looking-glass and arranging her toilet at the same time, her employment will not then, I should fancy, be so pleasant to herself, neither will it be so profitable to her employer.' (1886)[58] 'I can't see women taking up a course of training, when they have all their troubles, marriage and what else.' (1980) 'There's not a girl who goes to the trade with the idea that she is going to earn her bread in it . . . and she will not apply her mind to it.' (1907)[59] 'Girls have got a different attitude to work. In general. Sound like a chauvinist pig don't I. They are, to be quite honest, fly-by-nights.' (1980)

There is bad faith in such arguments however, and sometimes the men admit it. Women's work is much less gripping and satisfying than men's work. The men admit they would not want to be telephone receptionists or office typists. In their non-working life, women's orientation towards marriage is positively desired by men as being to their own advantage. There are historical reasons for this orientation – reasons that men have contributed to constructing. Again, men also have their own time-honoured techniques of 'soldiering', of giving the employer as little as possible in return for the wage. It is true that this practice is in tension with craft pride. But it weakens the men's protests at what they represent as a characteristically female disregard of the work ethic. It was interesting to hear one contemporary compositor suggest that changes in the industry and technology were teaching men to have a similar attitude. There is no point any longer to looking for a job that will last forty-five years: 'We haven't got the long-term outlook now either, can't have.'

As a result of all these assumptions about women's nature, they are represented by men to each other as partial workers, not whole ones. They are variously incomplete workers, temporary workers, choosy workers or flawed workers. They may have nimble fingers but they are not all-rounders, like the craftsman. In a study of women in the printing industry in 1904, J. Ramsay Macdonald pointed out that women were frequently taught extraordinary competence in narrowly defined tasks but were never taught the whole job.[60] 'Dexterity' is a concept used politically by the men. They can praise a woman safely enough for natural dexterity, 'her fingers fly along the keyboard, she can type at twice the speed I can' etc., since they themselves lay claim to something greater.

If women *can't* do certain work because they are weak, unintelligent or temperamentally unsuited, the resulting economic advantage for men needs little emphasis. There are political advantages as well, however. A man, being relatively competent, becomes relatively powerful.

Much of men's self-respect depends on the idea of being able to do work that men alone are fit to do. There is much bitterness in the references by men in the Edinburgh dispute to being reduced to 'picking up the crumbs from the women's table'. 'I felt degraded following in the footsteps of generations of compositor-forefathers before me, at having to descend to such vile practices' as competing with women for work. (1886)[61]

A young comp told me in 1980 how he felt his work would be spoiled by women entering it:

> Some of the shine would go out of the job for me. Prestige might not be exactly the right word, but it carries what is known as a macho bit, composing. It's man's work. If you hear of a man secretary, a lot of people raise a few eyebrows. Well, it's the same with a woman working alongside a man doing *his* job. They would say – even though a woman is doing what has been a man's job, they would tend to think that because the woman is there, the man is now doing a *woman's* job. You might only have *one* woman working with nine men. But if I said to my mates I was working with a woman, they would feel, say, oh, he's doing a woman's job – because they can see that a woman *can* do it. They wouldn't think to say that she is the one who is doing a man's job.

He is saying that the presence of woman, one woman, any woman, is enough to destroy the mystique that women could not do the work and its corollary, that men must be superior because they can. 'Oh, it's nice to see the girls going past,' another said. 'But women, if they worked in here, they would see – they would find out the weaknesses. It would dispel the myth of what composing is about. It wouldn't do anyone any good, honestly.'

Men feel that everything a woman touches turns to dross. Part of what they are reflecting is the real-life fact that women have only been allowed to enter or remain in relatively degraded work. They are right in associating the entry of women with the deskilling of jobs in both mechanised typesetting and electronic photocompositon. Partly, however, it reflects the low value men put on women. In nineteenth-century printers' chapels, when a journeyman acquired a baby son the other members of the chapel would donate a shilling. If a daughter was born to him the sum was only sixpence.[62] Women are worth-less.

Now that compositors are being obliged to do (and indeed to be grateful to be allowed to keep) work they think of as 'women's work', it is not surprising that they feel trapped. In fostering an ideological correspondence between 'women's work' and 'degrading work' they have, as it turned out, been digging their own grave.

'She shouldn't do it'

There have been appeals to two principles in arguing that women *should* not do a compositor's work (even if she could). The first is the principle that it is proper and logical for the male head of the family to be its breadwinner, earning enough on his own efforts to keep a wife and children. The second is that women, visualised as sexual creatures, would be exposed to bad moral influences by entering a male occupation – or indeed any paid work outside the home.

During the last half of the nineteenth century there was a pronounced decline in the proportion of married women going out to work. At the census of 1851 a quarter of married women had occupations distinct from housework; by 1901 this proportion had fallen to one in 10. Compositors were, as we have seen, among that group of men, the better-paid and more secure workers, who were able to sustain more effectively than the rest the privilege and status-symbol of a wife in the home, devoted solely to servicing him and his children, both practically and emotionally. 'If you can support the family on your own earnings it gives you a better life at home. So long as she is happy to be at home, it's better. Keep the place right, for you, for the family. Great. Fine.' (1980)

The question of the male breadwinner and the family wage was at the forefront of the Edinburgh struggle. There was anger against women who were prepared to accept, for much of their lives, the support of another wage earner, yet who nonetheless appeared ready to take the bread out of men's mouths when they found an employer ready to take them on. A comp addressed a woman typesetter in the columns of the *Scottish Typographical Circular*, 'Let me ask you, were you a father, which you are not, of course – would you feel rather pleased to serve seven years to learn your trade, then get dismissed, or starved, to let newmade compesses do men's work, at less than half the wage?' (1886)[63]

The fact is, of course, that many women at the time did work all their lives. Many did not marry. It is interesting to note that only two of the many women printers passing through the Women's Printing Society in London in its first *eighteen* years, married.[64]

A brave woman calling herself 'Ella – Type-lifter' had a poem published in a trade journal in 1886. In the following extract she makes the point that women, too, often worked to keep dependents:

> We'd fain live at peace with all men – and all printers
> And be rid for ever of sneerers and hinters:
> State broadly and fully wherein we are sinners;
> Remembering that many of us are bread-winners
> For mothers and sisters whom we must assist, hence
> We claim with yourselves equal right to existence.

She adds a sharp little bite at the end:

> And tho' we *were* all wed, or 'bespoke' like new clothes,
> That would not release us from work, or from woes.[65]

During the twentieth century, critics have increasingly exposed the illogicality of 'the family wage' as a concept. Not all men have dependents. Eleanor Rathbone calculated, around the time of the first world war, that the 'family wage' was paid on behalf of about three million wives and 16 million children who were mere 'phantoms', the non-existent responsibility of bachelors. Worse, not all women were supported by men, and one-third of all women workers were wholly or partially responsible for the keep of other people. But skilled craftsmen, such as the compositors, continued within the labour movement to resist the introduction of state family allowances which alone could have made a more equal distribution of income. The artisan defended his right 'to keep half the world in purgatory because he enjoys playing redeemer to his own wife and children'.[66]

Women have, despite this prevailing ideology, increasingly evaded a housebound life. Nearly all the men I interviewed were married, and half of their wives were currently working outside the home. Most of the remainder had had a job when younger, but given it up on the arrival of children, or with an increase in earnings and status of her husband. Many of the wives I met made it clear how much they valued the chance to go out to work, to 'get out of the house', earn their own money. But with barely an exception the men gave me to understand that, while they too now recognised that it was 'good for the marriage', a kind of therapy, that the wife should 'have her own interests', nonetheless her earnings were seen by them as peripheral to their own. And it seemed to be felt as a relief to be able to make that clear.

To be the male breadwinner, supporter of a comfortable household, has helped to give men as a sex both ideological and economic strength. A compositor in interview told me, 'I think a lot of the masculinity of work was related to the fact that the man was the only person that brought the money in.' Another said, 'A man has got to be a breadwinner, I think. A woman won't respect a man unless he earns his living. He has to be the protector, yes. A man has got to be a flicking *man*, whatever that means. He has to fight for his family, for his wife.'[67]

The theme of 'wife to the home' is given new impetus by the current recession. Some men can still say, bitterly, as one compositor did to me: 'When I see chaps out of work, a compositor, say, and other chaps in work *and* their wives working too, not to put bread on the table or keep the wolf from the door but to have a holiday in Majorca . . . that gets up my nose.' But the contradictions are being more keenly felt. Some of the compositors, during the *Times* lock-out, when their own earnings were sharply reduced and their security in doubt, had been momentarily dependent on their wife's earnings. Some of the wives had gone back to paid work during that crisis and for one, I was told it had been a turning-point, for the better, in her own life.

Although the social security benefits are still posited on a women's dependence on a man's wage, the tax system and child benefit provision have recently been reorganised in such a way that a woman, in place of a man, receives direct relief in respect of children. Such intervention by the state has undermined men's confidence in their old rights. The equality legislation has had a similar effect. Logically, equal pay and 'a family wage' are incompatible principles. Equal pay legislation therefore catches compositors in a painful contradiction. It makes sense industrially because women can no longer be used by employers to undercut men. Besides, its fairness, at one level, is irrefutable: 'Why should you, working alongside me, be paid any less than the rate for the job?' Nonetheless it means that a wife, in place of being represented as the burden of a grown and responsible man, can now be seen as an equal, and indeed a benefit to a man: source of doubled earnings. The men are thus caught in a pincer movement: their own reduced job security and status, and women's assumption of an equal right to work and to an equal wage. 'When a man was the sole provider it gave him a false sense of importance, if you like. In fact, it wasn't false, he *was* important. Now that has changed and it knocks the old dominant male syndrome down a bit. It changes outlooks – it's changed the social structure of men.'

If 'the family wage and the male breadwinner' is the first principle flouted by women who seek after compositors' employment, the second is *sexual morality*. The historical evidence shows the men arguing that women would be coarsened by working alongside men, they would hear language that was not good for their ears, they would lose their sweet femininity (even perhaps their virginity) in the course of abrasive contact with the masculine world of paid work. In the late nineteenth century, the London firm of Bowden & Brown, for instance, felt that it had to defend its position to the Children's Employment Commission: 'No doubt there are dangers, in a moral point of view, from having the two sexes working together. We however are always on the spot ourselves and see that all is right; indeed Mr. Bowden's daughter worked here for some time.'[68] Today it is taken for granted that unmarried girls work (though not of course in the composing room). One comp's worry had shifted to the propriety of married women mixing with men. 'You would have the problems of involvements. Suppose you had married women working here . . . they might start coupling up with the chaps at work, purely for the fact that they are with them for so many hours. It would have a bad effect on family relationships.' (1980)

In the Victorian period there was a strong feeling against women doing night work or being out on the streets at night. 'In very hot weather, some printer women said they should prefer to commence work at four in the morning instead of six, and to have two hours longer to rest in the middle of the day. The employer agreed. They arrived at the workshop at four but had been noticed by the police who reported them to the inspector, who put a stop to the practice.' (1896)[69] 'When I worked with women I had to do all the late shifts because they didn't want to walk around London late at night. Oh,

I don't blame them, in the climate of violence. But then again, if you are going to talk about equality, it's got to be equality all the way, hasn't it?' (1980)

It is true, of course, that women are unsafe on the street at night, now as in the nineteenth century, and that they are subject to physical and emotional harassment at work, now as then. The contradiction arises for men, however, in the fact that, while it is possible to argue 'the family wage' in class terms alone, disguising any specifically male interest in it, once the sexual and moral argument is introduced one is no longer within the class problematic alone: it is irreducibly clear that the source of danger for women is *men*. Deep within men's expressions about this problem is a glimmer of recognition that there is something illogical about dealing with men's rapaciousness not by restraining or changing men, but by confining women.

Men appear to have a strong need to visualise and to make meaning of women in two incompatible ways. First, they need to see women as pure and unsullied beings. The men continually represented women to me, for instance, as *not* swearing. One man, noted for his crude language at work, admired as one who could curse along with the best of the fellows, claimed that his wife would say, 'I've never heard him swear.' Women should be clean. A real woman is, 'somebody who looks like a woman, who smells nice, you know, that kind of sexual aura, makes you feel protective towards them,' as one comp put it. No ink under *her* fingernails. This is the way the man wants 'his' women, his wife and daughters, to be – kept and clean. In the words of the nursery rhyme: 'Peter, Peter, pumpkin eater, had a wife and couldn't keep her, put her in a pumpkin shell and there he kept her very well.' In the pumpkin shell of the family the woman's sexuality is her husband's alone to define and to exploit.

On the other hand, however, men want women's sexuality as free currency. They want women to be like the communal bicycles in the Amsterdam of the libertarian revolt of the late sixties: there to be picked up, ridden and laid aside by any one at any time. This is the 'meaning' ascribed to women in compositors' workplace culture. As noted in the previous chapter, the men's relationship with each other is mediated through the coinage of women, in which women are handled and besmirched routinely. There is a cultural rape in progress much of the time. The pleasure in this process, though (and it is of course only partly pleasurable, being partly also a fear of women) comes precisely from the contrast between the pure and the sullied. This becomes an unresolvable contradiction for men if women share the workplace in *unsegregated* occupations, on equal terms, in the same room. Exposure to their own male-male intercourse would damage women in men's eyes and then they would not be nice to know in any real social sense. 'There is one woman copyholder in our reading room,' one of the men told me, in Fleet Street where a woman copyholder is a freakish novelty. 'I was working with her the other night. I personally thought that she'd got a skin like a rhinoceros. Because you work in a room with a lot of men who treat you as if you were just one of them, language flies around, they have a pretty animal-like attitude to life. She must have a pretty thick hide to survive that.' In other words: she is spoiled for me.

To hold in tension *both* of the two meanings ascribed to women depends on the separation of the spheres of work and home. Men have different standards of behaviour for the two. As I have noted, the workplace walls are unashamedly covered with pin-ups. But a man who brought out his Pirelli-style nudes calendar for me to see at home, said that while it was his practice to get it out now and then when friends visited, ('To search the girls over and say – she has a lovely pair, don't think much of those'), he kept it in a cupboard because 'his wife would shoot him' if he hung it up in the house.

The separation of work and home is taken to be a feature of capitalist production and capitalist relations alone.[70] Within the context of capitalism, however, it has developed a significance within sex-relations as well. When a women turns up, in the flesh, in the man's workplace demanding and expecting essentially human treatment, that is to say neither being idealised nor defiled, she presents a startling dilemma for men. Implicitly she asserts her own estimate of her worth and her own definition of her sexuality, in defiance of his. In doing this, she spoils both his games: by becoming a competitor she has to be taken seriously, which is incompatible with being a sexual pawn. She drives a man to fight against her and this hurts *him*, since he likes to think of her as something to protect and cherish. This little poem which appeared in a compositors' publication in 1891 neatly counterposes the indulgence and the aggression.

> Oh Woman! In our hours of ease
> You are so soft and nice to squeeze
> And hold, as something ever bright
> To minister to man's delight.
>
> When in our daily work you dare
> To boldly ask that you may share
> We fail to see your special use –
> And straightway send you to the deuce![71]

'Aggression', a comp explained to me in 1980, 'is to do with the relationship between *men*. A woman – I feel compelled to *protect* a woman.' It was painful to him, he said, that she does not need this now. In 1886, another correspondent wrote of the 'revulsion of feeling' he had against women, 'simply from the position men are forced to assume in a fight for the bare necessities of life' and how this had disabused him of 'the angelic sweetness of their tempers and their native loveliness of manner'.[72]

In the men's ideology of sexual difference, behind the split that they have constructed and manipulated between the 'pure wife and daughter' and the 'nice piece of skirt', the age-old dichotomy of the virgin and the whore, lies another organising principle. It is the principle of complementarity. A man is the mirror image of *both* his women. In discussing men and women, compositors sometimes used the phrase *'vive la différence'*. Sexual difference is celebrated, fêted. But it is not a random difference. The appeal to essential qualities in males and females forms them as complements to each other. The couple – a man and a woman together – makes up the true whole.

'Women are, from their more delicate organisations, really better adapted than the sterner sex for rapid work, yet they lack that stamina and application by which alone their labour can be made profitable,' wrote a compositor in 1886.[73] And today, 'It's a matter of physiology. Men can tackle some jobs better than women, women can tackle some jobs better than men.' 'Girls are natural typists – more suitable for it than us.' 'Girls can stand boredom, much better than men.' 'Women are patient, men are impatient.' 'Women are too temperamental to work with machinery. Machinery, that's a man's thing.' '*They are complementary to us. It's healthy.*' (1980)

Women threaten to obliterate complementarity when they seek to do the same work as men. It seems that as women destroy differences, men retreat and recreate them. A compositor told me:

> I've noticed, in our canteen, there's a table where the women sit. Eighty per cent of them smoke these days. Probably only 20 per cent of the men smoke now. To me this is symptomatic of something. Smoking was associated with something masculine. Maybe women are smoking because they can afford to smoke, now they are working and have the money. And perhaps the men are giving up smoking as a kind of reaction, because smoking is something that *women* do now. Maybe they don't want to do it for that reason.

The most graphic account of the ideology of essentialism and complementarity that I received during the course of the interviews was this:

> There is the sexual thing, though, this is the thing that . . . you see, you can have *equality* . . . this is the thing that I've often discussed with my wife. I do have to discuss it with her because she is a completely different type of person. But you get these very, very masculine-type women. I say masculine-type women, which is a confusion in terms really, but you know what I mean. I don't mean *sexually* masculine, butch or anything, lesbian or whatever. But they seem to identify almost aggressively with males. They seem to be in competition with them for some strange reason. They seem to resent the fact that they can have babies, resent the fact that they are supposed to push prams about, they want to do all the things that men do and they say they can do them just as well They don't see why they are any different at all. But of course basically the difference is *sex*, quite simply. Now I know that

there are lesbians, I know that there are butch types, but generally speaking we live in a heterosexual world you know. I've got no axe to grind against gay people or anything . . . but we *do* live in a heterosexual world in which it has been established that certain areas are male provinces, for good, bad or . . . or . . . I mean I . . . in most work areas. Take the army, you know, for instance. Though I know in the States women are flying helicopters, but they have said they won't be in combat duties and so forth. But, I mean the whole point is that there is a *difference* in my opinion between a man and a woman, an *essential difference* you know. The way they think, the way they feel. This is the essential difference. And that's something that, although they can do the job of a man or are as good as a man, some of them more intelligent than a man even . . . well, they are still a *woman*. And I'm thankful for it. Can you understand what I mean?

Oddly, two contrary positions emerge from the celebration of complementarity. One is that 'Women have an adverse affect on men. To be quite frank. *Men are not men in the company of women.*' The other is that men are more like men when they are with women. 'In the presence of women men behave differently. *More like men.* Men together behave more like women. They are narrowminded and spiteful. Women bring out the best in men.' While they appear contradictory, both these views are in fact organised around complementarity. Both imply that women are a catalyst to men, present or absent.

What is at stake for compositors today, therefore, is much more than an economic threat to their jobs. What they see as their whole world is sexually structured. The struggle over the entry of women to printing cannot therefore be compared directly with the struggle that compositors wage against the employer, or even that which they wage against less-skilled men. It cannot be unqualified rivalry. The female competitor is also, potentially, a man's lover, wife or daughter, close and cherished. Yet women do not appear to be honouring their side of the complementarity bargain, the domestic loyalty bargain. One comp described to me how he felt himself to be engaged in an escalating struggle as a worker and as a member of a trade union with newspaper owners, the bosses, while holding the lid on a growing rebellion from his wife. Along with other women, she could now use contraception to undermine men's power over procreation, cite the priority of her career over housework and 'wear jeans which she knows don't turn me on'. 'So what can a man do about it? We can't *attack* women!' The way out of this contradiction involves hard choices for men.

7. Class and sex: two power systems

The story of compositors in printing, as I have sketched it here, has unfolded within two major processes: developments in relations between classes and in relations between sexes. Although it has not been a fully-elaborated historical account, nonetheless instances from the past have been used to throw light on today, to show that we are always involved in a continuing process of making and being made.

Although the dominant class, the employing and ruling class, have made most of the running in the developmental processes of the mode of production, the working class has not been without initiative in history. The class relationship between the owners of the printing presses and their own particular proletariat, skilled and unskilled, is one of 'challenge and response, action and reaction, problem and "solution", threat and containment . . . : a pattern, in short, of struggle.'[1] The strategies of craft organisation and craft control, for instance, influenced the way newspaper capital went about its business in the past and is one of the causes of technological innovation today. Likewise, while men and male values may have been the dominant factor in defining what is masculine and what is feminine, in constructing our gendered selves and distributing power unequally between us, women have never been entirely passive. Whether working to shape their complementary part of the mould or seeking to shatter it, they have also influenced the development of society.

These two processes, that of class development and that of gender development, affect each other and often proceed, step by step, through the very same occurrences. The Edinburgh crusade against women typesetters, for instance, or today's struggle over computerised composition are incidents in *both* histories, that of class relations and that of sex/gender relations, that of capitalism and that of patriarchy.

The difficulty for most of us is to hold in sharp focus both sets of connections at one and the same time. Let's review briefly the class framework of the story. We have been looking in close detail at the activity and the consciousness of a group of men at work, and the first thing to recall (as Paul Willis has said) is that 'the working-class culture of the workplace exists in hard conditions set by others'.[2] That much is painfully clear to the newspaper compositor today. The working class in printing has experienced three or four decades of increasing concentration and centralisation of capital, in the printing industry, in newspapers and the economy as a whole. The years of this study have been a period of deepening recession, with unemployment climbing to over three million. Even compositors, long used to a shortage of labour not of jobs, now experience over 4 per cent unemployment. These things objectively weaken the position and shake the confidence of those who, like the compositors interviewed here, are lucky enough to be still in work.

The working-class man had become used to relying for the maintenance of his own and his family's standard of living on certain guaranteed, albeit ungenerous and often manipulative, supports: the health service, schooling, housing, benefits. Cuts in public expenditure, particularly under the hard monetarist regime of the Tory government elected in 1979, have thrown the worker back upon reliance on the earned wage. The support of a strong trade union has become more vital that ever before. Yet at the same time the Conservatives are imposing new legislation that limits the freedom and scope of the trade unions and makes many of their practices illegal. The NGA's campaign to black work originating in the 'unfair', i.e. non-unionised, shops will soon become unlawful. The closed shop, long the lynch-pin of craft organisation, is also under attack. Meanwhile, the judiciary and the police have gained in authority and are accorded a new high profile. While the balance of class power has thus tipped further against the working class, the employers have been able to revolutionise their methods of production and management and that indeed has been the state's purpose. In preparation for the moment when investment will once again become profitable, industry, not just in printing but much more widely, is attempting to wipe out the power of the skilled working class by nullifying its industrial competence.

As we've seen, even the compositor's old manual working-class identity seems to be melting away. Manufacturing manual workers are a dwindling proportion of the working population. It is not that the compositor is changing his place in the class structure so much as that the working class is being restructured around him so that he is merged with a more inchoate working-class whole. No doubt the class has its own new pattern, but it is not yet clear. The comps are being split up now, some heading for early retirement,[3] some to the dole queue, a few hanging on in the old craft occupation. Others are becoming computer operators, typists, data processors. Some might be called text processors or graphics personnel, less sure of the line that divides them from the journalist, the editor or the clerical worker, less sure too of just what those other occupations signify socially. A few are becoming mini-capitalists going into business on their own account, investing their redundancy money in the smaller and cheaper photocomposition systems, setting girls to work on *their* keyboards. The majority, though, continue to depend upon employment by 'big capital' that alone can invest in competitive technology. Accumulation is still the motive force and the working class (whatever its restructured composition) is still the crucial factor in its achievement. The history of capitalism, it is evident, has still a long way to run.

Seeing a sex/gender system

Class accounts of changes in the labour process, such as the foregoing, have been written many times before. Often, women have been slipped into the analysis here and there, demonstrating how sexual divisions play a part in class processes. Sometimes it is emphasised how the existence of the family and women's unpaid work in the home benefits the capitalist class economically.[4] Sometimes it is pointed out how a sexually-segmented labour market and a sexually-segregated labour force can serve capital.[5] The boisterously masculine culture of the male workplace can be shown to be an effective part of the workers' culture of resistance against capital – all part of 'the task of making fundamentally punishing conditions more habitable.'[6] There is nothing erroneous in these ways of seeing the world. All events, even gendered events, can be 'read' from a class perspective. What I have tried to do in this account, however, is to show that the same events can also be read from a different perspective, a sex/gender perspective, one from which they all reveal another side to themselves, the workings of another system. It is not just in order to tell us something about the position of women that we should make such an analysis. *The events themselves cannot be understood unless read from both perspectives.*

I have tried to make explicit throughout this account the significance of the events for *both* the development of patriarchy and the development of capitalist society. Thinking in terms of two systems at once is not easy, especially perhaps to marxists who have such a well-developed sense of the class system. In her article, aptly titled 'The unhappy marriage of marxism and feminism', Heidi Hartmann pointed out that when a feminist analysis and a marxist analysis are attempted at one and the same time it turns out, curiously often, that the feminist account becomes subordinated: all problems get subsumed under 'capitalism', and what men as men contribute to human exploitation and oppression goes unremarked.[7]

From long practice, our eyes can distinguish a 'mode of production' without difficulty. After all, we have had over a century of experience in teasing out this model from the mass of events we live through and read about. We *expect* to find an economic base, a set of practices that produce wealth and distribute goods. We expect to find political institutions – organisations for promoting a national interest, controlling class conflict, producing consensus. We expect to observe physical forces mobilised in class struggle: sources of energy, forces of production, insurrectionary bands, armed forces, prisons, police. In addition to these material expressions of a class system we also expect it to be manifest in ideology. We expect to find a climate of ideas and meanings, taking now solid form in the shape and practice of institutions themselves, and now a more abstract form in argument and discussion in the union meeting, in parliament, in the media. There have been periods when marxist thought has been narrowly economistic. Today, the totality of the capitalist relation has been rediscovered. Marxism at its best is a world view. It takes the world as its subject and writes an account of it from one perspective: a theory of classes defined by their relation to the means of production.

When we look for a mode of production, for capitalism, therefore, we know pretty well where to look and what to look for. When we start to look for a sex/gender system, however, it is difficult to know where to begin. Where *is* the system of sexual power that we have called patriarchy? All the institutions and practices we know of are already ascribed: to the mode of production and its class relations. Is the sex/gender system somewhere else, then, in the interstices of capitalist society, somewhere where capitalist relations are *not*? In answer to this question we used to say 'it's in the family', where men and women relate most intimately. But now that we understand that the family too can serve capitalism and be structured by it, we do not even feel confident of this.

We should not, I think, be looking for specific locations of sex power, any more than of class power. To say that patriarchal power is exercised only in the family or in directly sexual relations is as blinkered as to suppose that capitalist power is exercised only in the factory. The sex/gender system is to be found in all the same practices and processes in which the mode of production and its class relations are to be found. We don't live two lives, one as a member of a class, the other as a man or a woman. Everything we do takes its meaning from our membership of both systems. Families, factories, schools, trade unions – these are class institutions, true enough, part of the capitalist relation. Some, like the stock exchange, take their very *raison d'être* from capitalism. But they are all gendered too, their practices and processes are those of patriarchy as well as class. Feminism, like marxism, is a world view and its subject is the world itself: a totality. The two systems are, at bottom, conceptual models, each explaining different phenomena. We need them both.

It is as though we have in front of us one of those drawings used to illustrate optical illusion. We look at it one way and interpret it as a particular shape. Suddenly our perception switches and we see the same lines form another object, another meaning. One is the image of a class structure, the other of a sex/gender structure. We have to accustom ourselves to thinking of patriarchy as affecting most aspects of life, as being as tangible as a mode of production and even more extensive, more durable. Whether a person is male or female may well have as much impact on individual life chances as whether a person is a member of the ruling class or working class. To devote twenty years of life to rearing children in the seclusion of the home is dramatically different from spending the equivalent twenty years in the competitive social world of paid work. The different pressures of the lives of men and women produce different effects. In Britain a woman is more likely to need treatment in a mental hospital than a man; a man is very much more likely to go to prison than a woman. A sex/gender analysis is necessary if we are properly to explain our world.

We ought not, however, to expect to find exact parallels between the two systems. Although, as we have seen, even biological maleness and femaleness is partly a social construct, nonetheless there *is* a biological category onto which genders are mapped. This is not the case with class.[8] Another factor reduces the comparability of the class and sex systems. The paired nature of heterosexual relations, the domesticity of the family and physicality of sex relations, all bring members of the sexes into a particularly intimate kind of interaction, in contrast to class relations where the scale is usually larger and more institutional. A third factor is that, within the complex of material phenomena, the concepts of a mode of production and a sex/gender system have somewhat different emphases. Although marxism recognises that capitalism is a system of social relations backed by physical force, primacy is assigned to the *economic*. The sex/gender system, too, is material in the full sense of the word, with expression in economics among other things. But within the concept a special degree of importance adheres to the *physical* and the *social*, to sexuality, for instance, and the reproduction of human life. In important ways, however, a mode of production and a sex/gender system are analogous. Both have material form and that materiality has full phenomenal expression in economic, in socio-political and in physical reality.

Both, too, have ideological expressions.

A problem arises when we compare the manner and pace at which the two systems respond to the passage of time. The concept 'patriarchy', when loosely used to mean 'male supremacy', affords no sense of historical change. That is why, as mentioned in the Introduction, the term 'sex/gender system' is helpful, introducing as it does a sense of plurality and sequence, the notion that one 'mode' of sexual relations can succeed another. Too little is known, however, of the past to be sure that there were societies in which men were subordinate to women – and it is hope more than prediction when we suppose that there may be a sexually egalitarian society in the future.

What is clear, however, is that there have been historical changes *within* the structure of male domination. For this reason the term 'patriarchy' needs more closely defining as a society in which the material and ideological subordination of women is achieved through a cluster of specific means. These include, for instance, the authority of older men over younger; the economic and social dominance in the family of the male head of household; inheritance by primogeniture; individual (and often inherited) male power exercised through the ownership of the business firm; the 'family' values of a masculine Christian church; fraternal formalities within all-male societies – whether these are the gentleman's clubs or the craftsmen's societies. Victorian England was clearly the paradigm instance of one form of male-dominated society – and let us call it patriarchy.

Many details of this story of technological change and restructuring in the working class point to a dissolution of patriarchy in this sense. The 'man of the family' is feeling his power diminish as more women have independent earnings or social security benefits, as more women bring up their children without a male counterpart. One compositor suggested to me, philosophically,

> I think marriage is going to die off, actually. Now that women are progressing and getting more and more money, it's making them far more independent. The thing is that in a lot of marriages there is a good deal of tension. The women, to be honest, might do better to get out. The man may well be the

one who prefers things to go on as they are, because he has someone to cook and mind for him. He has more to lose.

The story of the printers in the nineteenth century and today has shown a similar shift of emphasis. The benevolent despotism of 'the family firm' and the fraternalism of the trade societies are dying out. For compositors, titles and ranks such as Imperial Father, the deference and discipline within the chapel, the rites of passage of apprenticeship, are all now little more than hollow form. As one compositor complained, 'All that male comradeship, "banging out", wayzgooses, wet chapels and what have you . . . it's all finished now. It's a tragedy, but there it is'.

The question remains however whether the end of patriarchy means the end of the exercise of male power in society. Marxist theory proposed that the dethronement of capital would melt away male supremacy.[9] Yet in those countries called socialist today, though women's legal and political status has improved and more women have been drawn into paid work, men have not taken on their share of caring tasks, homosexuality is still taboo and male dominance continues in society as a whole.[10] Freudian theory on the other hand proposed that men's rivalry and men's power over women hinge on the existence of the dominant father. Yet somehow, though the father is being eclipsed, his son in the school playground today seems to have lost none of his belligerence or his ability to intimidate and marginalise girls. His son on the street corner still possesses the ascendancy that can enable him to make any passing girl blush and cross to the further pavement. Those who have had little faith in the marxist or the freudian promise have said: men's power will only fall when women challenge it. There were waves of feminist activism in the nineteenth century, in demands for the right to work and to improved legal status, and in the early twentieth century over female suffrage. The 1970s saw a tremendous upsurge of self-definition and self-organisation among women.[11] And these things have contributed to the eclipsing of many of the features of patriarchy. But male power does not wither so easily. The power elites in the multinationals are men. Within the restructured labour force the knowledgeable and influential technician, scientist or computer specialist is still 20 times more likely to be a man than a woman. The threat of rape and violence to women and children is growing, not diminishing, so that women live in continual tension between accepting curbs on their own and their children's freedom or paying the price in anxiety and fear. We may indeed be in the process of building a sex-equal society, but it is just as likely that patriarchy is merely giving way to another form of male superiority: andrarchy perhaps? History certainly has more than one form of male supremacy up its sleeve.

The economics of male advantage

The time has come to stand back and see what difference thinking with the concept of a sex/gender system has made to our understanding of the story of printers experiencing technological change. Conversely, what instances has this history of a particular group of craftsmen thrown up that illustrate the extent and materiality of a sex/gender system? Since the scope of these material effects is very large I will refract them through the prism of the three instances: *economic*, *socio-political* and *physical*.

Let's recapitulate the material facts: the *economic* as a first instance. Men as a whole have benefited much more in the past from the capitalist development of the printing industry than women. More men than women have been drawn into printing employment and the jobs they have occupied have been better paid. It has often enough been noted that women's domestic ties adversely affect her chances at work.[12] It is less often noted that women's economic disadvantage in employment adversely affects her standing in life outside work. Having less money and owning fewer assets puts women at a severe disadvantage relative to men. The weekly pay packet of the compositor's wife (perhaps £30 or £40), the product of her part-time job in a hairdressing salon or as a secretary in some local business office, looks puny in the bank statement alongside her husband's thumping monthly salary cheque. (In the London news trade a compositor may well gross £2,000 a month in 1982.) If the wife has equal power to decide what the family will spend its money on, this is because the husband chooses to give her that power: it doesn't spring from economic equality. If she were able to earn as much as her husband, which she is not, she would be in a better position, if she wanted to, to suggest that he share the household responsibilities and that their life choices be determined as much by her career as his. So long as she cannot maintain the same standard of living on her wage as he can on his, this is not realistic. Some compositors are prepared to feel that their wives are unfairly paid for the responsibility they take or the effort they make. 'They pay her less just because she's a woman.' But sympathy does not compensate for sheer lack of economic initiative, within marriage and outside.

A compositor might well protest however, 'Is it my fault that women earn less than men, that my wife earns less than me?' When we shift the focus onto the newspaper workplace it is possible to see that the earnings differential between a craftsman and his wife is reproduced in that between the craftsman and the woman clerk or canteen assistant. Then we can see that men and their unions do share responsibility with employers. It is true that throughout the history of capitalism employers have tried to employ women at lower rates than men. But we've seen that men are implicated, in printing as elsewhere. Though they have sometimes paid lip-service to the idea of equal pay for women (as indeed most do today), they have never made it a part of their industrial strategy to demand that the employer not only observe the principle of equal pay but actively recruit women into the industry at male rates, and open to them the full range of occupations. If men had represented themselves and women to employers as an undifferentiated labour market, with undifferentiated skills and rights to work and pay, to challenge the employer's manipulation of labour, then the occupation and earnings pattern in the industry might look much less lop-sided than it does. More often, men have been glad to see the notion of equal pay result in the flushing of women out of jobs they wished to reserve for themselves.

Women's lower pay, while significant in itself, is also part of a rigid ladder of pay differentials that is the product and cause of rivalry between different groups of *men* in the industry. Men's class strategies against capital have been distorted by the fact that they took the form of the maintenance of a patriarchal hierarchy. 'Working-class organisation' and 'working-class action' are fine concepts. But they have all too often been used to give legitimacy to a centuries-long squabble over a male pecking order. The presence of patriarchy has never permitted the real working class, all its men and women, to have a total and actual common interest. That was never more than a hope for the future, as it is today.

Skill differentials and the unique right of men to 'a family wage' have been justified by trade unionists as the strong leading the weak: 'We demand more than you, we lead the way up the ladder but we all get more out of the employers that way.' A related practice has been to use industrial muscle at local or chapel level to boost earnings up high by means of merit money, bonuses and overtime, while neglecting to push up the national basic rate. As a result this yields low pay in the weaker areas. If such strategies have some plausibility in times of economic boom they have no merit at all in times of recession. Labour clearly needs to defend and advance the wage against the encroachments of capital on working-class living standards. But class interest does not lie in fighting over differentials, the elevation of wage leadership to a principle, while low pay continues to be endemic and women to feature significantly amongst the low paid. There is a danger that masculine interests expressed in industrial bargaining lead to overwhelming priority being given to the wage over other kinds of demand. Paul Willis has argued that 'the unholy interlocked grip of masculinity and the wage form . . . holds in check the other possibilities of shop-floor culture'.[13]

If unequal earnings is the simplest to detect, it is not the only economic facet of male advantage. Men's career achievements, including their earnings, have been predicated on women's domestic labour. Most of the compositors in my study, like most men in well-paid skilled manual work in Britain since the war, own their own house and aim to maintain, through their own salary alone, their wife and children. The expected arrangement, it seems almost too obvious to point out, is that the wife does the housework and looks after the children – work which has to be done every day and which imposes its own discipline. The man's role in the house is seen as contributing the do-it-yourself work as and when needed: painting, decorating and repairs. The wife, in an informal exchange for her daily domestic labour, is 'kept' by the husband to a high standard of living. He (and in many cases she as well) will say that in this way her domestic labour is paid for by the man. She does not, however, have any firm rights or expectations concerning the amount of money she receives for herself – as opposed to the household's budget. Such relations have been analysed in sociology, as they are discussed in daily life, to the point of tedium.[14]

The men I was able to talk to about their domestic lives made it clear that while most participated in the household 'chores' (as they often call them) on the basis of 'giving the wife a hand' or 'helping her out', all but a very few were able to engage or disengage on their own terms. One of my sample, exceptionally, had brought up several children single-handed after divorce. A few were bachelors looking after themselves. Needs must. But in no instance was a man who *had* a wife doing 50 per cent of the housework and child care, even when his wife was working full time. When a man has a wife she takes responsibility for servicing him (*and herself*, something which is often overlooked). Conversely the man does not need to plan, shop, wash clothes, clean, cook or mend for anyone, even himself. And of course, when the couple have children, then the sexual division of labour, which may have been interpreted lightly before, clamps firmly into place.

The men seemed to walk a tightrope in regard to marriage. They want their freedom but are very dependent on the family. They worry about their marriages – talk a lot about them. It is not surprising. By this time-honoured family structure a man obtains hard economic advantages. He is free to build up a remunerative career, which his wife is not. He gets domestic service on the cheap – he would have to pay far more to have a living-in housekeeper. He also of course obtains many emotional and physical advantages – an unmarried or widowed man, after a certain age, is an outcast in a hard world organised around the nuclear family.

There's more to 'material advantage' than money

If these are some of the economic advantages that men enjoy through their status as artisans in printing, what of the organisational strength they have developed through their engagement with the world: what we could call *socio-political* strength?

The fact that men and women pair and live in couples makes the subordination of women seem to us, sometimes, to be achieved by individual men, on a one-to-one basis. Sometimes, reminded suddenly of the full extent of women's subordination in the world, we look around and wonder how such an overwhelming and universal effect can be achieved by such negligible means. Surely this enduring physical, political and economic domination cannot arise from each individual woman being outfaced by a single man? It does not, of course. Patriarchal relations, like class relations, are organised and institutional. But where are the societies, the institutions, the armies that organise men's power? The answer is that they are right there in front of us: the same old newspaper firm, the same old printing chapel, the Fleet Street pub, the golf club in the leafy suburb.

In all such organisations men 'establish or create inter-dependence and solidarity that enables them to dominate women'.[15] In all the institutions of society men are more active than women. They build wealth within them, build competence, build rights and expectations. By this stage in our story there can no longer be any doubt that the craft unions of the printing industry and their predecessors, the trade societies, have made notable contributions to the advancement of male solidarity and strength. Women are relatively absent from this social and political sphere. They are obliged to give only a partial and conditional allegiance to work and union. They are mainly confined to the domestic world, which is characteristically isolated and private. A woman's life is not conducive to the mobilisation of social and political power – it has taken us a long while to learn how to relate to each other politically at all.

Beyond this, however, the focus on technology in this study has forced the recognition of another material aspect of male power that is very often overlooked: the *physical*.[16] The occupation of composing is one of many 'male jobs' that has contributed to the construction of men as strong, manually able and technologically endowed, and women as physically and technically incompetent. The emergence of a lad into a full-grown, trained and qualified craftsman is the end of a long process of social creation. When a compositor talks of the greater physical strength of a man, the strength that enables him to carry a printing forme, of the affinity for technology that differentiates a man from a woman, we need not accept his claim that 'it's only natural'. We have evidence enough that men have built their own relative bodily and technical strength by depriving women of theirs, and they have organised their occupation in such a way as to benefit from the differences they have constructed. The attributes of strength and skill have also been deployed competitively in the manoeuvring for status between men in the male hierarchy that dominates women.

The physical and technical competence of men, relative to women, has helped them onward and upward in their occupations. As with economic advantage it has also amplified their power in marriage, in home life and in society as a whole. It has been a process parallel to that which has turned the biological fact that women bear children into the social fact that they alone look after them. Small biological differences are turned into bigger physical differences which themselves are turned into the gambits of social, political and ideological power play. Females are born a little smaller than males. This difference is exaggerated by upbringing, so that women grow into adults who are less physically strong and competent than they could be. They are then excluded from a range of manual occupations and, by extension, from the control of technology. The effect spills over into everyday life: ultimately women have become dependent on men even to change the wheel of a car, reglaze a broken window or replace a smashed roof slate. Worse, women are physically harrassed and violated by men: women are first rendered relatively weak; the weakness is transformed to vulnerability; and vulnerabilty opens up the way to intimidation and exploitation. It is difficult to exaggerate the scale and longevity of the oppression that has resulted.

Economic, socio-political and physical – all these key material factors work together, interacting to produce advantage for men and disadvantage for women. Socio-political power organised within a trade union such as the compositors' societies wins the 'right' to certain physical competences and so secures greater earning power. Higher earnings make men more politically and socially powerful in domestic life. Physical and technical competence produces economic advantage for men but also enables them to control women physically. The circle is complete – and vicious indeed. What is more, this circle interlocks with another, with the exploitation of one class by its counterpart, in such a way that working-class women are doubly trapped.

Ideas and their effects

I emphasised the *material* ramifications of the sex/gender system first, leaving a discussion of ideology to follow. I did so because all too often it is believed that the problem of women in society is one that can be put down to ideas. It is 'male chauvinism', 'prejudice' or 'sexist attitudes' that are to blame. I wanted to show that there is a complex set of material circumstances underlying such ideologies. To think of changing people's ideas alone is impractical, because ideas are expressions of practices. The patriarchal system of relations also exists, however, at the level of ideas, just as the capitalist relations of class exist at this level. Meanings ascribed to 'men' and 'women', expectations of the way they will behave, an implicit definition of what is 'work' and 'skill' – these are real and influential. They arise out of material circumstances such has those we have considered, but they also bear upon them. Antonio Gramsci wrote of the hegemony, the leadership by force of ideas as much as by force of arms, that enables a leading class to hold sway over 'subaltern' groups in society. Bourgeois hegemony holds the working class into a spurious 'national unity'.[17] Male hegemony, by making alternatives unthinkable, is every bit as effective in holding women into compliance.

The evidence drawn from interviews with compositors and from a reading of their history revealed an ideological process that is persistent and influential, that both interprets the material world and acts upon it. Three features of this dominant ideology emerged as important within the sexual field. The first was the *essentialism* that sees men and women, by birth and by nature, as possessing particular sex-specific characters and potentials. The second was the appeal to *complementarity* that sees a man or a woman as no more than the interlocking half of a whole: the couple. The third was the *split*, in the men's images of women, between the pure wife, mother or daughter in the home and the sex object, notionally available to all men. I have shown how the maintenance of those ideas as plausible and workable has been threatened by the entry of women into the men's sphere of work in the wake of new technology.

It is not only men, of course, who contribute to ideas of sex-essentialism and gender complementarity. Many women choose an explicitly 'feminine' style. Some take a kind of pride in being incompetent at certain things that are defined as masculine, or speak up for the satisfactions of a committed domestic life, the importance of a home with a full-time mother in it, and so on. There are many good reasons why they should do so, not least of which is to reassert the value of women's work and feelings. But there is a negative side to this: patriarchy is not just a system in which men dominate women without consent. Like capitalist class hegemony, male hegemony is organised in the main by consent, by identification with the *status quo* and a belief in common interests or in inevitability.

In this respect, complementarity and essentialism are functional ideologies. Difference, if it is expressed as complementarity, can be represented as *not* inequality: you're as good as me, we're just opposites. Essentialism helps to make patriarchy, like capitalism, a system to which men and women find it very hard indeed to imagine a viable alternative. If there is no alternative in sight, you hurt no-one so much as yourself by resisting. Perhaps, though, such ideologies are not harmful? What, after all, is wrong with *difference*? Many of the men had the answer to this themselves, speaking out quite strongly against sexual stereotyping.[18] A few more showed a confused worry and awareness of the harm it can do. They recognise sometimes that complementarity produces 'oppositeness' but that that is not at all the same thing as range and variety. There is a strand of resistance to patriarchal relations woven into the problematic as men define it to themselves: it is not just an idea in the heads of discontented women. There is a recognition that breaking of the 'yin-yang' syndrome need not mean a freakish androgyny, some sort of sexless uniformity. It could mean that the young comp who wanted to be a hairdresser could have been so without suspecting himself and being suspected by others of 'being a poufter'. Men could work in the same room with women, even work under their supervision, without loss of self-respect. Homosexuality would invite no slur. A girl who grew up to find herself more interested in a career than in having children need not think of herself as a crank – or indeed even have to discard one possibility for the other. Difference is, if anything, constrained and limited by complementarity.

Some men would really welcome women as colleagues because it would relax the rigorous standards of masculinity demanded by work today. After all, one reason that is given for women being unsuited to life in the composing room is that 'a girl couldn't stand toe-to-toe with the men and trade punches without dissolving into tears, or blushing or running away'. This speaks of a hard world, hard for the woman but also hard for the sensitive man. As one comp put it, 'Often I wish there were women around. It would tend to simmer things down.' Not all men deride women's activities. Some would like to feel free to do some of them. One man said, 'I am interested in cooking, you see. I admit it, perhaps I want to embrace a lot of these things.' But his wife felt threatened by this invasion of the only field in which she was supreme and he understood that she had fewer ways than he of gaining self-identity. Men are torn over what they want their marriages to be. Partly they want complementarity – especially since they get the best deal out of it: 'I like to pop down to the pub for an hour or two, play darts. She has little jobs she likes to get on with in the house.' But pulling against this is the idea of a relationship between similars, an equal friendship, something ideal, undistorted by sexual stereotyping, economic necessities or the demands of children. 'She's my best pal, really, I suppose.'

Sometimes, talking about their daughters, the men managed to escape from the miserable dichotomies of sexual roles and show a generosity and hope for them and their futures, that they could not allow themselves to feel for women in general. These, their own female children, would be given the best education, they would be encouraged to express themselves, they would be free to choose. When a father imagines his daughter falling to the demands of another man, he can see the attractions of autonomy for women.

The movement of women, a few women, out of the strait-jacket of the feminine sex-stereotype quite reasonably makes many men envious. The fact is that womanly activities are, in the dominant ideology, repellent to a man. Even if sex roles break down, few men can see themselves taking up the new options. So, they may be jealous that a woman can take on a man's capabilities without losing her own, reaching a new wholeness. They may feel bitter that a woman can 'go out to work if she wants to but she can also still stay at home and be kept by a man if that's what she wants'. One man had had the experience of ocean sailing with an amateur crew that included young married women. He noted that the women enjoyed the physical work, that they were quite tough and competent, but he also noted that they were attractive and fun, absorbed in 'chatting to each other about nail varnish and fashion'. They seemed to him to be getting the best out of everything. It is not surprising that some men feel envy mingled with admiration when they say 'the potential of women is limitless'.

It may seem that the fight against patriarchal ideology is something that has to be carried on at an individual level, in the painful privacy of encounters between men and women. But ideological effects are organised and get expression in very material forms. One of these media is 'the media' itself – including the newspaper, which the compositor is involved in producing every working day.

When you talk to a comp about the newspaper, he expresses no surprise if you suggest that the product is something that has political and ideological significance in class terms. He is quick to say, himself, for instance, that his paper is an 'establishment paper'. He may say, 'It puts about ideas that are damaging to trade unions' or, in the case of the *Daily Mirror*, 'they claim to take a working-class view but . . . ' He recognises that the ownership of the paper is significant, that a newspaper confers political power on its owners and makes wealth (when it is properly managed) for the corporation that invests in it. Try, however, suggesting to him that the paper he produces is political and ideological from another point of view in that it confers political power on men. The compositor will look at you in surprise.

Yet newspapers are an important part of the processes by which the hegemony of masculist ideas and values is sustained. Male rivalry, competitiveness and prowess are given a daily boost in the sports, war and crime reporting. There is a strident assumption that the reader is heterosexual, with the matching assumption that if you are not you are a misfit. The family, with its paraphernalia of love, marriage and babies (royal and common) is a subject of continual celebration, but its contradictions crop up painfully in the cartoons, such as Andy Capp. The double standard fills the tabloids: here a chat piece with a bereaved mother, there a full-page nude in leather boots. As Anna Coote and Beatrix Campbell have pointed out, 'during the 1970s . . . the idea of a "newspaper" became inseparable, in the minds of many millions of British readers, from the idea of naked female breasts.'[19] Page 3 of *The Sun*, with its huge photos of 'lovelies', 'dazzlers', 'sizzlers' and 'tantalisers', has become a catchword in musical comedy and offstage. Women's bodies feature equally in the advertising pages, as bait for male buyers. And the stereotype of the wife and mother is exploited in other adverts attempting to sell products for use in the home. In these respects, all that has changed since the fifties is that the porn threshold has risen: images appear on the breakfast table now that would not long ago have been shocking in a sex magazine.

The media expresses the dominant ideology of the sex/gender system as it does that of the class system, making both appear inevitable and irresistible. Women's own efforts to redefine them-selves and to hit back with an alternative ideology are systematical-ly misrepresented in the newspapers, trivialised and ridiculed as 'women's lib' and 'bra-burning'.

As we've seen, the compositor has always refused responsibility for the content of the newspaper he helps to produce. The press owner, says the craftsman, wants it this way: 'We tell it, you spell it, we sell it.' This has been elevated to a law of nature, or at least a law of class power: that the craftsman has a *necessary* distance from the ideological implications of the newspaper. There is more to it than this, however. Men have vested interests in the sexist aspects of the press today – it is their power that is being amplified and their sexuality addressed. Many a comp turns in expectation and plea-sure to Page 3 for his daily dose of skin. When he says, 'After all, I'm only human', we have to hear, 'I'm only a man'.

8. Men and the making of change

We arrive then, at the final chapter of this book, holding in our hands the fragments of the working class with which we began the first. It still seems that these shards must have the makings of a historic whole, but they continue to repel each other and keep their distance. Skill is a human capability to make and heal, but it is used to divide us. Trade unionism, which could bind the class together, often appears to organise its fragmentation instead.

The skilled white, male working class is not the only impediment to working-class unity. Other analysts in other books have chosen to point the finger at the manipulative role of capital and the state, or the historical accidents of religion and language, and they are right in doing so. This book has had a more limited and certainly more painful approach: it looks simply at some of the divisive forces acting within the working class itself.

I began this research with a question at the back of my mind, underlying the more easily researchable concrete phenomena of technology and skill. It was 'How do people change?' In this chapter I want, first, to explore some of the mechanisms of change as my reading of compositors' experience suggests them to be, and to consider technological innovation as a catalyst of change. Beyond that, however, I want to suggest that a future expressive of working-class interests, indeed any future at all, may depend on an abdication by men, or their removal, from a position of power over women. I will explore the relationship of male power and masculist ideology with the right-wing and authoritarian option in society, and the alternative working-class strategy that becomes a possibility only with the fusing of socialism with feminism.

Contradiction: the motor of change

How does social and political change come about? Often we see nothing but inertia around us. Many people feel defeated. But many others are comfortable filling a slot in a hierarchy of class or sex: responsibility is minimised; set procedures and rules, limited expectations, all reduce the risk of suffering and disappointment. If getting beyond capitalism or patriarchy means a disastrous moment of disruption, it is not surprising that people settle for what is there. Men, particularly, before they win the long-term gains, have a lot to lose in the short run from the kind of changes we are talking about. For women too, given the world as it is, there are many attractions in the gender role that complements the more active role of men. Women are cocooned in their 'essential' femininity. Many feel it would make them unpleasant and strident people, especially to men, if they were to protest and compete – and they are right.

In part, material circumstances are such that they represent a realistic deterrent to change. The contradiction betwen capitalism and patriarchy catches us for a start. As Rita Liljestrom has said, for instance, 'What is to be gained if symmetry amounts to inflicting on fathers the same guilty feelings about the children that mothers have, or letting women share with men the mental risks in the mad scramble for upgraded pay rates and careers?'[1] Again, because traditional women's work is good and worthwhile and because it is undervalued, some women put their energies into celebrating it, even at the cost of endorsing the sexual division of labour.

In part, the problem is that people are blinkered by their material circumstances. The point has already been made that many office workers look down on male manual production workers as being their social inferiors – though the latter may earn twice their own white-collar wage. The culture of office life makes a person a ready prey to such ideas. The housewife whose horizon ends at the local shopping centre is hindered from developing any loyalties beyond those of the family, or any aspirations beyond those of being a good wife and mother. This is the sense in which 'life is not determined by consciousness but consciousness by life'.[2]

As well as these material constraints, ideologies push and pull the individual, telling her/him what it is normal and acceptable to think and feel and what is cranky or extreme. Yet individuals are surely 'more than the passive points of intersection of a plurality of discourses', as Terry Lovell complained. Of course history is not made in sovereign freedom, she said, but it does not follow from that that the individual collective action of men and women has nothing to do with it.[3] How do we make sense, make up our mind?

The replies of compositors to my questions, their painstaking exploration of their situation and their feelings about it, are what Gramsci called 'common sense', or what a more recent tradition of cultural studies terms 'culture'.[4] They are ideologies in the little sense of the word, the thoughts and feelings that arise from daily experience. Over and against these, we are aware of ideologies as organised, sustained philosophies that endure and develop over time, take expression in written texts, in institutions, policies. These big ideologies offer authoritative, though competing, versions of the world.[5] They do the work of integrating, dominating and resisting in class struggle. They are at work in creating and challenging the sex/gender system as well. Though feminist ideology arises now and then to contest it, patriarchial or simply masculist ideology helps to maintain the dominion of men over women by consensus. Physical violence is only one of the ways women are kept down.

Ideologies are 'of the mind', they are not material. 'Ideology may be the object and instrument of . . . practice but it does not constitute the practice – it is merely an important element within [it].'[6] Nonetheless, ideologies are grounded in material conditions and practices and have material effects. A particular design of type face, the linotype machine or the computer can be seen to be material forms structured by ideologies, making ideologies active. 'Ideology is thus both mental and concrete, a creation and creator of social practice and produce.'[7] Marxism has in the past tended to conceive of the material conditions in which class ideology is grounded as *economic* conditions: the 'base' as against the 'superstructure' of politics and ideas. A perspective on the male power system leaves no doubt that sex/gender ideologies too are materially grounded, in economic and physical conditions and in organisation. It is the very interaction between material circumstances and ideological forces that makes any system so powerful and enduring. Our imagination is fettered, as our lives are fettered. The result is often a stalemate. As Friedman says, workers 'must act as though capitalism were permanent for most of the time'.[8] And women are certainly obliged to act as though patriarchy were.

However, ideologies may invite and command, but they are not all-powerful. The subjects they address always have their own ideas, tentative though they may be. Their experience, their decisions, play a part in outcomes. 'To neglect the moment of self-creation, of the affirmation of belief or the giving of consent . . . would return us to "pure mechanicity" . . . It is what distinguishes the force of ideological social relations from relations of political coercion or economic necessity.'[9]

Working people do erupt into organisation and resistance; women do protest and hit back. Individuals change their minds and start off on different tracks. The determinist strand in marxist thought suggests that material circumstances fetter our free will. But material circumstance, including the material pressure of external ideologies, can never permanently or wholly govern us because it is riven with contradictions and therefore pushes and pulls us in contradictory directions, making choice a possibility, even a necessity. *What truly can be said to determine the limits of individual free will is not material circumstance itself, but the presence or absence, the severity or insignificance of contradiction.*

The three explosive contradictions in the situation of compositors are the fundamental ones of capitalism, of patriarchy and of the relationship between the two systems. Capital's inability to escape from the law of value produces extremes of wealth and poverty. It destroys human rights and dazzles us with a spectacular flowering of productive forces while denying us the ability to enjoy them. Patriarchy offers men the advantages of power, and in so doing robs them (and women) of the warm and creative relations that sexuality continually promises. And men are torn between a working-class identity and a masculine one – all too often subordinating the former to the latter. While contradictions such as these can be contained, no change will occur. When they become explosive, individual choices will add up to societal change.

Throughout this story I have given special emphasis to contradiction. Wherever people have felt tension between different interpretations of events, been undecided 'what to make of it all', I have allowed that tension to have full expression. What we have seen is contradiction between practices and meanings (what a person is doing or experiencing belies what they say about it); between alternative meanings (conflicting interpretations of events and practices); and between alternative practices (doing incompatible things).[10]

Let's look at some of the contradictions provoked for compositors by change in the newspaper industry and the ways they are finding to resolve them. (These instances are composites, each drawn from several real-life cases.)

First, the vexed question of power relations between men. The comp rejoiced in the possession of skill and this enabled him to think of himself as better than the common man. Indeed he found psychological advantages in considering the Natties as essentially inferior, because that justified him and his union in organising to keep them out. Now the employer introduces photocomposition. The comp find himself doing work that feels much less skilled. Indeed, during the industrial dispute leading up to its introduction this comp did temporary work on a milk round: he felt degraded. Now his old set of ideas concerning his difference from and height above the unskilled man are inconsistent and discrepant. *It is people like himself he scorns.* This is unpleasant. He broods on it for a while. He may evade the issue more or less permanently in bitterness and cynicism. Or he may begin to deal with the discomfort. He may organise a new meaning out of work to accord with the old ideas: dressing up an association with the computer, perhaps, into something affording status. Or he may change his ideas about the essential difference between skilled and unskilled men, allowing a submerged thought to come to the fore: 'We are all brothers, really'.

A second instance: the issue of women and work. Let's suppose a compositor emerges from his apprenticeship as a young man with untroubled ideas about a woman's place in the printing industry: women do lower paid work. Men have a natural right, because of their 'family responsibilities' (and just perhaps because men are the important people in society) to jobs that bring security and high rewards. Composing is such an occupation. Then the compositor marries. He loves and admires his wife and wants the best in life for her. She is educated and gets satisfaction and identity from her work. He is proud of her. She is every bit as clever and deserving as he. He can't help wanting to support her in her struggle for equal status and equal pay. He is angry with those other men who want to cheat her of her due. But at work, he and his union are facing problems from women seeking access to craft jobs and to equal pay. He believes it is in everyone's interest that this should be resisted, especially in time of recession when men's jobs are under threat. *Now, it is people like himself he is angry with.* Holding such conflicting ideas and feelings makes him feel dishonest. There are several ways he may move to ease the discomfort. He may be let off the hook by the fact of his wife having children, staying home and taking on a domestic personality, relinquishing claims to equal working status. Or he may carry his ideas from home over to work – and help change union policy towards women. Perhaps, though, he will defiantly stick to a double standard and hang the anxiety – and it is tensions like this that produce neurosis, illness and violence.

Finally, let's think about the confusions, not common to compositors alone, about the electronic revolution and ideas of technological progress. The compositor worked for years in an unchanging craft occupation. Technological change was 'out there', in the offing, but not yet threatening him personally. His ideas were influenced by the papers and TV: the development of science and technology represents the steady path of human progress. Now the computer invades his work. It promises enormously increased productivity. At first, he applies his 'progress' ideology to the problem: it will be all right because we will produce and sell more copies of bigger newspapers containing more advertisements. Jobs will be gained, not lost. But the recession intervenes. When the price is survival, the firm has no loyalty to its craftsmen any longer: redundancy and unemployment follow. *He is now the victim of people who think as he does.* What will he do? He may stick to a belief in progress, narrow his loyalties, fight to be one of the privileged who get good jobs. He may adopt a sceptical detachment and agnosticism. Or he may realise his fears for the future, make a critique of technology and its uses, begin to think about the issue of control and to reassess 'skill'.

These individual choices have significance when multiplied many thousands of times. They change institutions and they make history. Of course, they are made under the pressure of material circumstances. The presence or absence of a compelling ideology or organisation pulling one way or the other also plays a part in the choice. The labour movement, the anti-war movement, the National Front, the women's movement heighten the sense of contradiction, offer alternatives and amplify individual choices. But, less publicly, the future is forming out of other material: the illogicalities, inconsistencies and circularities in individual lives and the sense that individuals make of them. Human beings have a great need to be rational and consequential. They do not always succeed. But it is in the struggle to make satisfying meanings of things and to bring behaviour into line with beliefs that change in the individual occurs, if it occurs at all. And change in many individuals adds up to change in trade unions, in political parties and in society.

Technological innovation as catalyst

There are moments of history when disruption opens the way for dramatic change in political orientation and prospects. The technological innovation that is transforming many industries today could precipitate events on this scale. Computerised composition has hit the compositors' craft a terrible blow, shaking the class and gender relations that have been developing over hundreds of years, throwing them into a maelstrom of confusion. And they are not alone: throughout society, patterns of work and consumption are being affected.

New technology is a force acting from without on established social relations. But within that set of relations, as we have seen, are many tensions. The effect that new technology will have will depend not only, or even mainly, on the force of its impact but on the pattern of tensions within the social structure. It is an open question, therefore, whether technological innovation will jolt the printing craftsmen and other skilled male workers into a critical consciousness, or whether capital will succeed in regathering them into continued acceptance of the governing terms of capitalist society.

It is a moment of peril for working-class interests: redundancy, unemployment, the hands of the unions tied by new laws. Trade union membership in Britain has fallen from 13½ million in 1979 to 11½ million in 1981.[11] Many men, and not just older men, threatened with redundancy due to new technology have been happy enough to accept what seems a generous pay-off, to live well for a while and trust to the future to provide. After all, employment is often tedious, tiring and unhealthy. 'Leisure' can be appealing, even if it means selling a job back to the employer for ever. Nor is it inevitable that the consciousness and militancy stirred up by the moment of technological innovation will survive even among those who stay on in work, in a modernised occupation. They may well settle down again to become the trusty hands at the controls of the new technology.[12]

There is much, after all, that pulls the employee into loyal identification with the firm or with 'British industry'. This is not just 'false consciousness' on the part of the worker who fails to see that his or her real interest lies in resistance. It is a real contradiction for the worker:

> Since labour can only gain access to the means of production through selling its labour power to capital, it has an interest in the maintenance of that relationship and therefore the viability of the unit of capital which employs it. Hence labour too will have a direct interest in developing the forces of production within the factory, but again in contradictory fashion, since it will not wish such development to be used solely to benefit valorisation but also to increase wages or provide more pleasant jobs.[13]

The firm positively plays on this fact, of course, by saying 'we need new technology in order to survive'. The newspaper firms were saying to the men, it's not *our* choice. It is the pressures of the market, it's what the advertisers demand, what the readers want. In this way the employer sidesteps responsibility and the employees are confronted directly with the customer and the market. The men are persuaded to identify with the inevitability, the common sense of technological progress. The individual craftsman risks dispossession and the working class risks renewed co-option.

A crisis of technological innovation, however, is also a risk *for capital*. When people are brought to question their class position there is a danger that they will reject their day-to-day accommodation with capital. Late capitalism could be, as Ernest Mandel put it:

> A great school for the proletariat, teaching it to concern itself not only with the immediate apportionment of newly created value between wages and profits, but with all questions of economic policy and development, and particularly with all questions revolving on the organisation of labour, the process of production and the exercise of political power.[14]

As deskilling and restructuring goes on apace, this argument goes, the worker may well wake up to her, or his, situation, organise and rebel.[15]

Of course, the capitalist is caught in his particular contradiction concerning labour: to develop the forces of production, capital cannot get away with merely deskilling those workers it cannot trust. It has also to re-equip some workers with new abilities. It cannot reduce all of us to the idiocy of robots because someone has to design and maintain the idiotic labour processes. Capital needs some labour that is intelligent, resourceful and imaginative if innovation and accumulation are to continue. Can the restructured new-style workforce, building its knowledge of machinery and labour process, be trusted to stay loyal to capitalism? Some think that advanced technology carries the seeds of revolution within it. Serge Mallet, for instance, has suggested that the archaic industries, like coal mining, building and textiles – and perhaps we should include letterpress printing among these – cannot any longer develop a revolutionary ideology and behaviour in their workers. Their struggle will 'necessarily take on reactionary, corporatist and Malthusian aspects, as did that of the English weavers of 1840 . . . It can no longer formulate the *avant-garde* themes of the movement'.[16] In contrast, however, the restructured working class of the modernised industries – including we should suppose, the new newspaper and media workers – will be the ones most likely to develop a critical frame of mind: 'It is only in the social groups within the active population integrated into the most advanced processes of technical civilisation which are in a position to formulate the manifold forms of alienation and envisage superior forms of development.'[17]

The baleful contest, then, between skill and technology may precipitate changes in political perspective. It is not enough, however, to note the moment and the mechanism of change. We need to examine what the substantive possibilities are: what is the best, what is the worst, that could happen? I do not think it is scaremongering to suggest that the worst is a totalitarian, inhuman and war-ridden world.

The family, sexism and the right-wing option

I have argued that a sex/gender analysis, in harness with a class analysis, helps us to understand the past and the present. It remains to suggest that it has something also to say about the future: *only if masculinity ceases to be a factor determining working-class orga- nisation, action, and imagination, will we avoid a fascist future and achieve a fully human one.*

London printers are no strangers to the organisations of the extreme right. While there have always been committed anti- fascists and anti-racists, in Fleet Street and outside, there have also been craftsmen who hold dual membership of both a trade union and a right-wing extremist party. The anomaly, of course, is always possible where a closed shop obtains, because a man may hold a union card merely in order to get access to the occupation and to defend his sectional interest without necessarily having any com- mitment to the principles or philosophy of the labour movement.

It is among the petty bourgeoisie, rather than the working class, that fascism is generally held to find its most fertile ground. When male manual workers are converted to white collar occupations, however, as is happening to compositors today, their class identity becomes less clear and asks for some kind of resolution. Wilhelm Reich long ago suggested that, 'degradation of manual labour (which is a basic element of the inclination to imitate the reaction- ary white-collar workers) constitutes the psychological basis upon which fascism relies as soon as it begins to infiltrate the working class. Fascism promises the abolition of the classes.'[18] Especially, it promises to abolish *proletarian* status, and this may be appealing to the ambitious or confused blue-collar worker, wanting to turn the losses of deskilling into some kind of social gain. Fascist authoritarianism can appear as a solace to men whose status in the skills hierarchy can no longer afford them identity and security. The ideological mechanism by which the unskilled man is seen as a natural social inferior is, as we saw, not dissimilar from that of racism, and the exclusiveness of craft echoes the exclusiveness of nationalism.

Marxist studies of fascism normally assume that the determining factor in a social group's political orientation, in determining whether it is likely to adhere to the left or the right, is class consciousness. There is another determinant, though, that is often neglected: sex/gender identification.[19] Men who give primacy to the patriarchal family form of domestic and sexual relations, with dominant husband and subordinate wife, who benefit from a strong domestic division of labour, and who give priority to a man's wage and a man's right to superior work, will never be out of the reach of fascism. As Reich pointed out, family life and sexuality, factors ignored by marxist theory, rank equally with the economic factors in anchoring the social system: 'We must pay more, much more attention to these details of everyday life. It is around these details that social progress or its opposite assume concrete forms, not around the political slogans that arouse temporary enthusiasm only.'[20]

'Family' is central to rightist ideology and rhetoric. Adolf Hitler called the founding of families, 'the noble mission of the sexes . . . the origin of the natural and specific gifts of providence'. The family, he wrote in *Mein Kampf*, is 'the final goal of genuinely organic and logical evolution . . . It is the smallest unity, but also the most important structure of the state.' It has been pointed out that the Nazi regime had a more clearly defined and more self-conscious attitude towards women than perhaps any other modern government. It was avowedly illiberal and protective in its aims, emphasising motherhood and the home as part of its paternalistic and eugenic purpose.[21] It is cautionary to reflect on the enthusiam for the family, the 'good housekeeper' ethic, of the Thatcher and Reagan administrations today. 'Family policy' has always run in harness with class conservatism within the Labour Party too, as can be seen in the Fabianism of the Webbs or postwar 'welfarism'.

Essentialism and the ideal of complementarity find their fullest expression in fascist thought. Benito Mussolini addressed the nation's women as 'illustrious, prolific mothers' and he himself, as head of state, became the archetype of the patriarchal head of household, the father, the sturdy worker, with his 'male vigour' and militarism. 'In fascism sexual difference is imposed to an absurd degree,' wrote Maria-Antonietta Macciocchi:

> The sex struggle is denied, like the class struggle, since fascism takes as its point of departure the subordination of one sex to another, in so far as women voluntarily accept the 'royal attributes' of femininity and maternity. In the same way that in the fascist corporation the proletariat is forced into a relation of agreements and social peace with the boss, so women are involved in the social contract between them and society. Ownership of women is the same for all men, who precisely because they own this chattel, woman, which cannot be expropriated, are considered, from boss down to worker, equal to one another and with the same rights.[22]

The series of decrees and measures which aimed to resolve the Italian economic crisis of 1929 effectively made women pay the bill. Many women were dismissed from work, especially from the professions and from teaching. Women students were deterred from higher education by being required to pay double fees. It was decreed that women should not exceed 10 per cent of the workforce of both state and private institutions. In Britain today, too, the Conservative government is combining anti-working-class measures with anti-woman measures, making it clear that women are expected to relinquish paid work in the interests of men and of the nation, to take back from the state many of the responsibilities of caring for young and old, and return to their proper place in the home.

The same association of men and distancing of women from

technology, that we have seen occurring in printing history and in the compositors' ideas today, is present too in fascist thought. In an article entitled 'Machine and Woman', Mussolini asserted that women and machines were incompatible. He said that any such relationship degraded male virility, robbed men of their work, prevented births and masculinised women.[23]

Rightist ideology, then, first constructs sex essentialism and the duality of masculine and feminine – amplifying them to the point of caricature. Then it devalues the female. Hitler, for instance, characterised the political backwardness of the working class as typically *female*: 'The people in their overwhelming majority are so feminine by nature and attitude that sober reasoning determines their thoughts and actions far less than emotion and feeling.'[24] Fascism represses sexuality in general: 'The body of fascist discourse is rigorously chaste, pure, virginal. Its central aim is the death of sexuality.'[25] But in particular it involves the suppression of *women's* sexuality, which is incompatible with their social and economic role. As Reich wrote:

> More than the economic dependency of the wife and children on the husband and father is needed to preserve the institution of the authoritarian family. For the suppressed classes, this dependency is endurable only on the condition that the consciousness of being a sexual being is suspended as completely as possible in women and in children . . . Sexually awakened women, affirmed and recognised as such, would mean the complete collapse of the authoritarian ideology.[26]

For woman to escape from the split personality still imposed upon her by men today, to denounce the falsity of both the 'angel in the home' and 'slag in the street', and to step forward, clad in her own definition of her own sexuality, is a necessary precondition of progress on any other front. In the same way, demands for free and safe abortion and contraception, full rights and recognition for homosexuals, provision of social child care, the access of women to work and to technological work in particular, are all fundamental political demands for the left. They are not extras, something in the interests of women or 'minorities' alone. Their inclusion in the programme of trade unions, their presence in the aims of individual men and women, is a crucial guarantee against a drift to the right. Men are caught in a contradicition between their status as working-class people and their status as the male sex. If it is resolved, as so often in the past, in favour of sexual power the door will remain open for class as well as gender tyrannies.

The alternative option

The rights and powers of skilled working-class men of the old industries, such as compositors, are being challenged on three fronts: by employers divesting themselves of the constraints of craft control; by the state through anti-labour legislation (briefly, too, in the early seventies, through pro-woman legislation); and by women themselves in pursuit of their own liberation. Men are likely to respond in one of two ways: by hitting back, reasserting sexual primacy with whatever means are to hand; or by accepting the dismantling of the hierarchies of male power in favour of a more egalitarian way of living and organising. In the foregoing section I sketched some of the negative implications of the former choice. The latter, in contrast, opens up many invigorating possibilities for trade unionism and, beyond that, for working-class social movements. This is not fantasy. We are propelled towards change by the heightening contradictions of advanced capitalism and advanced technology. If we want to take advantage of the shake-up which capital has forced upon us and turn it to our own advantage, the possibility is there.

A single union for all those who work in the press and the printing industry, in radio and broadcasting, does now seem likely to emerge in the next few years, nudged into existence by advanced technology and actually predicated upon it. Such an industry-wide trade union would have more than half a million members: both men and women, 'mental' and manual workers, technicians and office employees, skilled, semi-skilled and unskilled. As a member of the National Union of Journalists today I would be a member of that big union too: in this sense the men in printing are my 'brothers', and what has been to this point a detached analysis of past and present becomes a shared responsibility for the future. Let's suppose that the 'Media Union' does become a reality soon.

What might its strategies be? How might it differ from any of its constituent parts today?

First, such a union could embody a much *wider class conscious-ness*, a new concept of what is meant by the working class and what are genuinely working-class goals. As Andrew Friend and Andrew Metcalf have pointed out, it will be perverse indeed if unions continue to institutionalise and even cherish distinctions between skilled and unskilled, intellectuals and manual workers, men and women, at the very moment when the evolution of the capitalist mode of production is laying an objective basis for overcoming such divides.[27] A single union for the media (or for any other industry) will be little better than numerous competing unions if sectarianism and hierarchy are simply shifted from without to within in such a way that well-paid 'craft' sections and low-paid 'women's sections' continue to exist in reality if not in name.

This wider class consciousness would entail many changes in union organisation, demands and initiatives. One would be a commitment to end both the sexual segregation of work and the sexual division of labour in society. Some of the steps towards this have already been formally adopted as policy by the Trades Union Congress and some unions. But the commitment is as yet more rhetorical than real. The 'Media Union' would, for instance, make 'equality officers' in chapels and branches mandatory, as they are now in the National Union of Journalists. It would set up an Equality Council, Women's Conferences and women's trade-union education. It would encourage women to apply for training and jobs normally thought of as men's jobs. Conversely it would encourage men to move into 'women's work' and seek to increase the status of this work (though that tends to happen automatically when men enter it). This would involve many men in training for and moving into typing, child care, catering, cleaning and sewing jobs. We should not blind ourselves to the fact that this might, in the short run, mean an overall reduction in average male earnings. The union would give as much importance to campaigns for employer support for nurseries, for improved maternity and paternity leave and for flexibility in hours of work, as the unions today give to the annual wage round. It would continually press the state for free and safe abortion and contraception. For their own part, of course, women who come into the industry have an equivalent obligation to join the union – and indeed they are much more likely to do so if it has many active women members and espouses women's interests.

Another facet of this wider class consciousness would be a sharper awareness of the impact of the union's actions on people who fall outside its charmed circle. Trade unions urgently need to stop looking after their own membership alone at the expense of other working-class people outside. The unwaged will always lie beyond the protective walls of the 'Media Union', and a high proportion of them now are women. Their relation to the economy is not through the wage but through the provision of the state, and their interest in the product is less as producer than as consumer, reader or viewer. Trade unionism, in spite of efforts to shift it, has remained stubbornly 'workerist'. And workerism is peculiarly masculine:

> Because of the centrality, in the lives of working men, of the shop-floor struggle for control, and because of the power of men in the family and community, the masculine rhetoric of the workplace comes to dominate every aspect of working-class politics. It is enshrined within the Labour Party and the trade-union movement – a language of 'brotherhood', a preoccupation with the right to work and an emphasis on wage struggles.[28]

Workerist ideology blinds us to the effects of our own work on others, or even of our own chosen tactics of struggle on others' struggles.

Among the unwaged are the unemployed. It is a paradox that (as Mandel put it), 'The compulsion to *save* the maximum amount of human labour in the factory or the company leads to increasing *waste* of human labour in society as a whole.'[29] For every one worker who is made more productive by new technology, a second person is relegated to the total unproductiveness of the dole and a number of young people find their work opportunities shutting down before they are even ready to reach out for them. For those of us in paid work, our goals have to go beyond the survival of our jobs, or even our union, to the survival of those in other occupations and unions and even in other countries. For every success story of British industry there is a comparable tale of unemployment or increased exploitation in some other country. Our perspective has to extend not merely beyond our own workplace to our own society but beyond that again to the world. It has to be international in a way to which trade unionism has often aspired but which it has seldom achieved. This is not mere altruism: our own interests depend on it too. To take an instance from the media: new technology has enabled Reuters, the news agency, to create a world-circling electronic news link that can by-pass and isolate any group of workers who strike in any of its many workplaces. The 'Media Union', then, born out of advanced technology which has the effect of melting away boundaries, could weigh in its policy-making the interests of more than its membership alone – and would ultimately find that its own interests lay in doing so.

One implication of the broadening of the horizons of trade unionism would be a *redefinition of work*. Work is already being rewritten for us and against our interests. The vast increase in productivity promised (or threatened) by the microprocessor is throwing into question the whole relationship between work and non-work, cajoling us into an enjoyment of a future 'leisure society'. The unemployed quite rightly complain that unemployment is not the same as leisure.

There is, however, a missing dimension from this problematic. 'Work' is not paid work alone. For every hour that one worker puts in in production and distribution, another hour's labour or more is contributed unpaid by a worker in the home – in human and social reproduction. This work of cleaning, buying, making and mending, cooking and caring, watching and minding should remind us of the inadequacy of the term 'production': we are all involved in transformative labour wherever we do it and however we subsist. Some in the Labour left and outside are preparing an Alternative Economic Strategy (AES), for implementation by a future left Labour government. Its main goal is 'full employment'. By this the authors mean 'no unemployment'.[30] But we need to look beyond the concept of 'full employment' to see that the most fundamentally important human work is reproducing the human race and human relations, and that the factor of the unpaid labour that this requires has to be put into the equation *before* we see how employment in production and distribution matches up with labour supply. Once those terms are added, it becomes clear that an equal sharing of both productive and reproductive work by men and women would mean a public economic strategy, and union support for it, involving some quite unprecedented innovations.

In the first place it would involve a reduction of the unpaid working day for women, together with an increase in the unpaid working day for men. It would involve an increase in access to paid work for women. It would require a marked reduction in the length of the standard paid working day, particularly for men, who now work the longest hours, in order to bring full-time work nearer to part-time hours. Though print unions have always backed a reduction in the length of the standard working week, this has all too often meant that men continued to work the same hours as before but were paid more of them at overtime rates. This has simply increased men's relative earnings and given them a continued reason to be well clear of the house when child care and domestic work needs doing.

If the union put limits on overtime working, if overtime payment were banned and 'time-off *in lieu*' (time-and-a-half, or double-time, of course) instituted instead, this would both create jobs and equalise the circumstances of men and women. It is worth emphasising too that what we need is a reduction of the working day, rather than of the working week. Child care and domestic responsibilities happen every day. They do not cluster conveniently into the three-day weekend now achieved by the compositors in this study in exchange for the relatively longer hours they work on the remaining four days. Finally, it would also mean greatly increased social services, including social provision for child care and care of the infirm and elderly, under our own control.

The 'Media Union' could and ought to develop a *new approach to pay*. Printing trade unionists have described the pay bargaining system in the newspaper industry as 'dancing a conga', in which the leaders prance on, pulling along behind them in a snake of diminishing earnings the less-skilled or less-organised groups of workers.[31] It needs little imagination to see that whether real earnings overall grow in this process or diminish, the inequalities between people remain. One aspect of the inequalities is lower pay for women. The 'Media Union' would need to put its strength behind demands for a toughening of equal-pay legislation – for instance to include a mechanism for defining equal work as work of equal value. But we would need to go beyond this to escape once and for all from capital's own evaluation of labour: more for intellectuals, less for manual workers; more for clean and enjoyable work, less for dirty and hard jobs; more for men's work, less for women's work. The concept of 'the family wage' too will have to go. As Bea Campbell and Valerie Charlton have pointed out, 'To date the Labour movement has managed to combine a commitment to the family wage with a commitment to equal pay. You can't have both.'[32] Women's pay, however, is only part of the bigger problem of low pay in general. Low pay is exacerbated by the 'smash and grab' of free collective bargaining, which has now been criticised by many women.[33] On the working-class side of the collective bargaining process the 'collective' needs redefining in such a way that wage *leader*ship would give way to an equalising movement focused on increasing basic pay and ending low pay altogether.

We will need to rethink, in the context of the 'Media Union', *the political uses of skill*. The craftsman has always been in advance of others in the importance he ascribed to control over the labour process by the worker. We've seen how craft control, however, became inseparable from craft elitism. Along with skill, capital has for the moment disturbed some components of the hierarchical structure organised around it. The way is open for a reassessment of *all* our skills, for a reinstatement of women's traditional skills and a new assertion of collective control based on the *collective* labourer's closeness to the technologies of production, rather than a control built upon the special knowledge and status of a few at the expense of the rest.

Somehow we have to keep the best of the old skill ethic while discarding the worst. Pride in the ability to produce must stay, but in the form of a pride in being collectively responsible for the making of a socially useful product. This is not without precedent: the Lucas Aerospace combined shop stewards' committee is perhaps the best-known instance of workers lifting their sights to the shaping of industrial policy. Their alternative corporate plan makes proposals for socially desirable products as alternatives to weaponry.[34] Professional and technical skill must be recognised to be no real human skill at all, no more than a tarnished and twisted parody of it, so long as it is applied unquestioningly to the manufacture of anti-working class, anti-woman and ultimately anti-human products. While it is clearly not in the power of the employees of the media singlehandedly to determine the content of newspapers, periodicals, broadcasting and TV, it is undeniably in the power of unions to make that content a subject of struggle.

Finally, we need *a critique of technology* itself, going far beyond that developed by trade unions to date. The Trades Union Congress (TUC) appears to identify as closely with 'the performance of British industry', as does the Confederation of British Industry itself. Among the TUC's aims are to seek 'co-ordinated action . . . towards improving, expanding and modernising Britain's capital stock'. Its main concern is to ensure 'effective demand in the economy sufficient to employ both capital and labour'.[35] In this approach, the problem becomes one of steering technology without questioning it. The assumption is that technology is fundamentally benign: 'There is the realisation that new technologies . . . offer great opportunities, not just for increasing the competitiveness of British industry but for increasing the quality of working life and for providing new benefits to working people.' The challenge, in the TUC's eyes, is to ensure that 'the benefits of this change are distributed equally'. Many individual unions, not knowing which way to turn, adopt a similar attitude.

Scientific discovery and technological invention are not, however, progressive *of themselves*. They are not even all progressive in the right hands. Some 'advances', in the right hands, could liberate people, feed, clothe and educate them. But some, too, are of no use to anyone except those who seek to control society or to profit at the expense of others. It is usual to portray scientific discovery as historic flair, arising from a combination of chance and genius, and to suppose that the application of scientific knowledge in technology follows logically on from discovery. I argued in Chapter 3 that this is not the case. The policies of states and the corporate strategies of multinational corporations govern what aspects of scientific enquiry are funded and what applications are developed. Those decisions are not made in working-class interests. An independent evaluation is needed from within industry and who will make it if not trade unions?

In many cases we really are powerless to resist new technology, and it is no use pretending that we are not. But we do not need to rationalise our unwilling acceptance of technology by persuading ourselves of its beneficence. It is possible to admit defeat while maintaining and developing a critique. The ideology of 'technological progress' is extraordinarily pervasive and compelling.[36] Anyone who questions the advisability of advanced technologies is branded as reactionary. (Marxism has much to account for in this respect.) The very reasonable spirit of the original Luddites is dead in trade unionism and 'Luddite' has become a label that trade union leaders fear. As Dave Albury and Joseph Schwartz argue in their critique of the myth of scientific progress, 'The Luddite tradition needs to be reclaimed in order to overcome the monopoly presently enjoyed by capital in the development of new machines and processes.'[37] As it is, the ideology of 'technological progress' *is* contested, but not by the unions. The challenge comes from the peace movement and the ecology movement.

The individual member is often in advance of her or his union in expressing a healthy scepticism of progress. 'I don't look on new technology as progress,' a compositor said. 'You have to ask, is it conducive to a better society or a better atmosphere? The way they are introducing it, it is not. They are taking no account of people.' Many compositors have come to see that computerised photocomposition poses questions that cannot be answered within the terms common to traditional trade unionism. 'Is it going to be like some of those films where you get overlords and slaves? Because where is the money coming from to pay for those who aren't working? It will only be those with a very high IQ who will be needed to develop and operate this equipment. The rest will be scrapped.' 'We're looking for a utopia, really, you know, talking about chips, automation and all this sort of thing. A utopia whereby people will do nothing and machines will do everything. It can't work. You kind of wonder what's going to become of people.'

For many individuals, however, as for their unions, the answer is still to be found in 'economic growth'. Compositors often say that the massively increased productive potential of computerised composition is no problem 'so long as we can go on selling more papers and getting in more advertising'. What more advertising means, in fact, is more of every other kind of production and consumption. If 'growth' is the price of advancing technology, the implication is a ballooning of consumption on a lunatic scale.

The growth ethic is a natural partner of the ideology of capitalist competition, but it has also been taken on board by post-capitalist societies, caught up either in international competition (such as the USSR) or struggling out of under-development (such as Cuba). Continual, exponential growth of production and consumption is incompatible with the long-term management of the planet. The interests of life as a whole impose constraints on economic activity:

> The fact is, all humanity cannot live like the privileged 20 per cent of North Americans and Europeans, whose consumption style is the – unattainable – standard for the rest of the North Americans and Europeans as well as the world. There are not enough mineral resources, air, water or land for the whole world to adopt 'our' rapacious ways of production and consumption.[38]

More energy-saving ways of producing may help us, but they will not dissolve the limits beyond which growth becomes destruction.

One factor in the ready acceptance of new technology by the trade-union movement may well be that the unions are so male-dominated. Insofar as any of us have an interactive and influential relationship with technology it is men. It is interesting to look more closely at Serge Mallet's scenario (mentioned above) of the new working class in its future technological employment and space-age enterprises.[39] He supposes these white-coated workers to be pulled by the advanced technologies towards an advanced social and political consciousness. But Mallet's new workers are no less in love with their computers than the craftsmen were with their tools. They have no critical detachment from the technical and scientific forces they set in motion for capital. 'It is in the immediate interests of the modern working class that technical development continues, together with its consequences,' he writes. These consequences, for him, are only good ones: 'substantial reduction in working hours, job revaluation, mobility and more varied activities.'[40] This might be a manufacturer's advert for computerised photocomposition equipment. Mallet's protagonists are, of course, male and they are propelled into their supposedly revolutionary consciousness by 'the contradiction between the integration into *an interesting technical universe which man* [sic] *naturally aims to understand and dominate* and the structure of command, the price system, the decisions which exclude almost all those who help in the functioning of this universe.'[41] (My italics – C.C.) Mallet saw himself as an optimist: but a male revolutionary class without a consciousness of the Promethean fire they hold in their hands is no cause for optimism.

Micro-electronics, the familiar genie of the newspaper industry, is one of a numerous family of new technologies that includes nuclear fusion and fission, laser technology and genetic engineering. And technologies of production are tightly linked to technologies of destruction: nuclear power produces plutonium for bombs; genetic technology produces biological weapons as well as medical remedies; micro-processors guide missiles as well as composing newspapers. To leave investment decisions to business interests is clearly nonsense. To leave them to men, trade unionists though they may be, still amounts to leaving a notorious arsonist with a box of matches.

What is suggested here may seem to go beyond the accepted role of trade unions. Indeed, my critique, in the very first chapter, of the nineteenth-century craft union's narrow male view of the world may prompt the same complaint: Unions are what they are. But what other organisational resources do we have? Of the trio of Labour parliamentarism, community action and trade unionism, the latter alone is close enough to the labour process and to technological decision-making to provide a lever for re-evaluation and intervention.

In the past it has been the practice of a certain group of trade unions, predominantly men, to sequester the technical knowledge arising from the labour process. But knowledge is not property. In future, trade unions must surely become educators, in the widest sense. Initially, those of us who are in trade unions must educate each other, deepening and passing on knowledge. We must see that it is opened up to those formerly defined as unskilled, particularly to women. Besides, printing, broadcasting and communications know-how is urgently needed by working-class movements.

Ultimately, men and women together, we have to ensure that technical knowledge becomes common knowledge. Decisions over what to produce and how to produce it should be made by all who are affected. The only perspective that can bring into view all the implications, for good or ill, of new invention is that of a diverse, united and fully-informed working class.

Afterword

At the beginning of the 1980s, when I did the research on which this book is based, London newspaper compositors, these old-style skilled artisans, were even then no more than shipwreck survivors clinging to a life-raft. Since that time the raft too has foundered and slipped beneath the waves. The men and their craft control, their union's closed shop, have been scuppered by the employers, aided by new technology and a decade of Conservative government. In this epilogue I will trace some of the events in the industry in the ten years to 1991, look at their effect on the industrial muscle of skilled print workers and the position of women in the industry, and set these findings in the context of broader trends in the relations of gender.

The 1980s were Margaret Thatcher's decade. Under her leadership the main thrust of government policy was to stifle socialist impulses in British society and curb the influence of the labour movement. The Conservative Party's proclaimed mission was to free capital's entrepreneurs and managers from the constraints imposed by organised labour and confer on them an untrammelled 'right to manage'. It was a goal the government approached with a dual strategy: monetarist economic policy and anti-union legislation.

The legislation was put in place by stages. Building on the Industrial Relations Act of 1971 came the Employment Acts of 1980 and 1982 and the Trade Union Act of 1984. Among the aims of the new laws were, first, to limit the circumstances in which workers might take industrial action without falling foul of the law, and to expose unions and workers to claims for large financial penalties for actions which until then had been lawful. They made it easier for employers in dispute to sack workers taking industrial action. Membership agreements were undermined. One of the most damaging innovations for the NGA was the illegalising of secondary action: in future the union might take industrial action only against the one employer with whom it was in dispute. Gone were the days when a print union could act nationally against an employers' federation as a whole, or freely picket the distributors or suppliers of the products of a firm with whom it was in dispute.

The combative Tory position against organised labour was characterised by the banning in 1984 of union organisation at GCHQ, the headquarters in Cheltenham of the government's secret communications operation, which precipitated a prolonged struggle. It was epitomised in the 12-month long coal mining strike of the same year in which it became apparent that the government's intention was not merely to win the dispute but to weaken the National Union of Mineworkers beyond the point at which it could any longer be an industrial or political force. Circumstances, then, were hardly auspicious for the National Graphical Association in the period of its engagement with the owners of the press as they launched their long-awaited offensive to break the right of the union's compositors to be the sole keyboarders of text – a struggle that unfolded with increasing intensity from 1983 onwards.

The printing and publishing industry was one of the few manufacturing sectors to sustain its level of employment in the 1970s and 1980s. During the 1970s it had expanded. During the 1980s, after a setback in the recession years of 1979–82 and before a new recession took hold in 1990, it experienced a period of prosperity and forward movement. There was a 58 per cent increase in the rate of capital invested in printing and publishing between 1980 and 1987, while investment in manufacturing industry as a whole remained static. From 1984 the publishing and printing share price index performed consistently better than the *Financial Times* industrial index, and in September 1988 the *Financial Times* proclaimed printing in the 'top ten' league of manufacturing industries.[1] Behind this success story was technology.

A Printing Industries Research Association forecast of 1982 described an array of new technologies available at steadily falling prices, waiting for a hitherto cautious printing and publishing industry to buy.[2] The developing technologies affecting all aspects of printed media touched compositors in two ways. Quite simple and relatively cheap equipment of the kind available to the smallest firm – word processors, desk-top publishing – enabled many more of the customers of the printing and publishing industry to do their own origination work, bypassing the composing rooms of the general printing trade. How to retain 'data capture' for the NGA was an intensifying problem. Threatened in the 1970s, this process of 'work bypassing the composing room' was increasingly common in the 1980s. By 1987 the NGA had been obliged to back down on its automatic refusal to handle material originating with non-print typists or non-unionised typesetting firms. 'Blacking' of such 'work from unrecognised sources' was no longer a remotely feasible industrial goal.[3]

Secondly, a more sophisticated version of this technology, as we have seen in the foregoing chapters, enabled newspaper publishers to have their telephone copy-takers and journalists input text directly without the intervention of a compositor. This 'front end' technology became rapidly more intricate and powerful in the 1980s, with such innovations as raster image processors, enabling the combining on screen of text, graphics and half-tone images; electronic full-colour page composition; and digital design and repro ('depro') all widely available by 1990. A sign that printing and publishing employers were thinking overtime about the new technologies was the fact that the industry spent 75 per cent more on capital expenditure on computer equipment than other industries and employed 50 per cent more computer specialists than the national average in the late 1980s.[4] The editor of *Printing World* reviewing the PIRA forecast warned the NGA's members in terms that 'couldn't have been expressed more starkly... the new technology will mean a reduction in the total numbers employed'.[5] The group most threatened by new technology, in the 1980s as in the 1970s, were the pre-press men, the originators, the compositors.

The comps in the newspaper industry were always better organised and better placed to resist threats to their status than those in the printing industry more generally. We have seen how in the late 1970s and early 1980s in two London region provincial newspaper publishing houses and in two Fleet Street companies the compositors dealt with the challenge of technological change, managing to sustain a traditional division of labour and 'follow the machine'.

They were retrained for computerised photocomposition despite the redundancy of their 'second keystroke'. What the following ten years have shown is the fragility of this hold on past privileges. First the provincials, then the nationals, geared up to shake their new technology free of the old compositors.

The intensification of the struggle was signalled in 1983 by *Project Breakthrough*, an initiative of the Newspaper Society, federation of the provincial press proprietors. The document laid the groundwork for an attempt to negotiate an industry-wide agreement over the implementation of direct text input – an attempt the NGA fiercely rejected as a threat to de-unionise newspaper production. The union was nonetheless obliged to respond with its own alternative strategy: *The Way Forward*. They offered, with what could be seen either as historic generosity or desperate realism, to share organisational jurisdiction in origination with the two other unions involved, SOGAT 82 and the National Union of Journalists. The whole origination area, including advertising, marketing, administration, editorial and composing, would, in the NGA's proposal, be viewed as a single entity and the total labour force distributed equally between the three unions. There would be direct input, but under union control. A member of any union might thus set type. Redundant comps would be retrained for editorial or journalistic work. The unions would run a combined chapel.

While the journalists went along with the NGA proposal, SOGAT 82 deemed it unacceptable. In any case, the Newspaper Society rejected *The Way Forward* in 1984. Newspaper owners were emboldened by declining profitability in the early 1980s and growing competition as advertising media from free-sheets and independent radio. The following year a number of provincial newspaper companies moved to direct input either without union agreement, or by splitting the movement and signing single-union agreements with either SOGAT 82 or the National Union of Journalists. Symptomatic disputes broke out as Eddie Shah threatened to de-recognise the NGA at the *Stockport Messenger* group, and the giant *Wolverhampton Express* and *Star* announced they were aiming for a completely electronic newspaper, without NGA participation, by 1986. Failures of solidarity between the three unions encouraged other firms, including the *Leicester Mercury*, the *Kent Messenger* and *Midland News* groups, to plunge into the fray.

While the NGA did move to scotch the divide-and-rule strategy of the employers with a TUC-sponsored 'accord' with the NUJ in 1985, this did little to avert the disarray and mutual disloyalty afflicting the three unions. From December 1985, however, when three new technology agreements were signed for direct input in the spirit of the NGA-NUJ accord, other provincials pressed ahead. By 1988 around 80 such agreements had been signed. But 15 other companies had gone ahead to direct input without any agreement with the unions, and a further 12 had reneged on agreements they had made.[6] Though a handful of comps remained in drastically reduced composing rooms, and some comps had been retrained for new work, many of the 14,000 NGA employees in the provincial newspaper industry had taken redundancy.

In the early years of the new technology battle in the provincial press, company priorities of expanding output, market protection and reduction in unit cost had made the actual exclusion of the union, given the continuing strength of the NGA, neither feasible nor necessary.[7] However, as the union was progressively weakened by the industrial relations legislation (for which printing and publishing employers had been among the persistent lobbyists) more and more the struggle shifted from mere control of the keystroke to total derecognition of the unions. The Conservative government was encouraging a move to local rather than national collective bargaining, to individual contracts rather than chapel agreements. Some individual employers resigned from the Newspaper Society, others simply ignored agreements signed between the Society and the NGA.

In 1990 the Newspaper Society formally scrapped the national agreement. Reviewing these processes in that same year Peter Smith and Gary Morton concluded that incremental changes in the provincial press in the 1970s and early 1980s had been followed thereafter by a radical shift in the pattern of employment relations in many companies. 'This has involved the dismissal of NGA pre-press workers (craft trained and overwhelmingly male, white and over 40) and their replacement by labour (often female and juvenile workers) employed at approximately half the previous rate for an extended week of 40 hours and a reduced holiday entitlement.' [8]

The cases of the two London provincials described in Chapter 3 illustrate nicely the strategies used by the press owners against the comps. At *Croydon Advertiser* the NGA avoided the worst-case scenario. The company had been a family firm. The family sold out in 1982 to the important Portsmouth and Sunderland Newspapers group. The new owners moved the printing of *Croydon Advertiser's* newspapers to Portsmouth. They went to direct input within the terms of the NGA/NUJ accord. Five NGA men, those considered most apt for the new work, were retrained as journalists. But the price was two rounds of voluntary, and a third of compulsory, redundancy.

By contrast, at King and Hutchings, the 1980s spelt disaster for the comps – even without direct input. The story illustrates the way technological and organisational restructuring may be used for similar ends. Westminster Press sold the company to a pair of entrepreneurs who soon declared all production staff redundant. They farmed out both printing and typesetting to sub-contractors. They assisted in setting up a typesetting company, Visual Sector, that employed some of the old King and Hutchings comps to continue setting the papers. The men were obliged to accept lower rates of pay and worse terms and conditions of employment, and to work alongside many new entrants to typesetting – mostly young men and female typists, some working part-time. Most of these newcomers saw little point in paying expensive subscriptions to join a union that was clearly unable any longer to protect its members. As time went by NGA comps were gradually outnumbered by the single-skill incomers who could be paid at a lower rate. In 1990, when only 20 NGA members remained in Visual Sector, the company withdrew recognition from the union. In a final ploy it claimed bankruptcy, made all its employees redundant, and re-engaged selected individuals for a 'new' typesetting enterprise, offering individual contracts involving yet further reduced wages, shorter holidays and increased hours. The former Father of Chapel at King and Hutchings told me 'when you did the research in 1980 nobody could have imagined the disasters that were to come'. As Smith and Morton conclude, 'the NGA's longstanding suspicion that direct input would be the occasion for the de-unionisation of the industry is in the process of realisation with a vengeance... '[9]

The mid-1980s marked a turning point: the national press barons now stepped into their own headlines, taking over from the provincials as a subject of media attention. As agreements with the provincials began to flow, the nationals on the contrary heightened the industrial aggravation.

At the *Daily Mirror*, as we saw in Chapter 3, the NGA in 1981 maintained control over all input to the system. With Times Newspapers Ltd temporarily tamed and Express Newspapers and the *Observer* also signing compromise agreements over input, the union believed the 'reasonable' behaviour of Mirror Group News would set the pattern for the other dailies, all now impatient for the much delayed move to computerised composition. But this was not to be.

Eddie Shah's News (UK) Ltd was the first to take on the unions, seeking to force through production of his new title *Today* with a single union, no strike agreement. This gave a lead to other proprietors. Rupert Murdoch, the new owner of *The Times* and *The Sunday Times*, as well as the *Sun* and the *News of the World*, was, as we have seen, by the early 1980s in any case well on the way to his long premeditated confrontation with the unions. It was no secret that between 1980 and 1983 he had been building a purpose-designed £100 million print plant in Wapping, in London's docklands. His first published intention was to transfer there the *Sun* and the *News of the World*. In January 1986 he announced abruptly that most of his *Times* and *Sunday Times* employees at Gray's Inn Road and Bouverie Street faced termination of their contracts. A residue of employees would be hand-picked by management from the old workforce and offered new individual contracts. The unions had been offering their 'accord' terms, plus binding agreements, something they had never before conceded to a national. Murdoch was unimpressed. He wanted direct input on his own terms. He made it clear that he considered the unions were defending three times the necessary level of staffing in Fleet Street and five times the level of wages. It was clear by now however that his main aim was less to get direct input than to break once and for all the influence of trade unions in his newspapers.

Murdoch set out four non-negotiable requirements as the price of recognition. They were an abandonment of the closed shop, total and unfettered right of management to manage, legally binding agreements on individuals and unions, and a commitment to no industrial action under any circumstances. The unions saw it as a 'serfs charter'.

On January 24 1986, 5,500 News International print workers went on strike. Murdoch countered by issuing dismissal letters. Among those affected were more than 500 women, mainly clerical, catering and cleaning workers. It was a dispute that would continue in unrelieved bitterness for 13 months. On more than one occasion the union, in the words of its leaders, 'offered an olive branch' only to be 'beaten over the head with it'. Inside the Wapping plant, fortified by high fencing and a ring of razor-wire, a militant Murdoch produced his papers using scab journalists and members of the electricians' union, the EETPU. The Battle of Wapping saw new excesses of state violence as police in riot gear and on horseback harassed the pickets attempting to prevent papers leaving the plant. Murdoch used to the full the weapons provided to employers by the Tory anti-union legislation. For example, the law now limited workers to picketing their own place of employment. Murdoch had ensured these buildings were now empty shells. He had moved the action to Wapping where the strikers could not legally follow it. When first SOGAT 82, then the NGA, capitulated to Murdoch in February 1987 it was largely because the unions were in peril of financial ruin from court actions in pursuit of a dispute that they no longer saw any chance of winning.

Murdoch's victory in the News International dispute had repercussions throughout the national newspaper industry. One after another the nationals withdrew their editorial offices from Manchester to consolidate in London. Secondly, they moved their origination and printing presses to cheaper and less visible sites in docklands or elsewhere. By 1989 the exodus was complete. The moves were accompanied by the introduction of direct input and a drastic reduction in the number of NGA members employed in the companies. At Mirror Group News, which Robert Maxwell had bought from Reed in 1984, origination and production were both moved from London. Despite Maxwell's claim to be supportive of trade unionism, only a tiny rump of NGA comps remain in his newspapers today and chapel power has been greatly reduced. Indeed all the unions suffered from the heavy cuts in staffing that accompanied the dispersal of production of the nationals. Many women as well as men lost their jobs in the process. the *Financial Times* shed 26 per cent of its staff, the *Observer* and Associated Newspapers, publishers of the *Daily Mail*, both cut theirs by 50 per cent, and the *Daily* and *Sunday Telegraph* by as much as two-thirds. For the print unions, it was 'the end of the Street'.[10]

What became of the men ousted from the Fleet Street composing rooms? Many were elderly and took early retirement with a good redundancy settlement. Some went into the general trade as typesetters either in London or in the provinces, at greatly reduced pay. Some went on the unemployed 'call book' and long remained there. There was besides now little recourse for a man's ego in the union itself. The pre-eminence of the newsmen was gone. They had been 'knocked off their perch' as one member put it, and the union too was back on its heels.

What the debacle of the 1980s brought home to the unions beyond all else was the damage they had inflicted on their own interests by sectionalism. The union that in 1982 had become SOGAT 82 had been the product of more than 30 previous amalgamations. Yet still it remained primarily the semi-skilled and unskilled union in the printing, publishing and paper industry. The NGA, also as we have seen, the product of many amalgamations, had remained the skilled men's union. The great craft/non-craft divide therefore lived on. So did the gap between journalists and the rest. The 1980s saw several fruitless attempts by all three unions to come to sufficient agreement to amalgamate into the dreamed-of Media Union, on which I speculated in the foregoing chapter. They failed. Meanwhile the employers used every chance to exploit the rifts and rivalries, using one union to defeat the others. In this situation, elitism and sectionalism, the negative side of the proud craft identity of the NGA (and even more of its news comps) was a stone that weighed heavier and heavier around the union's neck. Meanwhile the European Single Market projected for 1992 was focusing minds. With European capital becoming more unified what possible hope could there be for divided trade unions? The talks between SOGAT 82 and the NGA began again and this time they bore fruit: a new combined union, the Graphical Paper and Media Union, was due to come into existence on September 30 1991.

The GPMU will be a step towards the industrial union print and media have long needed. But it will be a marriage of drastically weakened unions. The last ten years has been, as an officer put it, a process of 'overseeing retreats, some orderly, some disorderly'. The membership of SOGAT 82 is only two-thirds of what it was when it formed. Over the same years the NGA has lost 10,000 (8 per cent) of its members. The new union will only deliver its promise to the mass of print workers if it becomes an industrial union in fact as well as in principle. The NGA merged with the Amalgamated Society of Lithographic Printers (ASLP) in 1968, yet even today it is common for separate 'ASLP' chapels to exist side by side with other NGA chapels in the same firm, never meeting. In ten years time will the union structure still place barriers to progress in the way of its own members who want to upgrade from one machine or section to another? Will there still be separate chapels for ex-NGA and ex-SOGAT members?

Above all, will male and female continue to represent two unequal classes of member? The printing and publishing industry has feminised fast since the year I finished writing *Brothers*, reversing the masculinising trend I noted on p. 160. Between 1982 and 1989 the number of women in the industry increased by 9 per cent, while the number of men declined by 7 per cent.[11] Most of these incoming women have joined their sisters in semi-skilled and unskilled work as clericals or in print finishing. Here, though women's work is often far more skilled than it is formally evaluated as being and, though the jobs women do often call for more sustained and exhausting effort than those of their brothers, women continue to see less reward for their labours. Besides, in the binderies and other print finishing areas, new technology in the 1980s has also caused high rates of deskilling and job loss.

The increasing numbers of women in print have therefore not greatly changed women's status relative to that of men. In SOGAT 82 today the great majority of men still continue to be Class 2 to the NGA's Class 1 men. Class 3 is where the women cluster. The earnings discrepancy in printing and publishing is still greater than that in the economy as a whole. Recent figures showed little change from those cited on p.163. Manual women earn only 56 per cent of manual men in print, against a national differential among manual workers of 62 per cent. Non-manual printing and publishing women earn, pro rata, 57 per cent of their equivalent men, against 60 per cent in other employment.[12] The sex difference reflects large differences in basic pay, exacerbated by shift and overtime earnings mainly accruing to men. Print pay is still one-fifth higher than the national average – yet it is men, not women, who profit by that industrial advantage.

Some women however have entered formerly masculine trades. There are now some 500 women machine minders, mainly operating small offset presses. Where before 1960 you could count the women in the 'skilled' print jobs on your fingers and toes, today there are an estimated 10,000 women employed in areas that were once journeymen strongholds.[13] It is doubtful however whether one should any longer identify some of these as the old 'masculine' trades. In many cases the labour process, the pay and the terms and conditions of employment have deteriorated as women have come into them. Pursuing the theme of our story, there are for instance many women typesetters – indeed of women in fulltime jobs in the printing industry over half are in photocomposition. With the weakening of the unions however, they are characteristically employed on only a routinised part of what was an all-round compositors' craft at a fraction of the former male rate of pay. Training provision, especially to upgrade unskilled and semi-skilled employees of the industry, is in any case poor, and little of it reaches women. The tradition in the industry, as we have seen, has been for training to occur only at entry, and entry to occur on leaving school at the minimum school-leaving age. The old apprenticeship system has given way to modular training. But where such training occurs access to it is still controlled by agreement of employer and chapel, and as one woman member put it 'both are liable to think "boy".' As a result less than 6 per cent of BPIF trainees in 1987 were female and of these 90 per cent were in origination, mainly keyboarding. Despite a commitment to equal numbers, in the industry's contribution to the MSC's school-leaver training schemes only 5 per cent are girls.

As long ago as 1980 equal opportunities clauses were inserted into the national agreements of both SOGAT and the NGA. But as Krysia Maciejewska has remarked, what ensued was a decade of inaction. 'The skilled jobs, the unions and the management of the industry are still largely in the hands of men. Women form most of the workforce in hand finishing and office work. They work in in-plants and instant print, and are generally confined to the lower tiers of management. At a time when the industry is crying out for skilled workers and dynamic managers, it has been out to lunch to half the population.'[14]

The old cultural processes of exclusion continue, it seems, little changed. In a series of articles run in *Lithoweek* in 1988 women told of their experiences trying to break into 'male' trades. A machine manager said she had started the City and Guilds course three times and on each occasion lasted no longer than five weeks, 'because of the abusive behaviour of other students and the failure of staff to do anything about it... I can put up with a lot but this was intolerable.' A typesetter reported as being met with 'a mixture of disbelief and hostility... They see you first and foremost as a woman and therefore as an intruder.' A four-colour planner said 'Some of the blokes I worked with would pester me from the moment I got in until I went home. For the whole eight hours they used to try and embarrass me.'[15] Racism compounds sexism. An article in *Printing World* in 1990 reported a sympathetic employer admitting that a young black woman had been put through a second stringent interview and a machine test too, 'because she was the wrong colour and the wrong sex. If I had got this wrong we would never have been able to take on another woman or member of an ethnic minority again.'[16] Every minute, these women were saying, when you apply for a job and when you get it, 'you've got to prove, prove, prove you can do it.' Fortunately, many young women can produce the needed evidence of being better. Helen Marshall, for instance, aged 18, won the Apprentice of the Year Award in 1985. The irony of her situation however needs no comment: the only woman on her compositor day-release course, she got her comping job by mistake. She had applied thinking it was a receptionist vacancy.

Helen Marshall may be the new face of the printing workforce – sucked into print despite herself by the flow of the economic and political tide. The old masculinist forms however do not cede ground easily. The banging out of apprentices for instance still appears to continue. Under a headline 'becoming a man and a real printer' an article in the NGA's journal as recently as 1988 showed a young man strapped to a model toadstool, wearing a gnome's hat. His workmates were shown first tipping a bucket of glue over his head, followed by a tub of printers' ink and other chemicals and shredded paper. He was then carted off and positioned by a roadside as a source of amusement to passing motorists. And still the lad managed a wan smile.[17] This ritual, as we have seen, goes back a very long time. Today however the contradiction between such manhood rites of passage and an 'equal opportunity' society does not go without comment. The paper later published a letter to the editor by Ruth Taillon, a woman member, ridiculing both the ritual and the way it was reported. 'Are we to draw the conclusion', she mocked, 'that only men are real printers (and never eat quiche?).'[18]

In the National Graphical Association the numbers of women have continued to increase. In 1991 there were around 8,000, just under 8 per cent of the membership. The number had almost doubled in ten years, though women continued to lack commensurate influence within the union. The Women's Committee formed in 1981 now had a majority of women on it, affording a somewhat more autonomous voice for women in union affairs. But motions for 'reserved seats' to ensure women's presence on both national and regional councils have been defeated, and it was only in 1991 for the first time that women were nominated and elected to the National Council. There is still only one woman among the paid officers of the union at national, regional or branch level. At the Biennial Delegate Meeting in 1990 women were only 15 out of the 345 delegates – though it has to be said that this dismal figure marked a steady climb from none at all in 1978.

The biggest change in print trade unionism is entailed by the impending amalgamation of the National Graphical Association and SOGAT 82. Women on both sides of the fence look forward with some trepidation to this event. Both foresee losses as well as gains. The NGA women may be few in number but they are, nominally at least, partakers of the higher status, subscriptions and benefits of a skilled union. They are joining a union where women have historically been a segregated and inferiorised sex. The record of achievement of women among the authoritative positions in SOGAT 82 is, the election of Brenda Dean as General Secretary notwithstanding, little better than in the NGA, and the NGA have had to fight hard to get their Women's Committee carried over to the GPMU. On the other hand NGA women will benefit from the overall boost to numbers – around a third of SOGAT 82's membership is female. They will besides inherit the annual women's conference newly won by SOGAT 82 women.

All told, women officers in both unions reported, there is more conviction and energy among women today than ten years ago. Yet they are still only poised to achieve a breakthrough that was already promised long since. Things have changed in the trade union movement since the miners' strike of 1984, when women in the coal mining communities played an important role in the struggle (and got short shrift from the National Union of Miners at the end of it). In recent years it has indeed often been the imagination and energy of women that have held things together. A SOGAT 82 woman officer I interviewed recently, said, looking back on the decade, that she felt men were no longer a historic force. 'Women feel men have nothing new to say. It's women that are holding it all together. Men haven't got the mental stretch. They have a lot of catching up to do.' At the beginning of the 1980s women were battling for the right even to express their views. By the early 1990s, even though equality of outcomes in practice is as distant as ever, there is a certain legitimacy in the idea of equality of treatment and of opportunity for women workers. If the men's age-old fear of employers' use of women to degrade their occupations has become a reality, it is a possibility they now know, in their heart of hearts, that they themselves helped to create.[19]

The 1980s was a decade of change for gender relations in Britain, but change of an ambiguous kind. The energy of the new feminism, which in the 1970s had been a widespread and self-conscious liberation movement, drained away. Feminist projects of many kinds lived on, however. The Equal Pay Act 1970 and the Sex Discrimination Act 1975 had been products of that movement. They had been intended as levers with which to dismantle male supremacy in employment, in organisations and in society more generally. But they proved flimsy tools, and by the end of the 1970s it was clear that the law, even backed by a movement of angry and determined women, was not going to change matters greatly. Women's average earnings as a percentage of the male average rose a couple of points in the mid-1970s, due more to the Labour government's incomes policy than to the new Acts. They then settled down to the level (between two-thirds and three-quarters of male earnings, depending on how they are calculated) at which they have remained since. A handful of pioneering women broke into traditionally male jobs, aided by the Sex Discrimination Act. But looking at employment overall, occupational sex segregation did not notably diminish.[20] Indeed there has been an incentive for employers in the new legislation to keep women apart from men at work: there is less likelihood they will be able to find a comparator to use in an equal pay case. Thus the Equal Pay Act 1970 led some employers to make new distinctions between women's and men's occupations and some responded to the 'equal pay for work of equal value' amendment of 1984 by setting up separate companies (such as typesetting subcontractors) to avoid intra-firm comparisons.

Disappointment with the results of equality legislation and the return to Whitehall of a Conservative government in 1979 combined to draw women's activism off the streets and into the institutions. Women's autonomous single-issue campaigns, such as those for reproductive rights and against male violence and war, continued through the 1980s, but now many feminists joined the Labour Party, sought jobs in left-Labour local authorities such as the Greater London Council and directed their efforts to changing things in and through trade unions. Led by these organisations, other employers began to initiate 'positive action' for sex equality and some feminists looked for employment as equality officers or women's officers inside the institutions.

The National Graphical Association was not the only union to set up a Women's Committee in the early 1980s. Many unions, especially those in which women were a much higher proportion of the membership, went further. In 1979 the Trades Union Congress had published a ten-point charter to press the unions along the road to sex equality.[21] A TUC survey showed that five years later 40 unions (about half of those affiliated to Congress) had national women's or equality committees.[22] Some, like APEX, had equality committees at lower levels too. Twenty-five unions had appointed equality officers, including USDAW, the NUJ and ACTT. Some, like the GMB and the NUJ had made provision or requirement for equality officers at area, branch or even shop level. Increasingly unions were running conferences and day schools for women members, providing nurseries to help women attend.

It proved easier to shift the structures than the practices of unions however. Collective bargaining was resistant to change. Women activists in the GMB demonstrated that official union limitation on pay differentials (notably those between grades largely inhabited by males and those inhabited by females) was simply not being achieved in at least half the union's agreements. Job evaluation schemes actually approved by the union were flawed with bias against women.[23] Unions led by men also, it seemed, found it hard to give priority to 'equal pay for work of equal value' claims under the amendment to the equal pay legislation that became effective in 1984. In an enquiry I conducted in 1987 I heard many women say the outcome of positive action for women had been disappointing.[24] Though they still supported the idea of women's advisory and equality committees, they were running into trouble. Some were dominated by men, often appointed by the executive. Cut off from the main structure, lacking the legitimacy of being elected bodies, some were kept marginal to power. They were isolated from the mass of women, had no clear guidelines and were starved of funds. Some unions, it seemed, had even moved into reverse, dropping reserved seats for women on decision-making bodies in spite of – or perhaps because of – the fact that they can be very successful in increasing women's influence.

It is not only in the unions that 'equal opportunities' met with impediments. I have written elsewhere of the ways in which men, by means of their institutional influence and all the little social interactions of workplace culture, limit the effect of women's equal opportunities strategies.[25] Even male managers and union officers who support the new measures, and indeed enable their introduction into their organisations, often have a more limited agenda than their women colleagues, one that involves minimum change: a cleaning-up of recruitment and promotion procedure to reduce bias. Organisations therefore rarely follow the logic of equality to its conclusion: that there must be provided all the means necessary to achieve equality of outcomes, rather than a notional equality of chances.

Men's privilege has, it seems, been successfully defended against women's incursions into the organisations in the 1980s. A few token women made it to the boardroom; we see a few more women television news presenters. But men remain massively dominant in all significant positions in society and what, perhaps, is more damaging, feminism has been anathematised. While the rhetoric of sex equality has entered everyday use, legitimacy for equality appeared to come with a price tag: 'drop the feminism.' Women activists say they must be careful to avoid being identified with feminism if they are to maintain credibility in their trade unions and their places of employment. Certain demands are difficult to raise because they are associated with feminism. Women cite, for instance, the negative response to calls for 'quotas' of seats for women on public and party committees, and for separate provision for and organisation by women. Feminism itself is represented (and viciously denigrated) as being a front for political lesbianism and extreme leftism. Feminists, lesbian and otherwise, who would like to work for transformative change alongside men in organisations such as trade unions, while they are heartened to encounter a few male allies, say they more often find themselves up against overt or covert resistance.

On the other hand women emerged as important actors in the struggles of the 1980s. An autonomous women's strand animated the peace movement, particularly in the resistance to the siting of cruise missiles in Britain. The imagination and resilience of women of the mining communities was an inspiration in the miners' strike. Yet men's action and organisation seemed little influenced by women. In the women's liberation movement of the 1970s and 1980s women developed a new model for society. But it was not taken up by the left and the labour movement, which continued little changed. There has after all been much to reinforce masculinism. The enterprise culture of the Thatcher regime favoured the combative individualist. The militarism and jingoism of first the Falklands War, then the Gulf War, fostered a violent expression of masculinity.

Individual men have shown signs of discomfort with the masculine norm. Trends in consumer fashion, with a softer and more colourful image for men (though a cynic would suppose it exemplifies little more than the multinationals' quest for a new advertising gimmick) may reflect a real wish for gentleness among some men. There were probably more men at the end of the 1980s than there were at the beginning willing to be seen wheeling a push-chair or shopping in the supermarket – indeed finding pleasure in these domestic relationships.

We know more than we did about the way men feel, not only because some men are more willing to talk about their feelings but because men have started to turn themselves into the subject of academic study. The decade has produced a proliferation of new literature on men.[26] *Brothers* is no longer a lone instance of a study of the relationship between skill, technology and masculine identity – although I believe it is still one of the more deeply researched. We know more than we did about the fragility (and pain) of masculine identity; about the part played by work, sport or science in the social construction of masculinity; and we know that masculinity has many variants produced by different cultures and different historical periods.

What has become increasingly clear, however, from the work of men in men's studies and the continuing findings of women in feminist studies, is that male dominance continues to be a reality.[27] Caution may be called for in use of the term patriarchy, as noted in Chapter 7. We know the sex/gender systems of different cultures have shown different patterns of domination. Western European imperialism and racism have cut across and diversified the sex/gender system of colonial societies. The communist USSR and formerly communist countries of Eastern Europe have their own variants of male dominance. Historically, change has occurred within Western Europe, where today the rule of the 'brothers' is a more recognisable concept than the rule of the 'fathers'. Perhaps, as Carole Pateman suggests, we should call the prevailing system 'fraternal patriarchy' or 'fratriarchy'.[28] Yet women have no reason now, any more than at the beginning of the 1980s, to doubt they continue to live in the cramping confines of a male dominance system.

If male power is systemic, as the evidence in this book and many others suggests, one clear conclusion can be drawn for action and change. Individual women cannot – even less can individual men – escape from these oppressive and damaging circumstances by a simple act of will. Women climb out of their disadvantage only by exploiting other low-paid or unpaid women in their turn. Men may behave more sympathetically to the women in their lives; yet they cannot shed, just by wishing it, the authority and advantage that society ascribes to males. It is only a collective movement for change in the way we define, share and pay for work and in the way we relate to each other and to children, that can get us out of our gender fix. Women have analysed the needs, sketched some visions and created a few alternatives. Further change depends greatly upon men generating their own movement for a reconstitution of masculinity in the interests of a fairer and gentler world. Optimism may be appropriate with the millenium just around the corner

References

Place of publication is London unless otherwise stated. All typographical, printing and publishing periodicals may be seen at the St. Bride Printing Library, Bride Lane, London, EC1.

Introduction

1. Some of the sympathetic portrayals of working men that spring to mind are Huw Beynon's *Working for Ford* Penguin 1973; the description of workers in a chemical plant, *Workers Divided*, by Theo Nichols and Peter Armstrong, Fontana 1976, and Stephen Hill's study *The Dockers*, Heinemann 1976. The influential study of *The Affluent Worker* by J. Goldthorpe and others Cambridge: Cambridge University Press 1968, and Martin Bulmer's collection *Working Class Images of Society*, Routledge and Kegan Paul 1975, have helped to perpetuate the impression that the working class, problem or promise, is male.

2. Three recent contributions are Anna Pollert's study of tobacco workers, *Girls, Wives, Factory Lives*, Macmillan 1981; Ruth Cavendish, *Women on the Line*, Routledge and Kegan Paul 1982, and the collection edited by Jackie West, *Work, Women and the Labour Market*, Routledge and Kegan Paul 1982.

3. The theoretical work of the 1970s that has come to be known as 'the labour-process debate' has been characteristic of this revival. Several contributions to the debate are cited in Chapters 3 and 4.

4. Richard Johnson, 'Three problematics: elements of a theory of working-class culture', in John Clarke *et al.* (eds.), *Working Class Culture*, Centre for Contemporary Cultural Studies, Hutchinson 1979, pp. 110f.

5. The seminal article by Wally Seccombe, 'The housewife and her labour under capitalism', in *New Left Review*, no. 83, 1974, and Eli Zaretsky's *Capitalism, the Family and Personal Life*, Pluto Press 1976, are examples of this interpretation.

6. The source of this concept is Gayle Rubin, 'The traffic in women: notes on the political economy of sex', in R. Reiter (ed.), *Towards an Anthropology of Women*, New York: Monthly Review Press 1975.

7. Ann Oakley, *Sex, Gender and Society*, Temple Smith 1972.

8. E. P. Thompson, *The Making of the English Working Class*, Victor Gollancz 1963, p. 9.

9. *ibid*, p. 9.

10. Raymond Williams, *Culture and Society*, Penguin 1961.

11. Zillah Eisenstein, *Capitalist Patriarchy and the Case for Socialist Feminism*, New York: Monthly Review Press 1979.

12. Heidi Hartmann and others in Lydia Sargent (ed.), *The Unhappy Marriage of Marxism and Feminism*, Pluto Press 1981, represent this view.

13. In earlier times many London proof-readers belonged to their own trade society, the Association of Correctors of the Press. It recruited its members in part from among compositors (members of the London Typographical Society) and in part from among 'copy holders', the semi-skilled readers' assistants who were usually members of the National Society of Operative Printers and Assistants. The ACP merged with the National Graphical Association in 1965.

14. An exception is Colin Sumner in *Reading Ideologies*, Academic Press 1979. I am indebted to his exploration of the relationship between *practice*, the actions of the individual and her or his social context, and ideologies, the meanings ascribed to them. See note 10, Chapter 8.

15. See for instance, *Hegel: The Essential Writings*, edited by F. G. Weiss, Harper and Row 1974; F. Engels, *The Anti-Dühring*, Lawrence & Wishart 1975; Mao Tsetung, 'On contradiction' in *Selected Readings from the Works of Mao Tsetung*, Peking: Foreign Language Press 1971.

16. As Stuart Hall has noted, the discipline of sociology, heavily influenced from the USA, abolished the category of contradiction in the 1950s. S. Hall, 'Cultural studies and the Centre: some problematics and problems', in Stuart Hall *et al.* (eds.), *Culture, Media, Language*, Centre for Contemporary Cultural Studies, Hutchinson 1980, p. 20.

Chapter 1. Craft, class and patriarchy

1. Printing by movable type was introduced to Europe in the fifteenth century by Johann Gutenberg. It had been invented in China four centuries earlier.

2. I am indebted to Keith Snell for the observation that printing was one of the occupations that broke earliest from the household, perhaps because of the amount of equipment involved. There also appears to have been a higher ratio of journeymen to masters than in other trades, which may have led to their greater organisation and influence by the eighteenth century.

3. John Child, *Industrial Relations in the British Printing Industry: The Quest for Security*, Allen & Unwin 1967, p. 22.

4. *ibid.* pp. 28–30.

5. Joseph Moxon, 'Ancient Customs used in the Printing House', *Mechanick Exercises*, 1683. This and other excerpts from Moxon will be found in Ellic How, *The London Compositor*, Bibliographical Society 1947, pp. 23–27.

6. See A. J. M. Sykes, 'The cohesion of a trade-union workshop organisation', *Sociology*, May 1967; 'A study in changing attitudes and stereotypes of industrial workers', *Human Relations*, no. 17, 1964.

7. This privilege was confined to male children of legitimate patrilineal descent. An ordinance of The Stationers' Company in 1678 affirmed that no 'master or any other printer or workman shall teach, direct or instruct any person or persons whatsoever other than his or their own legitimate son or sons in the art or mystery of printing.' Cited in Felicity Hunt, 'Women in the nineteenth century bookbinding and printing trades, 1790–1914, with special reference to London', M.A. dissertation, Essex University, 1979.

8. Felicity Hunt, *op.cit.*

9. *The Country Journal or the Craftsman*, 24 May 1740, quoted by Ellic Howe and Harold E. Waite, *The London Society of Compositors, A Centenary History*, Cassell & Co. 1948, p. 41.

10. *Memoirs of the Life and Writings of Benjamin Franklin*, 1818, quoted in A. E. Musson, *The Typographical Association, Origins and History up to 1949*, Oxford: Oxford University Press 1954, p. 14.

11. John Moxon, in Howe *op.cit.*

12. *ibid.*

13. *ibid.*

14. John Child, *op.cit.* p. 35.

15. *ibid.* p. 54.

16. *ibid.* p. 39.

17. See Eric Hobsbawm, 'The tramping artisan', in *Labouring Men*, Weidenfeld and Nicolson 1964.

18. John Child, *op.cit.* p. 21.

19. Felicity Hunt, *op.cit.*

20. John Child, *op.cit.* p. 110.

21. J. Ramsay Macdonald (ed.), *Women in the Printing Trades, A Sociological Study*, P. S. King 1904, pp. 57–58.

22. Felicity Hunt, *op.cit.*

23. John Child, *op.cit.* p. 110.

24. I am indebted to Anna Davin for these and other insights into the history of women in printing in the nineteenth century.

25. Sarah C. Gillespie, *A Hundred Years of Progress: The Record of the Scottish Typographical Association, 1853–1952*, Glasgow: Scottish Typographical Association 1953, p. 102.

26. Jonathan Zeitlin, 'Craft regulation and the division of labour: engineers and compositors in Britain, 1890–1914', Warwick University thesis, Ph.D. 1980.

27. J. W. Seybold, *Fundamentals of Modern Composition*, Media, Pennsylvania: Seybold Publications 1977.

28. *The Sunday Times*, 1 January 1895.

29. For a description of the machine and the labour process see Chapter 2.

30. Report of the Delegate Meeting of the Typographical Association, Sheffield, 4 December 1893, St. Bride's Institute Library archive.

31. John Child, *op.cit.* p. 174.

32. G. Binney Dibblee, 'The printing trades and the crisis in British industry', *Economic Journal*, vol. XII, March 1902.

33. *ibid.*

34. The Webb Collection, E, Section B, LXXIV 50, London School of Economics Library.

35. *ibid.*

36. Jonathan Zeitlin, *op.cit.*

37. John Child, *op.cit.* p. 182.

38. The Printers Labourers Union was the forerunner of NATSOPA. Its first General Secretary was a compositor, a social-democratic propagandist. That compositors helped in its formation should not be seen, in any simple sense, as egalitarianism. It was to the benefit of craft compositors to see the unskilled grouped within a union, amenable to labour-movement pressure, yet separate and inferior to the craft societies.

39. Jonathan Zeitlin, *op.cit.*

40. See Margery Davies, 'Woman's place is at the typewriter', in Z. Eisenstein (ed.), *Capitalist Patriarchy and the Case for Socialist Feminism*, Monthly Review Press 1979.

41. Lenin's writings on imperialism and reformism within the labour movement condemn the 'traitor, opportunist and social-chauvinist' leadership of the working class (e.g. V. I. Lenin, 'Imperialism, the highest stage of capitalism', in *Selected Works*, Lawrence & Wishart 1968). Eric Hobsbawm reaffirmed the concept of an aristocracy of labour in 'The labour aristocracy in nineteenth-century Britain', *Labouring Men*, Weidenfeld & Nicolson 1964. More recent contributions to the debate include: John Foster, *Class Struggle and the Industrial Revolution*, Weidenfeld and Nicolson 1974; Gareth Stedman-Jones, 'Class struggle and the industrial revolution', *New Left Review*, no. 90, 1975; A. E. Musson, 'Class struggle and the labour aristocracy 1830–60', *Social History*, vol. 3, 1976; H. F. Moorhouse, 'The marxist theory of the labour aristocracy', *Social History*, vol. 3, 1978; Alastair Reid, 'Politics and economics in the formation of the British working class', *Social History*, vol. 3, 1978; Robert Gray, *The Aristocracy of Labour in Nineteenth-century Britain c.1850–1914*, Macmillan 1981.

42. A re-emphasis of the active role of the working class in the development of capitalism has informed much of the debate stimulated by publication of Harry Braverman's *Labor and Monopoly Capital*, Monthly Review Press 1974.

43. Stephen A. Marglin 'What do bosses do?', in André Gorz (ed.), *The Division of Labour*, Brighton: Harvester Press 1976.

44. Andrew L. Friedman, *Industry and Labour*, Macmillan 1977.

45. A. J. M. Sykes, *op.cit.* p. 160.

46. In his work on the labour aristocracy of Edinburgh in the late nineteenth century, Robert Gray emphasises the individualism in the ideology of craftsmen. He quotes a printer as saying, 'a fair field and no favour is all that is asked by average workmen in the struggle for existence; a right manly sentiment' (Robert Gray, in Frank Parkin (ed.), *The Social Analysis of Class Structure*, Tavistock 1974, p. 20.) The predominant ideology among London compositors was, on the contrary, one of co-operation and loyalty to the society. In fact the successful articulation of 'masculinity' with 'solidarity' and the embodiment of the two ideals in a trade union, while a boon for the struggle against capital, was a disaster for women.

47. The racism inherent in printers' craft identity has been more evident in the USA where, in contrast to Britain, a black urban working class has long existed. Andrew Zimbalist, 'Technology and the labor process in the printing industry.' in A. Zimbalist (ed.), *Case Studies on the Labor Process*, New York: Monthly Review Press 1979, p. 124.

48. Stephen Hill, *The Dockers*, Heinemann 1976.

49. Thomas Wright, *The Great Unwashed*, 1868, Frank Cass 1970, p. 151.

50. *The Scottish Typographical Circular*, December 1886.

51. Sidney Webb and Amy Linnett, 'Women compositors', *Economic Review*, vol. II, no. 1, January 1892.

52. Thomas Wright, *op.cit.* p. 31.

53. *ibid.* p. 41.

54. *ibid.* p. 134.

55. This theme, for instance, runs through the Minutes of Evidence to the Fair Wages Committee, Report to Parliament, British Parliamentary Papers, vol. 34, 1908, p. 622f.

56. Please refer to the discussion of this concept in the Introduction.

57. Christopher Hill, *The World Turned Upside Down*, Maurice Temple Smith 1972.

58. Barbara Taylor, 'The men are as bad as their masters: socialism, feminism and sexual antagonism in the London tailoring trade in the early 1830s', *Feminist Studies*, Spring 1979.

Chapter 2. Hot metal: craft control

1. London Society of Compositors, *Annual Report*, 1915.

2. *ibid*. 1916.

3. London Society of Compositors, 'After the war – a few queries for non-Society compositors', booklet.

4. *British and Colonial Printer and Stationer*, leading article, September 18, 1941.

5. *London Typographical Journal*, September and October 1941.

6. *ibid*. February 1959.

7. *ibid*. September 1959.

8. *Typographical Circular*, January 1950.

9. *Worlds Press News*, 5 January 1950.

10. *ibid*, 1 September 1950.

11. *London Typographical Journal*, August 1950.

12. *ibid*. Graham Cleverley, in his mordant description of industrial relations in Fleet Street, has described printing craftsmen as 'a self-confident and self-assured group of men who are over-trained, over-educated and over-intelligent for the jobs they have to do: a surplus of ability that they can afford to dedicate to their primary task of maximising their own well-being.' (*The Fleet Street Disaster*, Constable 1976, p. 125.) It is important to recognise, however, that printers were no more than characteristic of well-organised and skilled men generally. As Andrew Friedman has written, 'The strength of worker resistance has always been distributed unevenly among the working population. Often the result of this resistance has been to shore up or even augment differentials. The class often appears to be fighting among itself rather than for itself. A century after Marx and there has not yet been a single revolution in a country with a well-developed proletariat.' (*Industry and Labour*, Macmillan 1977, p. 6.)

13. Chris Aldred, *Women at Work*, Pan Trade Union Studies 1981, p. 98.

14. G. S. Bain and R. Price, 'Union growth and employment trends in the United Kingdom 1964–1970', *British Journal of Industrial Relations*, 10, November 1972.

15. *NATSOPA Journal*, October 1950.

16. *Worlds Press News*, 30 September 1955 and 28 January 1955.

17. *London Typographical Journal*, July 1955.

18. For a complete text on the technology and labour process of composition for letterpress printing see H.W. Larken, *Compositor's Work in Printing*, Old Woking: Unwin Brothers, The Gresham Press 1961.

19. Graham Cleverley *op.cit.* p. 119.

20. D. Lockwood and J. H. Goldthorpe, 'The manual worker: affluence, aspirations and assimilation', paper presented to the Annual Conference of the British Sociological Association, 1962.

21. Andrew Glyn and John Harrison, *The British Economic Disaster*, Pluto Press 1980, p. 5.

22. *ibid*, p. 49.

23. Prices and Incomes Board, *Report on Wages, Costs and Prices in the Printing Industry*, HMSO 1965.

24. Royal Commission on the Press 1961–1962, *Report*, Cmnd. 1811, HMSO, 1962.

25. British Federation of Master Printers, *Economic Study of the Printing Industry*, 1965.

26. British Federation of Master Printers, *Members' Circular*, December 1959.

27. *ibid*.

28. *Graphical Journal*, July 1965.

Chapter 3. Technological innovation

1. John Seybold, *Fundamentals of Modern Composition*, Media, Pennsylvania: Seybold Publications 1977, represents a thorough introduction to the new technology from inception to the mid-seventies.

2. Rex Winsbury, *New Technology and the Press*, (Royal Commission on the Press Working Paper No. 1) HMSO 1975.

3. *ibid*. p. 19.

4. Correspondence with Horst A. Reschke, Director, Union Label and Public Relations, International Typographical Union, USA, 1980.

5. Rex Winsbury, *op.cit.*, p. 10.

6. *ibid*. p. 10.

7. *British Printer*, January 1959.

8. All three Royal Commissions on the Press, reporting in 1949, 1962 and 1977, were prompted in part by anxiety over the trend to monopoly. See in particular N. Hartley *et al*, *Concentration of Ownership in the Provincial Press*, (Royal Commission on the Press Research Series 5), Cmnd. 6810–5, HMSO, 1977.

9. *ibid.* pp. 5–8.

10. Profit ratios improved steadily between 1970 and 1979 but for a dip in the depressed years of 1975 and 1976 ('Newspaper publishers 1974–80', Inter-Company Comparisons, Business Ratio Reports). National chains showed better results than the small family firms. As the third Royal Commission report made clear, the regional press is profitable precisely because much of it operates in monopoly conditions. (Royal Commission on the Press 1974–77, *Final Report*, Cmnd. 6810, HMSO 1977, pp. 30f.)

11. 'Court of enquiry into problems caused by the introduction of web offset litho', *Report*, ('The Cameron Report') HMSO 1967. See also L. C. Hunter, G. L. Reid, D. Boddy, *Labour Problems of Technological Change*, Allen & Unwin 1970.

12. Information provided by the Newspaper Society, 1981.

13. *Print*, Journal of the National Graphical Association, November 1980.

14. N. Hartley *et al*, *Concentration of Ownership in the Provincial Press*, *op.cit.*, p. 26.

15. The phase-one innovation involved King and Hutchings in purchasing a Fairchild web offset press and two Crosfield 713/10 Photon photosetters. These were advanced for that date, providing eight type faces up to 36 point in size and capable of producing 40 newspaper lines a minute. The photons were replaced in 1976 by Pacesetters capable of 90 lines per minute. Their input installation was a set of Datek keyboards producing 'idiot' tape for hyphenation and justification by an ICL 1901A computer. The experimental video terminals were Lumitype.

16. Phase two was a complete Itek system involving four times 64K computing capacity with Zentek Visual Display and Graphics Display Terminals.

17. Croydon Advertiser's installation centered round Whittaker Compugraphic photosetters (Videosetter V), offering a range of eight type faces. The computer came from Data General, the programmes from Comprite. The input facility comprised 16 simple Datek keyboards without screens, producing 'idiot' tape, and the VDUs were Datek and Compugraphic.

18. In 1975 the 'populars' managed a small aggregate profit but the 'qualities' made a loss equal to 6.5 per cent of turnover (Royal Commission on the Press, 1974–77, *op.cit.*, p. 30). A mild improvement was noticeable in the years 1976–79 when profit before tax, expressed as a percentage of sales (average for nine national newspaper houses), rose from 3.7 per cent to 8.5 per cent ('Newspaper publishers 1974–80', Inter-Company Comparisons, Business Ratio Report). The nationals' survival has been achieved by increases in advertising revenue rather than increases of sales to readers. Total circulation remained steady during the seventies ('ABC Circulation Review', Printing and Publishing Industry Training Board 1980).

19. Tom Clarke, 'Trade unions and the press', a paper to the Conference of Socialist Economists, July 1981.

20. See the reports of all three Royal Commissions on the Press, HMSO 1949, 1962 and 1977, and in particular *Industrial Relations in the National Newspaper Industry*, prepared by the Advisory, Conciliation and Arbitration Service for the third Commission, Cmnd. 6680, HMSO 1976. See also Economist Intelligence Unit, *The National Newspaper Industry – a Survey*, HMSO 1966; and more generally National Board for Prices and Incomes, *Costs and Revenue of National Daily Newspapers*, Cmnd. 3435, HMSO 1967; National Economic Development Office, *Signposts for the Future*, HMSO 1961; *Printing in a Competitive World*, HMSO 1970; and British Federation of Master Printers, *Economic Study of the Printing Industry*, 1965.

Such reports abound with complaints of over-manning, especially in the machine room, of the excessive number of casuals employed, of a variety of restrictive practices, demarcation quibbles and unstable and disputed pay differentials. The Fleet Street print workers were showing 'suicidal behaviour' and 'reckless disregard of peril' by causing disruption and loss of millions of copies per year.

21. During the 1978–79 dispute Times Newspapers attempted to produce *The Times* at a press in West Germany using non-union labour. The project was foiled by co-operation between the British and German print unions.

22. Economist Intelligence Unit, *The National Newspaper Industry – a Survey*, HMSO 1966.

23. For a tirade against both employers and unions see Graham Cleverley, *The Fleet Street Disaster – British National Newspapers as a Case Study in Mismanagement*, Constable 1976.

24. Royal Commission on the Press 1974–77, *op.cit.*, pp. 223–24.

25. *ibid*. pp. 218–19.

26. A more detailed account of the background to MGN's conversion will be found in Roderick Martin, *New Technology and Industrial Relations in Fleet Street*, Oxford: Oxford University Press 1981.

27. *Print, op.cit.*, April 1978.

28. Simon Jenkins, *Newspapers, The Power and The Money*, Faber and Faber 1979, p. 113.

29. The equipment purchased by MGN comprised two Prime computers, three Linotype Paul 606 photosetters capable of 100 pica output, 18 'blind' keyboards and a number of Linoscreen LSK boards with screens. The page-view terminals were also supplied by Linotype Paul.

30. See Roderick Martin, *op.cit.*, and Eric Jacobs, *Stop Press: 'Times' Dispute*, André Deutsch 1981.

31. *The Guardian*, 23 October 1979.

32. The Printing and Publishing Industry Training Board (PPITB) predicts growth for newspapers at 5 per cent per annum in the mid-eighties. Longer-term output is projected as climbing steadily. I am indebted to the PPITB for a number of internal reports (notably TRIS 23, 26 and 27 and their annual 'Industry Manpower Figures') on which I draw in this chapter.

33. While the wages bill as a percentage of costs remained more or less constant for manufacturing industry as a whole in the period 1973 to 1976, in newspapers and periodicals the proportion (which already started higher) continued to climb. At the end of the period it was 52.3 per cent compared with 49.7 per cent in general printing and publishing, and 48.7 per cent in manufacturing as a whole. 'In the next five years the threat to worthwhile returns in the printing industry will come not so much from lack of consumer appetite . . . but from cost factors.' (Printing Industries Research Association (PIRA) and Printing and Publishing Industries Training Board (PPITB), *Developments in Printing Technology – a Ten Year Forecast, Executive Summary*, 1979.)

34. For an example of how such labour shedding may be achieved consider the view of the third Royal Commission on the Press that publishers in national newspapers could reduce employment by some 2,500 compositors, by some 4,500 jobs in other areas and by some 2,000 casuals, so achieving a reduction in labour costs of about 25 per cent. Though the costs would be enormous in the short run (perhaps £30–35 million on redundancy hand-outs as well as £20 million on new equipment) they hoped that the savings would give the nationals the breathing space to find new markets and assure their long-run survival. (Royal Commission on the Press 1974–77, *op.cit.*, p. 43, p. 216.) As a result of such labour-'saving' multiplied many times, the long-term forecast is a drop of 22 per cent between 1981 and 1990, representing a loss of some 75,000 printing jobs (PPITB figures).

35. PIRA and PPITB, *op.cit.*

36. Advisory Council for Applied Research and Development, *Technological Change: Threats and Opportunities in the United Kingdom*, Cabinet Office, HMSO 1979, p. 7.

37. Mike Bruno, 'The status of printing in the USA', in 'Advances in Printing Science and Technology: proceedings of the 15th International Conference of Printing Research Institutes, USA, 1979'. (Cited in the National Graphical Association's *Research and Review Report*, no. 3, December 1980.)

38. For reasons that are still little understood the last two hundred years of capitalism have seen a pattern of growth and decline taking the shape of 'long waves' of approximately fifty years. Each long wave sees the destruction of one set of industries and the creation of one or more growth sectors based on new technologies of fundamental importance. Today we are seeing the scrapping of the existing organisation of production in the successful industries of the post-war upswing – car production and certain consumer goods. As the cost of computers and related electronic devices falls in price they promise to be the technology of the next upswing. (See Ernest Mandel, *Late Capitalism*, Verso 1978.)

39. Britain lagged behind the USA, Japan and certain European countries in investing in new technologies after the second world war – new printing technology among others. It has been suggested that one reason for this was that the British working class was more strongly organised and capable of resisting the introduction of new technology on terms that would weaken it. During the thirties, when other capitalist countries were forced to smash working-class organisation through fascist-type regimes, Britain avoided this confrontation due to the continued existence of large external markets in the empire. Britain was 'the only major proletariat in the world which suffered no serious defeat for the 30 years 1936 to 1966.' (Mandel, *op.cit.*, p. 179.

40. See for instance, Advisory Council for Applied Research and Development, *Technological Change: Threats and Opportunities in the United Kingdom*, HMSO 1979, among a host of official publications.

41. Stephen A. Marglin, 'What do bosses do?', in André Gorz (ed.), *The Division of Labour*, Brighton: Harvester Press 1978, p. 44. André Gorz himself wrote, 'Capitalist techniques were not meant to maximise the production and productivity *in general* of all workers *whatsoever*. Instead they were to maximise the productivity for capital of workers who had no reason to give of themselves, since an enemy had dictated the aims of their production. To make them bow to this will it was not enough that they should lose the ownership of the means of production . . . They had to lose what their professional and practical knowledge and skills had given them so far: the power to run the machines without the assistance of a hierarchical corps of engineers, technicians, maintenance experts, foremen and so on'. ('The tyranny of the factory: today and tomorrow', in André Gorz (ed.) *op.cit.*, p. 56.) Gorz, Friedman and other contributors to the flowering of 'labour process theory' during the 1970s build on Marx's analysis in vol. 1 of *Capital* of the necessity for capital to seek the 'real subordination' of labour by means of continual revolutions in technology and organisation.

42. Andrew Ure, *The Philosophy of Manufacturers*, Charles Knight 1835, reprinted by Frank Cass 1967.

43. André Gorz, 'The tyranny of the factory: today and tomorrow' *op.cit.*, p. 57.

44. Andrew Friedman has used the concept of an 'internal labour market' to describe what goes on at work. Just as men and masters haggle over the terms of employment in the external labour market, so 'the internal labour market is where workers and managers bargain over the terms of the realisation of labour from labour power.' What is a fair day's work? It is as endlessly negotiable as what is a fair day's pay. (Andrew Friedman, *Industry and Labour*, Macmillan 1977, p. 68.)

45. *Newspaper Owner*, 22 October 1910, cited by Jonathan Zeitlin, 'Craft regulation and the division of labour: engineers and compositors in Britain, 1890–1914', Warwick University Ph.D. thesis 1980.

46. The third Royal Commission on the Press for instance pinned its faith on the speculation that 'the introduction of new technology would involve *changes in working patterns and responsibility* among different groups of workers and *diminished authority for chapels'*. (My emphasis – CC.) ('Royal Commission on the Press 1974–77, *Final Report*, Cmnd. 6810, HMSO 1977, p. 222.)

47. Graham Cleverley, *op.cit.*, p. 152.

Chapter 4. Cold composition: change in the labour process

1. In the new *Financial Times* photocomposition installation the chapel have, conversely, insisted against management wishes on retaining the linotype lay.

2. Since 1939 there have been several attempts to produce a lay that reduces operator fatigue. One suggestion, for instance, is that the characters DHIATENSOR should form one line.

3. For an examination of hazards of working on keyboards and screens see *Office Worker's Survival Handbook*, by the Work Hazards Group, British Society for Social Responsibility in Science 1981.

4. Rex Winsbury in *Print*, January 1982.

5. Although it was intended at MGN that the readers should in the long run be trained for and integrated into the whole job, reading itself being a shared task, compositors' anxieties about possible surplus workers leading to redundancy led them to exclude the readers from integrated working in the short run, although they are NGA members.

6. Linotype Paul, manufacturers of photocomposition equipment, recommend (failing direct-entry) an integrated operation. Some chapels have resisted it.

7. Harry Braverman, *Labor and Monopoly Capital*, Monthly Review Press 1974.

8. Karl Marx, *Capital*, vol. I, Lawrence and Wishart 1954.

9. Braverman, *op.cit.*, p. 113.

10. Brighton Labour Process Group, 'The capitalist labour process', *Capital & Class*, no. 1, Spring 1977, p. 19.

11. Tony Elger, 'Valorisation and deskilling: a critique of Braverman', *Capital & Class*, no. 7, Spring 1979 p. 63.

12. 'What is it that forms the bond between the independent labours of the cattle-breeder, the tanner and the shoemaker? It is the fact that their respective products are commodities. What, on the other hand, characterises division of labour in manufactures? The fact that the detail labourer produces no commodities. It is only the common product of all the detail labourers that becomes a commodity.' Karl Marx, *op.cit.* p. 335.

13. *ibid.*, p. 398.

14. This phenomenon is a product of patriarchal sex relations and cannot be explained by reference to capitalist employment alone. As Michèle Barrett has said, 'The gender divisions of social production in capitalism cannot be understood without reference to the organisation of the household and the ideology of familialism', (*Women's Oppression Today*, Verso 1980 p. 186).

15. Anne Phillips and Barbara Taylor, 'Sex and skill: notes towards a feminist economics', *Feminist Review*, no. 6, 1980, p. 79.

16. For instances of this tendency see Angela Coyle, 'Sex and skill in the organisation of the clothing industry', in Jackie West (ed.) *Work, Women and the Labour Market*, Routledge and Kegan Paul 1982; and Jill Rubery and Frank Wilkinson's consideration of paper-box production, in 'Notes on the nature of the labour process in the secondary sector', Low Pay and Labour Market Segmentation Conference Papers, Cambridge 1979.

17. Karl Marx, 'The results of the immediate process of production', appendix, *Capital*, vol. I, Penguin 1976.

18. Bryn Jones, 'Destruction or redistribution of engineering skills? The case of numerical control', School of Humanities and Social Sciences, University of Bath, unpublished paper 1981. See also the work of Charles Sabel and Jonathan Zeitlin who argue that 'important elements of a model of decentralised, flexible production based on general-purpose machines and skilled workers were a significant, neglected *leitmotif* of early industrial history.' They conclude that 'choice and struggle count for more in determining the ways we work than dominant ideas allow.' ('Historical alternatives to mass production', King's College Research Centre, Cambridge, unpublished paper 1981.)

19. Andrew Friedman, *Industry and Labour*, Macmillan 1977.

Chapter 5. A man among men

1. Heidi Hartmann, 'Capitalism, patriarchy and job segregation by sex', in Z. Eisenstein (ed.), *Capitalist Patriarchy and the Case for Socialist Feminism*, Monthly Review Press 1979, p. 232.

2. Thomas Wright, *Our New Masters*, 1873.

3. Advisory, Conciliation and Arbitration Service, *Industrial Relations in the National Newspaper Industry, Summary Report*, (Royal Commission on the Press), HMSO, 1977, p. 2.

4. John Child, *Industrial Relations in the British Printing Industry*, Allen & Unwin 1967, p. 17.

5. Andrew Tolson, *The Limits of Masculinity*, Tavistock Publications 1977, p. 48.

6. Examples, among many others, are Stephen Hill's *The Dockers, Class and Tradition in London*, Heinemann 1976; Jim Cousins and Richard Brown 'Patterns of paradox; shipbuilding workers' images of society', in Martin Bulmer (ed.), *Working Class Images of Society*, Routledge and Kegan Paul 1975; and Huw Beynon, *Working for Ford*, Penguin 1973.

7. Paul Willis, 'Shop-floor culture, masculinity and the wage form', in John Clarke *et al.* (eds.), *Working Class Culture*, Centre for Contemporary Cultural Studies, Hutchinson 1979.

8. For discussion of a more literal male 'dealing' in women see Gayle Rubin. 'The Traffic in women', in R. Reiter (ed.), *Towards an Anthropology of Women*, Monthly Review Press, 1975.

9. From an extract included in Maxine Berg (ed.), *Technology and Toil in the Nineteenth Century*, CSE Books 1979, p. 185.

10. Paul Willis *op.cit.* p. 196.

11. *Typographical Circular*, June 1950.

12. Paul Willis *op.cit.* p. 198.

13. See Phyllis Chesler, *About Men*, The Women's Press 1978, for an insight into male/male fear and rivalry.

14. Dennis Gleeson, ' "Streaming" at work and college: on the social differentiation of craft and technician apprentices in technical education', *Sociological Review*, vol. 28, no. 4, pp. 745–61, 1980.

15. Paul Willis, *Learning to Labour*, Saxon House, Farnborough 1977.

16. I. C. Cannon, 'The social situation of the skilled worker: a study of the compositor in London', *Sociology*, vol. 1, 1967, pp. 165–85.

17. Ivan Reid, *Social Class Differences in Britain*, Grant McIntyre 1981, p. 4.

18. Printing Industries Research Association and Printing and Publishing Industries Training Board, *Developments in Printing Technology: a Ten Year Forecast, Executive Summary*, 1979.

19. Ernest Mandel, *Late Capitalism*, Verso 1978, p. 269.

20. This reflects a theme explored in several recent articles. For example, Joan Greenbaum, 'Division of labour in the computer field', *Monthly Review*, no. 3, vol. 28, 1976; and more recently Philip Kraft, 'The industrialisation of computer programming', Evelyn N. Glenn and Roslyn

L. Feldberg, 'Proletarianising clerical work', and Maarten de Kadt, 'Insurance – a clerical work factory', all in A. Zimbalist (ed.), *Case Studies in the Labor Process*, Monthly Review Press 1979.

21. Thomas Wright *The Great Unwashed*, 1868, reprinted Frank Cass 1970.

22. Nicos Poulantzas, for instance, drew a tight and exclusive boundary round the 'proletariat', defining it as manual productive workers, strictly productive of surplus value. (N. Poulantzas, *Classes in Contemporary Capitalism*, New Left Books 1975.) Erik Olin Wright (*Class, Crisis and the State*, New Left Books 1978) identifies in-between groups as inhabiting 'contradictory class locations'. Alan Hunt, in a diligent disentangling of class theory, nonetheless concludes that the key question remains the worker's relation to capital. (A. Hunt, 'Theory and politics in the identification of the working class', in A. Hunt (ed.) *Class and Class Structure*, Lawrence and Wishart 1977.)

23. André Gorz, 'Technology, technicians and class struggle' and other essays in A. Gorz (ed.) *The Division of Labour*, Brighton: Harvester Press 1976, p. 167.

24. André Gorz, 'The tyranny of the factory: today and tomorrow', *ibid.*, p. 57.

25. Mike Hales, *Living Thinkwork: Where do Labour Processes Come From?* CSE Books 1980.

26. André Gorz, 'Technology, technicians and the class struggle', in A. Gorz (ed.), *op.cit.* p. 167.

27. Royal Commission on the Press 1974–77, *Final Report* 1977, *op.cit.* and Trades Union Congress, *A Cause for Concern: Media Coverage of Industrial Disputes*, 1979.

28. See Brian Whitaker, *News Ltd., Why You Can't Read All About It*, Minority Press Group 1981; Raymond Williams 'The press we don't deserve' and Dave Murphy, 'Control without censorship' among other contributions in James Curran (ed.), *The British Press: a Manifesto*, Macmillan 1978.

29. See *Women in the Media*, UNESCO, United Nations, 1980; National Union of Journalists, Equality Working Party, *Images of Women*, 1981; Anna Coote and Beatrix Campbell, *Sweet Freedom*, Picador 1982.

30. Dave Murphy, *op.cit.* p. 171.

31. An instance of the compositors' myopia concerning the political significance of print is that during the bitter print strike of 1959 when they brought the print masters' presses to a halt, the London Typographical Society ceased production of *their own* journal, a much-needed source of information for the striking men, because 'it was deemed inconsistent with our own policy to publish'. Meanwhile, needless to say, the British Printing

Industries Federation, representing the owners, continued to print their circular by scab labour. (*London Typographical Journal*, September 1959.)

Chapter 6. Women: stepping out of role

1. This, incidentally, is not only the usage of craftsmen. The sociology of class too has often assumed that 'the working class' has wives and daughters.

2. Fair Wages Committee, *Report to Parliament*, British Parliamentary Papers 1908, vol. 34, pp. 623f.

3. The extent and bitterness of the differences between men and women over work is often muted in histories. For another instance of struggle see Barbara Taylor, 'The men are as bad as their masters: socialism, feminism and sexual antagonism in the London tailoring trade in the early 1830s', *Feminist Studies*, 5, no. 1, 1979.

4. Sarah Gillespie, *A Hundred Years of Progress: the Record of the Scottish Typographical Association*, 1853–1952, Glasgow: Scottish Typographical Association 1953, p. 203f.

5. A. E. Musson, *The Typographical Association, Origins and History up to 1949*, Oxford: Oxford University Press 1954, p. 120.

6. London Society of Compositors, *200th Quarterly Report*, 2 February 1898, Webb Collection, London School of Economics.

7. Statement by the Edinburgh branch on 'The Female Question', *Scottish Typographical Circular*, September 1904.

8. *ibid.*, May 1904.

9. *Scottish Typographical Journal*, February 1910.

10. *ibid.* May 1910.

11. Jonathan Zeitlin, 'Craft regulation and the division of labour: engineers and compositors in Britain, 1890–1914', Warwick University Ph.D thesis, 1980.

12. *Scottish Typographical Journal*, May 1910.

13. *ibid.* June 1910.

14. *ibid.* June 1910.

15. *ibid.* August 1910.

16. *ibid.* May 1910.

17. *ibid.* June 1910.

18. *ibid.* February 1910.

19. *ibid.* July 1910.

20. *ibid.* May 1910.

21. *ibid.* March 1910.

22. *ibid.* September 1910.

23. *ibid.* October 1910.

24. G. S. Bain and R. Price 'Union growth and employment trends in the UK 1964–70', *British Journal of Industrial Relations*, 10, no. 3, 1972.

25. These figures, which represent 'insured employees', both employed and unemployed, are drawn from Department of Employment, *British Labour Statistics Historical Abstract 1886–1968*, available on microfiche from HMSO.

26. John Child, *Industrial Relations in the British Printing Industry*, Allen & Unwin 1967, p. 302.

27. Department of Employment, *New Earnings Survey*, 1975 and 1980, Part E, HMSO.

28. Department of Employment, *British Labour Statistics Historical Abstract*, *op.cit.* and *New Earnings Survey* 1980, *op.cit.*

29. *New Earnings Survey*, 1980, *op.cit.*

30. Catherine Hakim, *Occupational Segregation*, research paper no. 9, Department of Employment, HMSO, November 1979.

31. Printing and Publishing Industry Training Board, (PPITB) *Equalising Job Opportunities for Women in Printing and Publishing*, an attitude survey and report, April, 1982.

32. Advisory, Conciliation and Arbitration Service, *Industrial Relations in the National Newspaper Industry*, Royal Commission on the Press, Research Series 1, Cmnd. 6680, HMSO 1976, p. 42.

33· PPITB Industry Manpower Figures annual, unpublished appendix on women's employment.

34. Royal Commission on the Press, *Final Report*, Cmnd. 6810, HMSO, 1977, p. 220.

35. PPITB Annual Statutory Returns.

36. PPITB Company Training Plans, 1976.

37. Department of Education and Science, *Statistics of Education*, 1975–78, HMSO, 1979.

38. PPITB Company Training Plans, 1978–80.

39. John Child, *op.cit.* Chs. XVII and XIX.

40. To take two early instances: in 1906 men's earnings in printing were 26 per cent higher than the average for the three textile trades of cotton, woollens and hosiery. Yet women's earnings in printing were only 33 per cent of men's, while in cotton the figure was 63 per cent, in woollens 51 per cent and in hosiery 45 per cent. In 1924, considering the newspaper industry alone, male workers' earnings were 88 per cent higher than the average for men in cotton, woollen and worsted industries. Female workers on the other hand were only 14 per cent higher. In general printing and bookbinding in this same year, male workers' earnings were 34 per cent higher than the textile workers, while women's earnings were 4 per cent lower. (*British Labour Statistics Historical Abstract*, *op.cit.*)

41. *New Earnings Survey*, 1975–79, *op.cit.* tables 54 to 57.

42. See Mandy Snell, 'The Equal Pay and Sex Discrimination Acts: their impact on the workplace', *Feminist Review*, no. 1, 1979; M. W. Snell, P. Glucklich and M. Poval, *Equal Pay and Opportunities*, Department of Employment, 1981; and *Annual Reports* of the Equal Opportunities Commission, Manchester.

43. *New Earnings Survey*, 1975–79 *op.cit.*

44. Of these, 171 women were working in old letterpress technology, some on linotype and monotype, many as proof-readers. A further 568 were small offset operators. New technology occupations accounted for 1,951 women, including 425 graphic designers, 1,002 on IBM and other QWER-TY-style keyboards and 299 in paper paste-up work. There were 552 secretarial, clerical and administrative women members.

45. *Print*, November 1979.

46. *The New Training Initiative*, Cmnd. 8455, HMSO 1981.

47. *Print*, November 1981.

48. *ibid.* August 1981.

49. Report of the Delegate Meeting of the Typographical Association, Sheffield, 4 December 1893, St. Bride's Institute Library archive.

50. Fair Wages Committee *op. cit.*, p. 737.

51. Vera Karsland, *Women and their Work*, 1891. I am indebted for this and others of the ensuing references to Anna Davin.

52. *Scottish Typographical Circular*, April 1886.

53. *Fair Wages Committee op.cit.* p. 737.

54. *Print*, February 1982.

55. Report of the Delegate Meeting of the Typographical Association, Sheffield, 4 December 1893, *op. cit.*

56. For a development of this argument see Cynthia Cockburn, 'The material of male power', *Feminist Review*, no. 9, 1981.

57. Fair Wages Committee, *op.cit.* p. 737.

58. *Scottish Typographical Circular*, December 1886.

59. Fair Wages Committee *op.cit.* p. 736.

60. J. Ramsay Macdonald (ed.), *Women in the Printing Trades, A Sociological Study*, P. S. King 1904, pp. 57–58.

61. *Scottish Typographical Circular*, June 1886.

62. A. E. Musson, *The Typographical Association: Origins and History up to 1949*, Oxford: Oxford University Press 1954, p. 13.

63. *Scottish Typographical Circular*, March 1886.

64. Margaret Bateson, *Professional Women Upon their Professions*, 1895.

65. *Scottish Typographical Circular*, February 1886.

66. Eleanor Rathbone, *The Disinherited Family*, republished as *Family Allowances*, Allen & Unwin 1949. For a contemporary contribution to the debate on the 'family wage' see Hilary Land, 'The family wage', *Feminist Review*, no. 6, 1980.

67. I do not wish to underestimate the burden to women that is represented by the 'double shift' of industrial work and housework, either in the nineteenth century or today. Given the sexual division of labour in the home it is reasonable that many women as well welcomed the ability of a man to support her and their children. Jane Humphries has suggested that the family-wage strategy of the artisan benefited the working class as a whole. (J. Humphries, 'Class struggle and the persistence of the working class family', *Cambridge Journal of Economics*, vol. 1, no. 3, 1977.) Michèle Barrett and Mary McIntosh argue, more convincingly in my view, that the family-wage system was in any case more of an ideal than a reality. Besides, it tends to enforce the dependency and oppression of women, to subject unsupported women, especially mothers, to severe poverty, to have no necessary effect on the value of labour power, and to divide and weaken the working class by reducing militancy, because it creates the conditions of conflict between men and women. They suggest that a preferable strategy for women is to demand that the cost of supporting non-labourers be met by the state. (M. Barrett and M. McIntosh, 'The family wage: some problems for socialists and feminists', *Capital and Class*, no. 11, 1980.)

68. Children's Employment Commission, *Fifth Report*, Parliamentary Papers 1866, XXIV.

69. Jessie Boucherett and Helen Blackburn, *The Condition of Working Women and the Factory Acts*, 1896.

70. See for instance, Eli Zaretsky, *Capitalism, The Family and Personal Life*, Pluto Press 1976.

71. Typographical Association of New South Wales, 1891.

72. *Scottish Typographical Circular*, February 1886.

73. *ibid.*

Chapter 7. Class and sex: two power systems

1. Richard Johnson, 'Barrington Moore, Perry Anderson and English social development', in Stuart Hall *et al.* (eds.) *Culture, Media, Language*, Centre for Contemporary Cultural Studies, Hutchinson 1980, p. 63.

2. Paul Willis, 'Shop-floor culture, masculinity and the wage form', in John Clarke *et al.* (eds.), *Working Class Culture*, Centre for Contemporary Cultural Studies, Hutchinson 1979, p. 187.

3. T. Rogers and N. Friedman in their detailed study of US compositors undergoing technological change (*Printers Face Automation*, Lexington USA: Lexington Books 1980) follow up a sample of compositors who opted for early retirement.

4. See Wally Seccombe, 'The housewife and her labour under capitalism', *New Left Review*, no. 83, 1974; Eli Zaretsky, *Capitalism, The Family and Personal Life*, Pluto Press 1976.

5. For instance, R. D. Barron and G. M. Norris, 'Sexual divisions and the dual labour market' in D. Barker and S. Allen (eds.), *Dependence and Exploitation in Work and Marriage*, Longman 1976.

6. Richard Johnson, 'Three problematics: elements of a theory of working class culture', in John Clarke *et al. op.cit.* p. 237.

7. Heidi Hartmann, 'The unhappy marriage of marxism and feminism', *Capital and Class*, no. 8, 1979.

8. The hierarchies of race are similar to those of sex in this respect. Those of sectarianism, as in Northern Ireland today, are dissimilar.

9. Frederick Engels, *The Origin of the Family, Private Property and the State*, New York: Pathfinder Press 1972.

10. See Nicola Murray, 'Women and the Cuban revolution', *Feminist Review*, nos. 2 and 3, 1979; and Maxine Molyneux, 'Women in socialist societies', *Feminist Review*, no. 8, 1981. Maxine Molyneux notes the continuation in many socialist societies of the sexual division of labour at work and at home. 'The result is that in effect women working outside the home have to perform the notorious double shift. Underlying this untransformed domestic situation is the failure to redefine men's roles in a manner comparable to the redefinition of women's roles.' (*ibid.* p. 29).

11. For a refreshing review of progress to date see Anna Coote and Beatrix Campbell, *Sweet Freedom, The Struggle for Women's Liberation*, Picador 1982.

12. Thus, 'Female wage labour is always premised on women's position economically and ideologically in the *family*', Lucy Bland *et al.*, 'Women inside and outside the relations of production', in Women's Studies Group, Centre for Contemporary Cultural Studies, (eds.), *Women Take Issue*, Hutchinson 1978, p. 55. See also Annette Kuhn, 'Structures of patriarchy and capital in the family', in A. Kuhn and A. M. Wolpe (eds.), *Feminism and Materialism*, Routledge and Kegan Paul 1978.

13. Paul Willis, *op.cit.* p. 198.

14. See, for instance, Ann Oakley, *The Sociology of Housework*, Oxford: Martin Robertson 1974, Hilary Land, *Parity Begins at Home*, Manchester: Equal Opportunities Commission 1981.

15. Heidi Hartmann, 'Capitalism, patriarchy and job segregation by sex, in Z. Eisenstein (ed.), *Capitalist Patriarchy and the Case for Socialist Feminism*, New York: Monthly Review Press 1979, p. 232.

16. Socialist feminist theory has tended to under-emphasise the physical aspects of women's oppression for a historical reason. Radical feminists of the early seventies gave priority to the part played by women's biology in

their subordination. Many feminists were uneasy with the essentialism inherent in this view, with its immobilising determinist consequences. As a result, marxist feminists subsequently tended to adopt an agnosticism about the physical differences between males and females. I suggest however that we cannot do without a politics of physical power and that it need not be politically negative. So much of men's actual physical advantage is socially constructed and so much of the power it confers is politically organised that the remaining small physical difference due to birth and biology can for practical purposes be ignored. For a further discussion of this point see Cynthia Cockburn, 'The material of male power', *Feminist Review*, no. 9, 1981.

17. Antonio Gramsci, 'State and Civil Society' in *Selections from the Prison Notebooks*, Lawrence and Wishart 1971.

18. For discussions by men of the harm they experience from sex-stereotyping, see Andrew Tolson, *The Limits of Masculinity*, Tavistock 1977.

19. Anna Coote and Beatrix Campbell, *op.cit.* p. 192.

Chapter 8. Men and the making of change

1. Rita Liljestrom, 'Integration of family policy and labour market policy in Sweden', cited in Hilary Land, *Parity Begins at Home*, Manchester: Equal Opportunities Commission 1981, p. 27.

2. Karl Marx and Frederick Engels, *The German Ideology*, Lawrence and Wishart 1970, p. 47.

3. Terry Lovell, review article, *Capital & Class*, no. 16, 1982, p. 139. The problem of the autonomy of the individual in marxist historical materialism has become a key theme in work on ideology, particularly since Louis Althusser's 1970 essay, 'Ideology and ideological state apparatuses' in L. Althusser, *Lenin and Philosophy*, New Left Books 1971. In Althusser's formulation, the human subject has the ambiguity inherent in the word 'subject' itself, being both subjected to ideologies that interpellate and command, but also an active subject of history, author of choices and responsible actions. Among many subsequent discussions of this problematic, see Centre for Contemporary Cultural Studies, *On Ideology*, Hutchinson 1977; Rosalind Coward and John Ellis, *Language and Materialism: Developments in Semiology and the Theory of the Subject*, Routledge and Kegan Paul 1977; and Colin Sumner, *Reading Ideologies*, Academic Press 1979.

4. Antonio Gramsci used 'common sense' to denote the varied and often contradictory meanings produced spontaneously by ordinary people. 'It is essential to destroy the widespread prejudice that philosophy is a strange

and difficult thing . . . everyone is a philosopher, though in his [sic] own way and unconsciously.' (Antonio Gramsci, 'The study of philosophy', *Selections from the Prison Notebooks*, Lawrence and Wishart 1971, p. 323.)

'It is important to retain "culture" as a category of analysis. By culture is understood the common sense or way of life of a particular class, group or social category, the complex of ideologies that are actually *adopted* as moral preferences or principles of life . . . The effects of a particular ideological work or aspect of hegemony can only be understood in relation to attitudes and beliefs that are already lived. Ideologies never address ("interpellate") a "naked" subject . . . Ideologies always work upon a *ground*: that ground is culture.' (Richard Johnson, 'Three problematics: elements of a theory of working-class culture', in John Clarke *et al.* (eds.), *Working Class Culture* Centre for Contemporary Cultural Studies, Hutchinson 1979, p. 234.)

5. Colin Sumner distinguishes between what I have called ideologies in the 'little' sense of the word and the 'bigger' sense, in this way: 'An ideology is a sign and involves a signification of the world of the social practitioner in terms of already available signifying units. Ideologies can become compounded, serialised or clustered in ideological formations such as conversational discourse, theory, law, theology and popular images.' (Colin Sumner, *op.cit.* p. 52.)

6. *ibid.* p. 29.

7. *ibid.* p. 22.

8. Andrew Friedman, *Industry and Labour*, Macmillan 1977, p. 54.

9. Richard Johnson, *op.cit.* p. 234.

10. I have found Colin Sumner's elaboration of 'social practice' and its relationship to 'ideology' useful here. 'Ideologies are important features of social practice since, (1) they define the purpose of the practice, (2) they define the actor's reasons for engaging in the practice and his mode of engagement (and disengagement), (3) they form part of the social context of the practice, (4) they will effect the shape of the product, (5) they will be generated within the practice and (6) they will be embodied (as past forms) in the material conditions (the raw material, the tools, the geography etc.).'

All this makes good sense if applied to the life and activities of the compositor (his practice) and to the meaning he makes of them (his ideology). And it is interesting that Sumner does in fact refer to newspaper production: 'Some practices will involve ideologies more centrally than others: compare brick-laying with news production . . . Clearly, where ideologies themselves are the tools and raw materials of the practice they have an exceptional importance in relation to the other elements. Thus the role of ideology in some practices is more complex than in others.' In Sumner's account of the relationship between ideology and social practice, however, the significance of contradiction is overlooked. (Colin Sumner, *op.cit.* p. 211.)

11. Trades Union Congress, and *Annual Abstract of Statistics – 1982*, HMSO 1982, table 6.27.

12. The skilled worker has been regathered in this way from even more rebellious moments that this one. James Hinton has recounted the history of the 'first shop stewards' movement', in the period during and after the first world war, when skilled engineers shed their resistance to dilution of their trade by women and less-skilled men and committed themselves to all-grades organisation in the workshops. For a while they were among the most militant workers in Britain, on the verge of leading a general strike against the pursuit of the war. The movement was defeated however, and by 1924 there had emerged a 'new and lasting accommodation of organised labour', the majority of engineers reverting to their craft separatism within the capitalist system of work. (James Hinton, *The First Shop Stewards' Movement*, Allen & Unwin 1973.)

13. Peter Cressey and John MacInnes, 'Voting for Ford: industrial democracy and the control of labour', *Capital & Class*, no. 11, 1980, p. 15.

14. Ernest Mandel, *Late Capitalism*, Verso 1972, p. 183.

15. 'Capital encounters a fundamental contradiction stemming from the fact that, step by step with the dequalification of work there is an increased social qualification of workers – a social disqualification (or devaluation) of all work as a productive force.' André Gorz, 'The tyranny of the factory: today and tomorrow', in A. Gorz (ed.), *The Division of labour*, Brighton: Harvester Press 1978, :p. 57.

16. Serge Mallet, *The New Working Class*, Nottingham: Spokesman 1975, p. 14.

17. *ibid.* p. 12.

18. Wilhelm Reich, *The Mass Psychology of Fascism*, Penguin 1980, p. 104.

19. The ideological affinities of patriarchy and fascism are often overlooked in marxist analyses of fascism. For instance, Nicos Poulantzas, in his major work on fascism, only refers in passing to the family (*Fascism and Dictatorship*, New Left Books 1974.) It is absent from Ernesto Laclau's analysis in 'Fascism and ideology', in Ernesto Laclau, *Politics and Ideology in Marxist Theory*, New Left Books 1977. It is also a missing dimension in Mihaly Vajda's *Fascism as a Mass Movement*, (Allison and Busby 1976).

20. Wilhelm Reich, *op.cit.* p. 103.

21. Tim Mason, 'Women in Germany, 1925–40: family, welfare and work', *History Workshop Journal*, no. 1, 1976, p. 86.

22. Maria-Antonietta Macciocchi, 'Female sexuality in fascist ideology', *Feminist Review*, no. 1, 1979, p. 77.
23. Article in *Il Popolo d'Italia*, 1934, cited in M. A. Macciocchi *op.cit.* p. 72.
24. *Mein Kampf*, cited in Wilhelm Reich, *op.cit.* p. 183.
25. M. A. Macciocchi, *op.cit.* p. 75.
26. Wilhelm Reich, *op.cit.* p. 138.
27. Andrew Friend and Andrew Metcalf, *Slump City*, Pluto Press 1981, p. 46.
28. Andrew Tolson, *The Limits of Masculinity*, Tavistock 1977, p. 64.
29. Ernest Mandel, *op.cit.*, p. 509.
30. See for instance Stuart Holland, *The Socialist Challenge*, Quartet 1975; Sam Aaronovitch, *The Road from Thatcherism: the Alternative Economic Strategy*, Lawrence and Wishart 1981; CSE London Working Group, *The Alternative Economic Strategy: a Labour Movement Response to the Economic Crisis*, CSE Books and Labour Co-ordinating Committee 1980. An attempt to adapt the AES in the light of discussions with feminists is to be found in Adam Sharples' paper for the Conference of Socialist Economists in Bradford, July 1982, titled 'Women and economic strategy'.
31. 'Aristocrats of Fleet Street', *The Economist*, 21 February 1981.
32. Beatrix Campbell and Valerie Charlton, 'Work to rule', *Red Rag*, 1978.
33. *ibid*; and, for instance, Anna Coote and Beatrix Campbell, *Sweet Freedom, The Struggle for Women's Liberation*, Picador 1982.
34. Hilary Wainwright and Dave Elliott, *The Lucas Plan: a New Trade Unionism in the Making*, Allison and Busby 1982.
35. Trades Union Congress, *Employment and Technology*, Report of the General Council to the 1979 Congress, p. 9.
36. The ideology of 'technological rationalism', as described by Ernest Mandel, persuades us that scientific and technical development has condensed into an autonomous power of invincible force, that traditional class rule has given way to the anonymous rule of technology, and because of its very technical rationality the existing social system cannot be challenged. Only more of the same can solve our problems. (Ernest Mandel, *op.cit.* p. 501.)
37. Dave Albury and Joe Schwartz, *Partial Progress: the Politics of Science and Technology*, Pluto Press 1982.
38. André Gorz, *Ecology as Politics*, Boston: South End Press 1980, p. 66.
39. Serge Mallet, *op.cit.*
40. *ibid.* p. 30.
41. *ibid.* p. 12.

Afterword

1. South East Economic Development Strategy, *Print Out: The Printing Industry in the South East*, Stevenage, Hertfordshire, 1990.
2. Reported in Roy Coxhead, 'The march of the microchip goes on', *Print*, June 1982.
3. *Print*, September 1987.
4. South East Economic Development Strategy, *op. cit.*
5. *Print*, June 1982.
6. Paul Smith and Gary Morton, 'A change of heart: union exclusion in the provincial newspaper sector', *Work, Employment and Society*, Vol. 4, No. 1, March 1990.
7. *ibid.*
8. *ibid.*
9. *ibid.*
10. Linda Melvern, *The End of the Street*, Methuen, 1986.
11. South East Economic Development Strategy, *op. cit.*
12. Average gross weekly earnings, Department of Employment, *New Earnings Survey*, H.M. Stationery Office, 1988.
13. John Gennard, *A History of the National Graphical Association*, Unwin Hyman, 1990.
14. Krysia Maciejewska, 'A decade of inaction', *Lithoweek*, 8 June 1988.
15. Krysia Maciejewska, *Lithoweek*, 8–27 June 1988.
16. Caroline Horn, 'Women still face discrimination', *Printing World*, 17 October 1990.
17. *Print*, April 1988.
18. *Print*, July/August 1988.
19. Old ideas die hard, however, and some men regret the passing of men's craft control. John Gennard, in his official history of the National Graphical Association records the following. In the 1970s, facing a threat from employers attempting to introduce female operators on the new typewriter-style composing keyboards, the union reasserted its pre-entry closed shop: only NGA men might input text. 'Dispensations to the policy were made only after exhaustive attempts to secure qualified NGA labour or suitable male labour from outside the industry had failed. Employers were required to advertise in the national, local and trade press and in the columns of *Print*, and then to examine the possibility of engaging males with the appropriate experience, such as telex operators. If this failed employers were to attempt to recruit disabled males. Only when all these avenues had been explored would the NGA accept the employment of women on keyboards...' This policy is recorded, without comment or regret, by an author who goes on to add, 'for a less than objective analysis of the attitude of craft compositors in national newspapers towards women, see C.Cockburn, *Brothers*, 1983.'

20. See C. Hakim, 'Job segregation: trends in the 1970s', *Employment Gazette*, December 1981.

21. Trades Union Congress, *Equality for Women in Trade Unions*, London, 1979.

22. Trades Union Congress, *Equality for Women within Trade Unions*, London, March 1984 and January 1989.

23. General, Municipal and Boiler Makers Union, *Eliminating Sex Bias in Labour Agreements*, Report to the Equal Rights Conference, P. Turner, 1986.

24. Cynthia Cockburn, *Women, Trade Unions and Political Parties*, Fabian Research Series No. 349, London, 1987.

25. Cynthia Cockburn, *In the Way of Women: Men's Resistance to Sex Equality in Organizations*, Macmillan Education, forthcoming 1991.

26. To name only a few titles from British publishers in recent years, see Andy Metcalf and Martin Humphries (eds) *The Sexuality of Men*, Pluto Press, 1985; Rowena Chapman and Jonathan Rutherford (eds) *Male Order: Unwrapping Masculinity*, Lawrence and Wishart, 1988; Arthur Brittan, *Masculinity and Power*, Basil Blackwell, 1989; Victor J. Seidler, *Rediscovering Masculinity: Reason, Language and Sexuality*, Routledge, 1989; and Jeff Hearn and David Morgan (eds) *Men, Masculinities and Social Theory*, Unwin Hyman, 1990. The list of such titles from the USA is considerable.

27. See Cynthia Cockburn, *Machinery of Dominance: Women, Men and Technical Knowhow*, Pluto Press, 1985; for a more optimistic analysis see Lynne Segal, *Slow Motion: Changing Masculinities, Changing Men*, Virago, 1990.

28. Carole Pateman, *The Sexual Contract*, Polity Press, 1988.

Index

advertising, 37, 231; freesheets, 69, 71; revenue, 69, 80; setting adverts, 50, 51, 63, 64, 70, 75, 115; personnel, tele-ad typists, 115, 119, 148

Alternative Economic Strategy, 226

andrarchy, 199

anti-catholicism, 127

apprenticeship, 113, 129, 131; end of, 166, 167; females, 158, 162, 164; intake, 20, 21, 38; practices, 15–21, 37, 38, 43–45, 198; *see also* National Graphical Association, new policies

aristocracy of labour, 31, 32, 237n., 238n.

Association of Correctors of the Press, 58, 235n.

Association of Professional, Executive, Clerical and Computer Staff (APEX), 165

Association of Scientific, Technical and Managerial Staff (ASTMS), 165

Astor, Lord, 79, 80

authoritarianism, *see* fascism

Bailey Forman, T., Ltd, 68

'banging out', 18, 198

biological sex, 6, 196, 204, 253n., 254n.

Bowerman, C., 28

British Federation of Master Printers, 56

British Printing Industries Federation, 248n., 249n.

Caledonian Press, 25

'call book', 'call office', 22, 30, 53, 104, 168

Cameron Committee, 68

Campaign for Press and Broadcasting Freedom, 149, 150

capitalism, 195, 206, 210, 213, 217, 218; development of, 19–21, 32, 86; relations of, 132, 192–94

Caxton, W., 14, 46

change, *see* political change

chapel: authority, 53, 54, 79, 90, 109–12, 245n.; organisation, customs, 16–19, 21, 32; relations within, 43, 45, 52, 53; role of FOC, 16, 53, 54, 79, 83, 89, 90

child care, *see* housework

class, 7, 32, 212, 218, 220, 244n.; identification, 193, 220; relations, 125, 141, 142, 150, 191–96, 205; structure and restructuring, 140–50, 191–96, 209; *see also* working class

clerical work, *see* office work

closed shop, 43, 53, 113, 121, 166, 171, 192

cold composition, *see* photocomposition

collective labourer, 118, 119, 148, 228

Combination Acts, 21

composition, *see* hot metal process; paste-up; stone hands

compositors: class identification, 33, 136, 140–50, 193, history of, 15–23, 31, 32, 236n.; and less skilled men, 123–29, 145–48, 155, 214, 237n.; and newspaper content, 148–50, 208, 209, 248n., 249n.; unemployment, 20, 30, 85, 143, 192

(*see also* 'call book'); and women (domestic), 34, 35, 133, 181–84, 199–202, 207, 215, (work) 17, 18, 23–26, 31, 36, 37, 41, 151–90, 199–201, 215
computer operators, programmers, 9, 109, 144–46, 148, 193, 198
computers, computerisation, 14, 61–64, 66, 85, 86, 91, 120, 121; *see also* photocomposition, installations
concentration of ownership, 55, 192; *see also* newspaper industry, concentration of ownership
Confederation of British Industry, 229
Conservative Party, 147, 192, 221
contradiction, 10–13, 172, 190, 211–17, 223, 235n.
control, *see* craft, control of production, labour supply; chapel, authority; technology, as control
corrections, 49, 100, 109
craft: control of labour supply, 21, 22, 28, 166, (*see also* closed shop); control of production, 29, 52–54, 58, 107, 112, 228; inter-craft relations, 40, 58; standards, quality, 49, 50, 100, 101, 106, 107; status and identity, 21, 32, 33, 52, 54, 59, 117, 118, 124, 129–32, 138, 220, 228; and technicians, 138
Croydon Advertiser Ltd., 71–74, 86, 94, 142
culture, 212, 255n.

Daily Mail, 83
Daily Mirror, 76, 77, 83, 95, 208
Daily Star, 122
Daily Telegraph, 28, 29
Dalton's Weekly, 47
demarcation, 68, 73, 124, 129, 242n.
dexterity, 24, 47, 51, 179; *see also* skill
dialectic, 10, 11
digitisation, 63, 82, 85
dilution, dilutees, 36, 37, 164
direct entry, 63, 64, 71, 76, 81, 82, 115, 143
disputes, 38, 39; Edinburgh, 33,

153–59, 191; *Times*, 81–83, 143
division of labour, 59, 112, 113, 119, 120; sexual, 116, 143, 224, 253n.; *see also* mental work, mental/manual distinction
Dixon, L., 78
dockers, 33
double shift, 252n., 253n.
drinking, 18, 169

earnings, 39, 43, 49, 55, 56, 73–75, 77, 82, 83, 201; *see also* pay differential
economy, 55, 57; cycles, 86, 87, 243n.; growth, 231
Edinburgh, *see* disputes
editors, *see* journalists
egalitarianism, 35, 126, 140, 173, 197, 223
electronic media, 64, 226
electronic technology, *see* computers; photocomposition; technology
Employment Bill, 166
engineers, 29, 30, 38, 256n.; *see also* technicians, technologists
English revolution, *see* revolution, English
environment, working, 52, 102, 106, 107, 117, 144
Equal Opportunities Commission, 162, 170
Equal Pay Act, 163; *see also* pay differential, sex

facsimile transmission, 77
Factory Acts, 34
Faithfull, E., 25
family, 20, 34, 35, 39, 44, 195; 'family wage', 35, 42, 181, 182, 185, 228, 252n.; ideology of, 209, 220; *see also* women, marriage and traditional roles
fascism, 210, 219–23
father of chapel, *see* chapel, role of FOC
feminism, 6, 7, 42, 157, 158, 194, 195, 198, 209, 210, 223
Financial Times, 245
Fleet Street, *see* national press; newspaper industry

flexibility, 111, 112, 148; *see also*
    polyvalent workers
'foreigners', 22, 128; *see also* racism
free collective bargaining, 228
Freudian theory, 198
front end systems, 63; *see also* direct
    entry

gender, *see* sex/gender
Gifts, The, 22
Guild of Young Printers, 46

health hazards, 52, 102, 103, 175, 176
hegemony, 205, 206, 208
homosexuality, 6, 137, 139, 188, 189,
    198, 206-9
hospital workers, 149
hot metal process, 14, 46-52, 54, 96,
    97, 101, 102, 105, 106; *see also*
    linotype; typesetting
hours of work, 71, 73, 79, 82, 201,
    224, 227
housework, 133, 201, 202, 206, 207,
    226, 227, 253n.
hyphenation-and-justification
    (H-and-J), 47, 61, 62, 82, 101

ideology, 10, 172, 181-90, 197,
    205-14, 225, 230, 235n., 255n.; *see*
    also meaning; sex/gender,
    essentialism and complementarity
idiot tape, *see* keyboard operators;
    hyphenation-and-justification
imposition, *see* stone hands,
    imposition
inkjet printing, 64
Institute of Printing, 66
integrated working, 9, 79, 81, 82, 95,
    108-12, 115
intellectual work, *see* mental work
internal labour market, 244n., 245n.
International Publishing Corporation,
    76, 142
International Typographical Union,
    65

Jarrett, A., 77
Joint Committee on Manpower, 56
joint negotiation, 57

journalism, journalists, 49, 103, 115,
    119, 139, 144, 145, 147, 193; *see*
    also National Union of Journalists

Kemsley, Lord, 80
Kemsley Newspapers, 43
keyboard operators, 9, 62, 70, 73,
    95-104, 109-12, 115, 119; *see also*
    linotype, operators
Keynesianism, 87
King, Cecil Harmsworth, 76
King and Hutchings Ltd., 68-72, 86,
    91, 94, 132

Labour Party, 31, 140, 221, 225, 226
labour process, *see* hot metal process;
    photocomposition, labour process
Labour Representation Committee,
    31
Lawson, Sir E., 29
letterpress printing, 14, 62; *see also*
    hot metal process
Licensing Act, 19
linotype, 27-31, 37, 45, 61, 70, 174;
    ninety-keyboard, 47, 61, 72, 96, 99;
    operators, 9, 29, 40, 41, 47-50, 54,
    62, 77, 79, 82, 94-104, 109, 112,
    114; *see also* typesetting
Linotype Company, 28, 29, 65, 66, 84
Linotype Paul, 99, 245n
London, *see* printing industry, London
London Master Printers Association,
    38, 39, 66
London Scale of Prices, 26, 29, 49, 75,
    77, 78, 82, 94; *see also*
    piecework-workers
London Society of Compositors, 26,
    28-31, 33, 34, 36, 38, 40, 41, 58, 66,
    129, 152-54
London Typographical Society, 58,
    66, 123, 124, 248n.
low pay, *see* pay differentials
Lucas Aerospace, 228
Luddism, 88, 230
Ludlow, *see* piece case

McCorquodale Ltd., 66
machine men, — managers, *see*
    pressmen

male: identification, 123, 134, 135, 138, 202, 203, 213, 223; organisation, 199, 202, 203; rivalry 135–37; *see also* masculinity

management, 39, 53, 54, 59, 70, 75, 81, 83, 88–91, 129

Manchester Guardian, 29

manning, *see* newspaper industry, manning

mark-up, 50, 104

marxism, 195, 196; and sex/gender, 5, 6, 194, 195, 198; and technology, 230

masculinity, 7, 31, 132–40, 238n.; and dirt, 52, 107, 108; and fascism, 219–23; and physicality, 107, 135, 136, 139, 203–5; and technology, 102–4, 135, 222, 231, 232; and work, 44, 52, 105–8, 133–36, 139, 224, 225

materialism, materiality, 6, 196, 199, 204, 208, 212, 213

meaning, 10, 11, 93, 214–16; *see also* ideology

Media General, 65

men, *see* compositors; masculinity; patriarchy

mental work, 146; mental/manual distinction, 44, 45, 139, 140, 143–45, 219; *see also* division of labour

Mergenthaler, O., 27

Mirror Group Newspapers Ltd., 76–80, 82, 86, 90, 91, 98, 99, 109–12, 119, 142, 177

mode of production, 194, 195

monetarism, 87, 192

Monopolies Commission, 67, 80

monotype, *see* typesetting, monotype

Murdoch, R., 74, 83, 142, 168

National Free Labour Association, 29

National Graphical Association, 9, 15, 43, 53, 66, 104, 109, 124, 126, 129, 152, 192; amalgamations, 58, 123, 124, 235n.; demarcation, 109, 128, 129; new policies, 120, 121, 164–68, 171; and photocomposition, 66, 70, 72, 74,

76, 81, 82; unemployment in, 85, (*see also* 'call book'); women in, 163–71

national press, 22, 38, 49, 50, 53, 56, 67, 73–83, 85, 108, 109; *see also* newspaper content; newspaper industry; and individual titles

National Society of Operative Printers, Graphical and Media Personnel (NATSOPA), 9, 27, 42, 50, 58, 82, 123–31, 139, 145, 155, 168, 170, 235n., 237n.

National Union of Journalists, 82, 123, 124, 149, 223, 224; *see also* journalism, journalists

National Union of Wallpaper Decorators (NUWDAT), 164

Newcastle Chronicle, 27

News International Ltd., 74

newsmen, news work, 21, 40, 51, 52, 59

newspaper content, 42, 43, 148–50, 208, 209, 229, 248n., 249n.

newspaper industry: circulation, 241n.; concentration of ownership, 67, 192, 240n.; growth, 243n.; labour costs, 74, 77, 243n.; labour process, 51, 52, 58; labour shortage, 36–38, 55, 160; manning, 38, 56, 68, 77, 83, 84, 106, 242n., 243n.; productivity, 56, 57, 73, 84, 85; profit, 55, 56, 70, 79, 80, 84, 241n.; women employed, 161, 162, 168; *see also* national press; printing industry; regional press

Newspaper Publishers Association, 65

Newspaper Society, 68

new technology, *see* photocomposition; technology

New Training Initiative, 166

Northcliffe, Lord, 76, 79

Nottingham Evening Post, 68

Officework, workers, 31, 73, 108, 140, 143–45, 164, 165, 171, 193, 211, 219; *see also* ASTMS; APEX; advertising, personnel

offset lithography, 39, 58, 62, 68

optical character recognition, 103

overmanning, *see* newspaper industry, manning
overtime, *see* hours of work
Owenism, 35

page make-up, *see* page-view terminals
page-view terminals, 64, 71, 78, 115, 119
part-time work, 169; *see also* hours of work
paste-up hands, 9, 62, 95, 104–9, 119, 164
patriarchal relations: in apprenticeship, 45, 46; in business firms, 68–72, 92, 197, 198, 203; among craftsmen, 33–37, 197, 203; between men, 125, 136; in pre-capitalist printing, 15–17, 236n.
patriarchy, 7, 8, 171–73, 197, 198, 210, 213; *see also* patriarchal relations; sex/gender system
pay differential, 41, 42, 124, 131, 132, 136, 166, 200, 201, 242n.; future of, 227, 228; sex, 41, 154, 162, 163, 170, 199, 200, 250n.; *see also* earnings
Pearson, S., and Son Ltd., 69
photocomposition: agreements, 70, 71, 73, 78, 82; installations, 70, 71, 73, 78, 81, 82, 241–43n.; invention and introduction, 39, 61, 64–67, 94 (in national newspapers) 73–86, (in regional newspapers) 68–74, 83–86; labour process, 61–64, 93–112; productivity gains, 65, 70, 73, 106, 115
photosetters, photosetter operators, 9, 62–64, 66, 86, 105, 109
piece-case, 9, 50, 109
piece-work, -workers, 26, 41, 53, 75, 77, 82, 94, 99; *see also* London Scale of Prices; piece-case
platemaker, platemaking, 9, 64
political change, 13, 210, 216–19
polyvalent workers, 148, 150; *see also* flexibility
pressmen, presswork, 15, 24, 27, 40, 58, 124

Prices and Incomes Board, 55
Printers' Labourers Union, 237n.
Printing and Kindred Trades Federation, 31, 57, 157, 159
Printing Industries Research Association, 85
printing industry: in London, 15, 20, 40, 129, 153; in provinces, 20, 39, 40, 129; in Scotland, 153–59; *see also* newspaper industry
productivity, 39, 55; *see also* newspaper industry, productivity; photocomposition, productivity gains
proof readers, reading, 9, 40, 41, 50, 109, 235n., 245n.; *see also* Association of Correctors of the Press
provincial press, *see* regional press

QWERTY keyboard, *see* typing, QWERTY board

racism, 127, 128, 165, 220, 238n.
random hand, 50, 104, 109
readers, *see* proof readers; Association of Correctors of the Press
Reading Evening Post, 66
real subordination, 244n.
Reed International Ltd., 76, 77
regional press, 56, 67–74, 80, 85; *see also* newspaper industry
relations of production, 93
reporters, *see* journalists
research method, 8–12
restrictive practices, 29, 56, 74, 84, 242n.
Reuters Ltd., 226
revolution: English, 19, 35, 122; revolutionary consciousness, 32–35, 218, 219; *see also* socialism
right wing, *see* fascism
Roberts, P., 77, 78
Rocappi Ltd., 66
Rothermere, Lord, 76

scientific discovery, 229, 230
Scotland, *see* disputes, Edinburgh;

printing industry, Scotland
Scotsman, 80
Scottish Typographical Association,
   26, 33, 153–57
Sex Discrimination Act, 163, 164
sex/gender: analysis, 5–7, 92, 152,
   219; complementarity 187–89,
   205–7, 221; essentialism, 173, 177,
   187–89, 205–7, 221; identification,
   213, 220; relations, 125, 126,
   132–40, 191, 196–209,
   (restructuring of) 173, 184, 189;
   system, 6, 92, 139, 191, 193–99,
   209, 212; *see also* patriarchy;
   patriarchal relations
sexual difference, *see* sex/gender,
   complementarity
sexual division of labour, *see* division
   of labour, sexual
sexual morality, 181, 184, 185
sexual segregation of work, 160, 180,
   193, 224
sexuality, 213, 220–22; *see also*
   homosexuality; women, sexuality
single keystroke, *see* direct entry
skill, 112–22, 210; deskilling,
   degradation of work, 58, 59, 95,
   112–22, 218; political dimension,
   113, 115, 120–25, 228; re-evaluation
   of, 228, 229; sex and, 24, 116, 117;
   see also hot metal process;
   photocomposition; labour process
social practice, 212, 214, 235n., 255n.
socialism, socialist consciousness,
   210, 218
Society of Graphical and Allied
   Trades (SOGAT), 123, 124,
   127–30, 170
Society of Lithographic Artists,
   Designers, Engravers and Process
   Workers (SLADE), 123, 124, 130,
   171
Society for Promoting the
   Employment of Women, 25
Southwark Offset, 142
Sporting Life, 76, 95
state: control of printing, 15, 19; and
   industry, 38, 55, 86, 88, 89; in
   restructuring, 192; services, 192,

224; and trade unions, 55
Stationers Company, 15, 19, 20, 236n.
Statute of Apprentices, 19, 20
stereotypers, 9, 40, 58, 148
stone hands, imposition, 9, 50, 51, 54,
   95, 105–9
Sun, 122, 209
Sunday Mirror, 76, 77, 95
Sunday People, 76, 77
Sunday Times, 74, 79–83, 90
swearing, 18, 134, 169

tappers, *see* keyboard operators;
   linotype, operators
technicians, technologists, 138,
   145–47, 198
technology: and class, 144; and
   control, 89, 91, 146; critique of,
   229–33; innovation, 210, 216–19,
   229; investment in, 55, 85–89; and
   sex/gender, 102, 138; *see also*
   computers; photocomposition
text input, *see* keyboard operators;
   linotype, operators
Thomson, Lord, 80, 83
Thomson Organisation, 90, 142
Times, 43, 74, 79–83, 90, 96, 168
Times Newspapers Ltd, 79–83, 86, 90,
   94, 109–12, 119, 142, 143, 168
Times Supplements, 81, 83
trade societies, 21, 153, 203
trade unions, 21, 130, 210, 217, 229;
   amalgamation, 58, 123–27, 129,
   130, 164, 223; future of, 223–33;
   and patriarchy, 33–35, 37, 158, 159;
   and skill, 21, 120–22; *see also*
   individual unions
Trades Union Congress, 165, 167,
   224, 229
Trafalgar House Investments Ltd., 74
tramping, 22
transformative labour, 121, 226
typing, typists, 31, 95–104, 114, 118,
   119, 164, 168, 193; QWERTY
   board, 61, 63, 85, 96–105
typesetting: early machines, 25–31,
   176; hand, 46, 47, 58, 155;
   Intertype, 65, 66, 70; monotype,
   30, 31, 36, 37, 45, 97, 155, 156, 158;

tele —, 61, 62, 72; *see also* linotype
Typographical Association, 26, 28, 30, 31, 33, 34, 40, 123, 124, 153, 154, 173

unemployment, 22, 143; *see also* 'call book'; compositors, unemployment
Union Society, 21
United States of America: printing industry, 38, 39, 65, 66; print technology, 56, 61, 62, 66
unskilled and semi-skilled workers, 9, 27, 30, 41, 62, 118, 119, 125–29, 145, 151, 155, 214, 220, 237n.
use values, 121, 122

VDU, VDT, *see* video screen
Victoria Press, 25
video screen, 63, 70, 71, 73, 78, 82, 96, 99, 110, 115
violence, 18, 137, 185, 199, 204, 212, 215, 232

wage: fetishism, 137; leadership, 57, 201, 228; strategies, 227, 228; structure, 57; *see also* earnings; pay differential
war time, 36, 37
Warehousemen and Cutters Union, 155
'wayzgoose', 18, 198
Westminster Press, 68–71
white collar, *see* office work, workers; mental work

Wilson, H., 55, 57
women: compositors, 23–25, 33, 37, 83, 153–59, 162, 168, 175; earnings, 162, 163, 170, 199, 250n.; marriage, traditional roles, 34, 35, 178, 179, 181–84, 191, 192, 197, 211; material disadvantage of, 199–204, 253n., 254n.; in the National Graphical Association, 164–71; objectification of, 19, 42, 43, 134, 135, 147, 185, 186, 209; in printing, 17–19, 23–26, 29, 31, 33, 37, 41, 42, 66, 83, 125, 151–71, 200, (apprentices) 158, 162, 164, (in newspaper industry) 161, 162, 168; sexuality, 185, 186, 222; and skill, 116, 117, 159, 168, 180, 228; split image, 185, 186, 205, 206, 222; supposed inferiority, 174–78; and technology, 92, 177, 188, 203–5, 222, 233; and trade unionism, 157, 159, 169–71, 224–33; and work, 20, 31, 42, 145, 215, 221; *see also* feminism; sex/gender
women's liberation, women's movement, *see* feminism
Women's Printing Society Ltd., 25, 175
word processors, 63, 85
working class: definitions of, 248n.; divisions in, 5, 22, 23, 31–35, 40, 43, 149, 210, 224, 239n.; identification, 213, 224; restructuring, 88, 118, 193, 218, 219; unity, 55, 148, 150, 201; *see also* class